In this wide-ranging and well-written study, Geoffrey Grogan provides a clear, scholarly and reliable account of the identity of Jesus ʿ za- reth. The fruit of prolonged thought about the New Tes⁺ ᶦ- ing, *The Christ of the Bible and of the Church'ᵣ* every page by clarity of exposition and reliᵇ have a careful and thoughtful sifting oᶠ conclusions which are in harmony wiᶦ

While familiar with trends in New 1 ᵤₑ past two centuries, and grateful for the work ᵢₐrs, Geoffrey Grogan has listened first and foremost to tᵢ ₔₛ of the apostles. He concludes that there is only one answer to ᵤₑ ancient question which Jesus himself asked them, 'Who do you say that I am?'

The result is this sturdy volume. Theological students, Christian min- isters and leaders will find it invaluable, but any serious reader to whom Jesus of Nazareth remains an elusive figure will also come to the con- clusion that this is a book well worth reading.

Sinclair B. Ferguson
Westminster Theological Seminary
Philadelphia, Pennsylvania, USA

This is an apologetic and theological study aimed at preachers, theo- logical students, thinking Christians and interested agnostics. It succeeds in its aims admirably.

Donald Macleod
Free Church College
Edinburgh, Scotland

This beautifully-written book is a feast of scriptural analysis and argument about our Lord Jesus Christ. With profound learning but with lightness of touch, Geoffrey Grogan discusses all the main lines of the presentation of Jesus in the Bible, and then skilfully relates these to the questions that trouble people today about him. So the book is an attractive combination of Christology and apology – explaining Jesus in a way that answers modern doubts and puzzles, cleverly arranged in alternating chapters. Hearts will be warmed and heads cleared by this book – and doubt and unbelief will be turned into confidence and faith.

Steve Motyer
London Bible College

THE
CHRIST
OF THE BIBLE
AND
OF THE CHURCH'S FAITH:
a Theological and Apologetic Study

Geoffrey Grogan

Mentor

Published in 1998 by Christian Focus Publications,
Geanies House, Fearn, Ross-shire, IV20 1TW, Great Britain
Printed in Great Britain by J. W. Arrowsmith Limited, Bristol

CONTENTS

INTRODUCTION 8

1. JESUS CHRIST IN THE GOSPELS 11

2. THE HISTORICAL ISSUE 30

3. JESUS CHRIST IN THE REST OF THE NEW TESTAMENT .. 50

4. THE THEOLOGICAL ISSUE 68

5. JESUS CHRIST IN THE OLD TESTAMENT 92

6. THE HERMENEUTICAL ISSUE 111

7. JESUS CHRIST IN HIS HUMILIATION 131

8. THE ETHICAL ISSUE 149

9. JESUS CHRIST IN HIS EXALTATION 169

10. THE SUPERNATURAL ISSUE 185

11. GOD INCARNATE 202

12. THE CREDAL ISSUE 225

13. THE UNIQUENESS OF JESUS 244

14. THE INTER-FAITH ISSUE 261

15. THE PERSONAL ISSUE 277

15. INDICES 284

THE NATURE OF THIS BOOK

Professor Howard Marshall[1] describes the teaching of the New Testament about the person of Jesus as 'a subject vast in scope, unencompassable in its bibliography and daunting in its problems'. For all these reasons, it is important that the reader should be clear as to what this present book is and what it is not.

It is not an exercise in Gospel Criticism
This is a very complex subject and there is a wealth of text-books on it. This book does not deal with the Synoptic Problem, nor, except in general terms, with the various problems that have been raised about the Gospel of John.

It is not a complete survey of Christological views
A great multitude of viewpoints about Jesus has emerged over the years and there are undoubtedly many current today. This book concentrates on the main issues. Some inadequate Christological views, long dead and gone, are not even mentioned, and some current today that are difficult to support and likely to be quite ephemeral in their influence are not included either.

What then is it?

It is a theological study
In the main, the odd-numbered chapters are theological. The first five of these set out the biblical evidence for our understanding of Jesus, while chapters 11 and 13 reflect on this theologically at a somewhat deeper level.

It is an apologetic study
This is the function of the even-numbered chapters. They deal with the main difficulties that have been and still are raised by those who are interested in Jesus but are not yet committed to him. It is to be hoped that they will also be of help to the committed. Each

of these chapters follows the theological chapter most closely related to it.

Much of the theological material (except that in Chapter 13) is an adaptation and extension of material originally published in my long out-of-print volume, *Jesus,* in the Kingsway Press 'What the Bible says' series.[2] Chapters 14 and 15 are based largely on a booklet of mine, *Inter-Faith Relations,* which was published in 1995 by the Baptist Union of Scotland, and which I have used for this purpose by kind permission of the convenor of the Union's Publications Committee.

Reading the book

It is hoped that the book will be useful to ministers and theological students. It has however been written in such a way that many Christians without theological training may be able to benefit from it, plus other readers who have not yet come to personal faith in Christ but are interested enough to read a serious book about him.

If you are new to theological study, it is suggested that you read the odd-numbered chapters first of all, followed by the even-numbered ones, whereas those with some familiarity with the subject already are advised to read it straight through.

References
1. *The Origins of New Testament Christology* , Leicester, IVP, 1977, p. 8.
2. Published in 1979. It was published simultaneously in the USA by Tyndale House Publishers under a slightly different title, as *What the Bible Teaches about Jesus.*

INTRODUCTION

People are fascinating. Julius Caesar, Francis of Assisi, Leonardo da Vinci, Garibaldi – there is a quartet of interesting and varied personalities you might study for years, and just from one country's history! It has been said that 'the proper study of mankind is man,' and we shall never exhaust that study.

One man stands above all others. Jesus, a carpenter, reared in an obscure town not even mentioned in his nation's literature before his day, has gripped the minds and hearts of people in a quite special way. His character and personality have fascinated all kinds of people for two thousand years. Far more books have been written about him than about any other human being. His life and the documents which record it have been subjected to scholarly research more intense than that devoted to any other life or record. All this tempts us to rephrase the old saying so that it reads, 'the proper study of mankind is the Man.'

We are living in times of great change, and the greatest changes of all are taking place in people's outlook and life-styles. In Britain, there has been a major reduction in church membership and church attendance (although this is not true on a world-wide scale) but this should not be misunderstood. It does not mean that there is less interest in Jesus himself as a person. Major television series featuring him are still likely to get large ratings.

It is striking how many leaders of other religious groups have found the life and character of Jesus especially interesting. Earlier this century, Jews like Klausner and Claude Montefiore, and Hindus like Gandhi took a very serious interest in him and his teaching, even though they did not become Christians, and he is still of great interest to people of other faiths. Even people who have written against traditional ideas of him have left their own testimony to his uniqueness. David Strauss, a sceptic if ever there was one, declared: 'Christ stands alone, and unapproached in the world's history.' Ernst Renan, another sceptic, called him 'the Incomparable Man', and said of him, 'Between you and God there is no longer any distinction.'

The influence of Jesus has been incalculable. We cannot over-estimate the extent of it on the history of civilization and human nature. W. G. de Burgh in *The Legacy of the Ancient World* [1] analyses the sources of modern civilization. Egypt, Babylon and others from the ancient world have each made their own contribution but there are just three major sources – Greece, Rome and Israel. The influence of the latter finds its focus in one man – Jesus of Nazareth. The history of western art cannot be understood at all without a study of the Christian faith, and there is much else in our culture that reflects his influence.

A Muslim parent once approached his son's headmaster with a complaint. There was no proper Christian religious education in the school and so his son was not getting the education he needed. 'But,' replied the astonished head, 'I thought you were a Muslim, not a Christian!' 'Certainly,' said the father. 'We are a Muslim family and we intend to stay that way, but we are immigrants, not just birds of passage in this country. How is my son ever going to understand Britain and the British unless he understands the religion that has moulded their culture all these centuries?'

Jesus of Nazareth has been changing people's lives ever since he came into the world. The New Testament tells the story of many of them. He does it still. We might expect to meet such people in church, but many readers of this book will have met them in the home, at school, at university, in the factory or the office. Their testimony to Christ's impact on them may be regarded by some people simply as an expression of personal preference in a world where there is a 'supermarket' approach to experience, including religious experience. This book will argue that this is a mistake, and that the claims of Jesus are so great and so universal that they should be accepted by everybody.

The approach is frankly conservative as far as the Bible's teaching about Jesus is concerned. The biblical teaching is taken seriously and rational arguments are given to support such an approach. Does this mean then that you need particular views of biblical inspiration to profit by this volume? No. The reader is asked simply to give the biblical writings the kind of respect primary documents deserve and normally receive. This does not mean that ques-

tions of inspiration are unimportant. It does mean you can get some-
where with the Bible witness to Jesus without starting off with a
particular view of Scripture.

A strange feature of the book for some readers who are not
familiar with today's theological scene lies in the fact that some of
the views combatted are not put forward by avowed enemies of
the Christian faith but by theologians. As David Wells says, 'The
theologian as doubter is a modern phenomenon. He or she is the
product, on the one hand, of a modern view of knowledge and, on
the other hand, of a radically shifting cultural milieu.'[2] His analysis is surely correct.

The writer of this volume is convinced that the Christian faith
in its historic form is not only still viable, but that the case for it is
immensely strong. It is in this conviction that this volume is written.

References
1. Harmondsworth, Penguin Books, 1953, in 2 vols.
2. David F. Wells, *The Person of Christ: A Biblical and Historical Analysis
of the Incarnation,* Westchester, Crossway, 1984, p. 3.

Chapter 1

JESUS CHRIST IN THE GOSPELS

Their Fourfold Witness to Christ

The New Testament contains four accounts of the life of Jesus of Nazareth. Most of us are so used to this fact that we have not stopped to ponder its significance. It is in fact a very unusual phenomenon and it is without extant parallel in ancient literature.

Perhaps the nearest we can find in that literature is the life of Socrates. It is true of both Jesus and Socrates that we have nothing written by either of them. For both we are dependent on the writings of others and in each case these were written by people who greatly respected them. Even this partial parallel is less marked than it might appear to be, however, for in the case of Socrates there are only two accounts that have come down to us, and Xenophon's has become completely overshadowed by Plato's. There is also difference of opinion as to how much of the teaching of Socrates given in Plato's *Dialogues* is really his and how much his utterances there are actually vehicles for Plato's own views.

Then too, while Plato and Xenophon are not uninterested in the life of Socrates and especially show great admiration for the courage and integrity he demonstrated in being prepared to die rather than to surrender his beliefs, there is little doubt that his teaching can be detached from his life and treated as important in itself.

When we turn to the Gospels we get the clear impression that the consuming interest of the writers was not simply in the teaching of Jesus but in Jesus himself. He is always at the centre of the picture.

This is true for all four Gospels, and yet of course they are not identical. The first three are known as the Synoptics[1] for all three present much the same kind of outline of the life of Jesus. There are however all sorts of differences in detail, and Matthew and Luke give much more of the teaching of Jesus than Mark does, while the two of them do not always present the same actual teaching material. In the case of John, the differences are more marked still, for this Gospel omits some events obviously regarded by the others as important while giving events and teaching not to be found in the others.

Yet the remarkable fact is that, for most readers throughout Christian history, these accounts have been viewed as harmonious and complementary rather than contradictory. They have each been seen as giving a somewhat different emphasis so that in reading them together we gain much fuller understanding of Jesus than we could obtain from only one. It is true too that most modern Christians view them in this way.

Striking also is the great emphasis each of them places on his death, the account of which is in every case followed by that of his resurrection. All of them, and most of all the Fourth Gospel, give considerable space to the events of the last week of his life. It would be difficult to find in the life-story of any other real person so much space and emphasis given to his or her death and the events immediately preceding it. In fact, it becomes obvious at a fairly early stage in the Gospels that the death of Jesus was gong to be important and eventually it is seen to have quite unique meaning. Yet here too there is no slavish copying nor evident contradiction. It is possible to put the various accounts together into a harmony, and this has often been done. It is not the easiest of tasks but this is exactly what we might have expected. The very first attempt at a general harmony of the four Gospels was made as early as the mid-second century in Tatian's *Diatesseron*.

The four appear to have been written with different readers in view.[2]

The Gospel of Mark

This is the best place for us to begin our study of the Gospels, and for two reasons. The first is that it is generally although not universally held by scholars that the Gospel of Mark was the first to be written.[3] Not only so, but it is the simplest. It can be read through in about an hour and in this short space of time the reader gains a vivid impression of Jesus. It is difficult to believe that there are serious-minded seekers after truth who have never taken time to do this simple thing.

'The beginning of the gospel about Jesus Christ, the Son of God.' In the very first verse of his book Mark indicates his purpose in penning it. It is important to realise that at the time of his writing, 'gospel' did not have the literary connotations it often has for us today. It simply meant 'good news'. He is not therefore defining the literary genre he is producing but indicating that he is a preacher bringing his readers good news about Jesus.

The method Mark employs in preaching Jesus is simply to tell us the story of his life, death and resurrection, but he begins with a theological assertion: Jesus is the Christ, the Son of God. It is true that 'Son of God' does not appear in all manuscripts of the Gospel, but its authenticity is accepted by most scholars.[4] Even if it should not be original, it simply expresses a truth about him that is amply witnessed to elsewhere in the gospel, including its first chapter. We find the term employed by Jesus (12:6; 13:32) as well as by others, and it is also spoken from heaven by God himself (1:11; 9:7). This latter fact gives it quite special significance.

The title 'Christ' means that he is God's anointed and promised King, for 'Christ' is the Greek equivalent of the Hebrew 'Messiah' meaning 'the anointed One'. The term 'Son of God' signifies that he has a special relationship with God himself. A passage like Psalm 2, which has a special position in the Book of Psalms as introducing the theme of divinely anointed kingship there, contains both titles (vv. 2, 7).

Because the Christ was promised, we are not surprised to find his forerunner, John the Baptist, introduced in the Gospel with Old Testament quotations (1:2,3). These come from Malachi 3:1 and Isaiah 40:3. They not only designate John as the forerunner of Jesus, but eloquently indicate Mark's high view of Jesus, for they tell of a way being prepared for somebody, and in their original contexts in the Old Testament the One whose way is being prepared is none other than God. Incidentally, it seems likely that the first readers of New Testament books would be expected to consider the contexts of the Old Testament passages they quote and to ponder their significance.[5]

The greatness of Jesus is also confirmed by the words of John the Baptist: 'After me will come one more powerful than I, the thongs of whose sandals I am not worthy to stoop down and untie. I baptise you with water, but he will baptise you with the Holy Spirit' (1:7,8). This shows that, although John's baptism was normally an expression of repentance on the part of those being baptised (1:4), this was not true in the case of Jesus. This is strikingly confirmed by the divine Voice which spoke from heaven (1:11). As God's Son, Jesus is assured of his favour by that Voice and now, as God's King, he is endued with his Spirit.[6] It was enduement by that Spirit which empowered not only kings but also prophets, priests and judges in Old Testament times, and it was so fitting that one who embodied these and other roles in himself, should be anointed in this way.

An important feature of the king's work in ancient times was to be as his people's war-leader. Already in the first chapter of the Gospel Satan has been revealed as an enemy (1:13), and this prepares us to witness a conflict between Jesus and Satan. Jesus shows his kingly authority, not only over nature, as represented by the wild beasts[7], but also over the evil spirits, Satan's agents,[8] and over all kinds of disease.

He comes, however, not only to cast out demons and heal the sick but also to preach and call for a verdict, expressed by the words 'repent' and 'believe' (1:14,15). He begins to gather followers (1:16-20; 2:13), for a king has a right to issue commands to his subjects. In fact enormous crowds are attracted to him (1:33; 2:2, 13; 3:7,8), drawn no doubt not simply by his teaching but by his healing and exorcising miracles. From among these followers he selects twelve for personal training, so that they may be with him and then go out to preach his message and express his authority over the demonic world (3:13-19).

As the story unfolds, it becomes evident that the enemy has many human agents. These are not only in expected quarters. It is not surprising to find them among the Herodians, the supporters of 'King' Herod who has no divine right to authority,[9] but we find them most markedly and frequently among the religious leaders of the people, the religious lawyers and Pharisees (2: 6,7,16, 24; 3:6, 22-30). We might have anticipated that these would have given Jesus a warm welcome, but this is the very opposite of the truth. In fact chapters 2 and 3 show him in spoken conflict with these men on one issue after another. He clearly believes it is his right to clarify important questions about man's relationship with God and the interpretation of the Old Testament, even though this puts him against the most respected theologians of his day.

One of his most striking sayings around this time is to be found at the close of a story in which his hungry disciples pick corn on the Sabbath day (Mark 2:23-28). We know from the Rabbinic literature that the Pharisees had interpreted such conduct as reaping and therefore condemned it as a breach of the law. On this occasion, Jesus interpreted the much-venerated Sabbath law, and concluded with the remarkable words, 'the Son of Man is Lord even of the Sabbath'. The Sabbath was a divine institution and it was meticulously observed by the Jews of his day. Such a claim strongly suggests that he believed himself to be more than a mere man.

The opposition of the religious leaders is not what we might have expected. Early on in the Gospel we are also warned to expect something worse still, his ultimate betrayal by one of his own men (3:19).

In chapter 4 there is a pause in the rapid succession of events as Jesus explains in the picture language of parables some basic principles of the kingdom of God, but the action starts up again at the close of that chapter. A king, as military leader, is called to save his people. This king is divine (4:41, 'Who then is this? Even the winds and the waves obey him!'), and so in four very different situations Mark shows the power of Jesus to save people when they are clearly beyond human help. He saves from drowning, from the power of demons and from disease, and he then restores life to the dead daughter of a synagogue ruler (4:35-5:43). Chapter 6, however, makes it clear that people can only know him as the Saviour-King if, setting aside all prejudice (6:3,4), they will believe in him and receive his messengers (6:10,11), whether these are his disciples or his forerunner (6:14-29). It is probably for thematic reasons that Mark has brought the story of the somewhat earlier death of John the Baptist into this context.

Just as Israel needed not only salvation from Egypt but a place in which to live and so God provided the land of Canaan for them, so Jesus, as the Shepherd-King, is Provider as well as Saviour of his people. This is made abundantly clear in two miracles of feeding (6:37-44 and 8:1-10). In fact, references to food are so frequent in chapters 6-8 that Mark must surely be making some emphatic point here. Perhaps he is underlining for his readers that Jesus is able to supply the most basic and urgent needs of human beings. Part of this passage, including the story of the feeding of the four thousand, concerns events outside purely Jewish territory (7:24-8:10), suggesting the thought perhaps that he came to save and feed people of every land, not simply his own. We might note in passing that the Fourth Gospel shows us that after he had fed the five thousand, Jesus went on to speak about spiritual feeding.

What have the disciples been doing up until now? They have been with him, listening and watching, but not always understanding. Their failure in comprehension drew from him a series of questions: 'Do you still not see or understand? Are your hearts hardened? Do you have eyes, but fail to see, and ears but fail to hear?' (8:17, 18). This is followed by the fascinating and unique miracle of the blind man given sight in two stages (8:22-26). This seems like an acted parable, and it shows what a marvellous sense of positioning Mark has, for it introduces the great confession of his messiahship by Peter but also the same disciple's refusal to listen to some most unpalatable teaching (8:27-38).

The disciples now know Jesus to be God's Christ but they have yet to realise that the Messianic teaching of the religious establishment, which they have learned from childhood, is all wrong. Jesus is to be no military Messiah but rather a lowly Sufferer. He has used the somewhat enigmatic term, 'Son of Man', of himself. It suggests humanness, as in Psalm 8:4, but also transcendent greatness, as in Daniel 7:13,14.[10] Now he uses it in a passage where he makes it clear that he has a destiny of suffering ahead of him: 'He then began to teach them that the Son of Man must suffer many things and be rejected by the elders, chief priests and teachers of the law, and that he must be killed and after three days rise again.' Peter's fierce rejection of this shows so clearly how completely the words of Jesus ran counter to what he and the other disciples had been taught in the synagogues.

As someone has said, employing a musical metaphor, Jesus transposed the messianic theme into a minor key. As another writer has put it, he also transposed it into a higher key, for the Christ is not merely a great man, as the Pharisees taught, but the Son of God. This is dramatically emphasised on the transfiguration mountain (9:2-8), where the power of the kingdom (9:1) is displayed in the glory of its King.[11] In many ways his transfiguration was like an anticipation of the glory of his resurrection.

On the mountain God reproves their failure to listen (9:7; cf. 8:32f.), while at its foot Jesus rebukes the lack of faith shown by the other disciples, for they have been impotent in the face of the powers of evil. On the road to Jerusalem the gulf in outlook between him and his men becomes starkly and disturbingly clear and this puts his uniqueness into high relief. He has called them to repent and believe (1:14), to follow him (1:17; 2:14), to deny themselves and take the cross as they follow (8:34). Now he speaks constantly of his coming sufferings and death while their thoughts are controlled by pride (9:34; 10:28), prejudice (9:38), presumption (10:13), and self-seeking (10:35ff., 41).

The important saying, 'the Son of Man did not come to be served, but to serve, and to give his life a ransom for many' is reminiscent of Isaiah 52:13 and 53:10-12. So it is now clear that for Jesus the terms Christ, Son of Man and Servant of God all apply to one person, that is to himself. What kind of Messiah then is he to be? Without doubt One destined for heavenly glory and universal dominion (Dan. 7) but this must be preceded by suffering and death for others (Isa. 52:13-53:12).

The reiterated cries of Bartimaeus (10:46-52) and of the Palm Sunday crowds (11:9, 10), in which Jesus is acclaimed as Son of David, remind us that a king, David's greater son, is coming to Jerusalem, David's city. He has, however, already delineated the true pattern of authority in terms of service, deeply costly service involving dying as a ransom for many (10:35-45), and the mode of his entry dramatises this vocation of service (11:1-7). Military kingship would have taken the horse for its symbol, not the donkey which Jesus chose. For contemporary Judaism, the role of the Messiah was largely seen in terms of judgement on the other nations, but by word (the cursing of the fig tree, an Old Testament symbol for Israel[12]) and deed (the cleansing of the Temple), he declares God's displeasure with Israel herself (11:12-33).

He has come to religious Judaism's geographical centre. Now, towards the end of chapter 11, we see its religious leaders crowding into the Temple with the clear intention of discrediting him before the people. Every question put that day either by them or by him has direct or indirect relevance to the meaning of his person. What authority does he have? That of a beloved Son. How does he relate to earlier revelation, to John the Baptist and the prophets?

He answers, in parable form, by indicating that he is the summit of all revelation, the final messenger (12:6). What then is his attitude to secular authority (Caesar), to Old Testament religious authority ('Which commandment is the first?')? Each of these questions is answered. At the end he focuses everything on the true nature of the Messiah by himself putting a question where previously he had responded to the questions of others. When they answer, he makes it clear that he is not just Son of David but Lord of all (12:35-37).

The teachers of the law would have been much in evidence in the temple courts giving teaching to the busy Passover crowds. He now contrasts them and certain rich people, whose religious giving was ostentatious, with the self-sacrificing poverty of a poor widow (12:38-44). He then makes it clear that the temple's beauty, greatly enhanced by work done under the authority of Herod the Great, cannot conceal the religious leaders' ugly rejection of God's Christ. It will be destroyed. This act of divine judgement will anticipate the return of the messianic Son of Man, whose kingdom takes the place of the troubled kingdoms of men, whose order replaces the religious and natural instability of the present age, and whose words will endure when even the present form of the universe will dissolve.

It is clear then that the King will ultimately triumph. But what is the way to that glorious end? This he has emphasised time and again. It is the way of suffering and death. Chapters 14 and 15 present the facts about his closing hours. There is plenty of Old Testament quotation and allusion in these chapters. God's purpose of atonement (10:45; 14:24) and vindication (8:31, 'rise again'; 9:9,31; 10:34; 13:26; 14:25, 28, 62) appears over against the malice of his enemies and the failure of his friends.

The result is a story shot through with irony. An unknown woman (14:3-9) and an unknown man (14:12-16) serve him before he is taken and two men, new to the story, do so in the closing scenes (15:21, 43), while an intimate disciple betrays him, another denies him, and they all leave him. He has come into the world for the very purpose of dying, yet his enemies send to arrest him a band of men armed to the teeth. Except with his close disciples he has kept the 'messianic secret' of his person (1:34; 3:11; 9:9) but he chooses to reveal it now when it seems most absurd, for he is apparently a helpless prisoner in his enemies' hands (14:61f.).

Pilate's question, 'Are you the king of the Jews?' (15:2) is probably highly sceptical. The Jews are under the Roman heel and hate it and yet, without realising the full implications of their action, they hand over their rightful King to the Romans. The irony continues, in fact it is now a double irony, for by mocking word and deed Roman and Jew call him king and saviour, which are in fact his rightful titles and give him the insignia of royalty, a robe and a crown.

Mark appears to have written his Gospel for a Roman readership. The Romans had taken over crucifixion from the Persians and used it to execute only those they most despised. On his cross Jesus asks in agony why God has forsaken him. Yet it is in such a setting that the very centurion in command of the crucifixion party confesses him to be Son of God!

So he is dead (note the emphasis in the last few verses of chapter 15), and the tomb is shut. But the Gospel contains sixteen chapters, not just fifteen! The promise of resurrection is gloriously fulfilled and at the end of the book Mark shows us, as Luke also does at his Gospel's end and at the beginning of the Acts of the Apostles, his ascent to the kingly place of universal Lordship (cf. 12:35-37; 14:62). So we see that Jesus is supremely relevant for all subsequent history, and his apostles are sent out to the ends of the earth with that message, while he provides living evidence of his own unconquered and unconquerable life.

Mark 16:9-20 is a passage not found in all manuscripts, and in some a different, shorter ending is given. Whether by Mark or from some other hand, however, the familiar ending certainly appears to be an authentic product of the apostolic age and thus a reliable witness to the facts.[13]

We can see the great value of this Gospel of Mark both for evangelism and for the teaching of Christians in the city of Rome. The picture of the strong Son of God and mighty Saviour would have an immediate appeal to the Romans, for they placed a high premium on authority and power and respected those who demonstrated them.

It might seem however that all this would be negated by the fact that Jesus was executed under Roman authority and by the method of crucifixion, for this was reserved for slaves and the worst of criminals. This is a salutary reminder to Christian preachers and to Christian witnesses generally, that in our declaration of the gospel we may be able to find points of contact in the minds and hearts of non-Christians, but also that there is bound to be a confrontational factor. Significantly a major climax point in the Gospel is the confession of Jesus as Son of God by the very Roman centurion who commanded the crucifixion party (15:39).

The Gospel of Matthew

Matthew's account of the facts follows the same general pattern as Mark, but he adds a lot of detail. It is very clear that he wrote with Jewish readers especially in mind. This explains why his Gospel was the favourite one in the early church when there were more Jewish in proportion to Gentile Christians than there have ever been since.

For a Jew, if you wanted to prove a person's right to kingship, as also to priesthood, it was important to know his family tree, for these two offices were restricted to those of the Judaean Davidic line and the Levitical Aaronic line respectively. Accordingly, Matthew starts by giving the genealogy of Jesus, and it is not surprising that he follows this with the story of his birth, in which Joseph is called 'son of David' (1:20). The birth of Jesus was a virgin birth, but this astounding fact would not have caused genealogical problems, for what was important was the acceptance of Jesus into Joseph's family which found confirmation when Joseph gave him a name (1:25).

The Jews would want to be quite sure that someone who claimed to be the Christ really did match up to the Old Testament prophecies, and so Matthew gives us a great many of these, especially in his first four chapters. These chapters might well make a deep impression on a Jewish reader with any degree of open-mindedness.

Chapter 2 shows a strong geographical interest. In it the story moves from the (undefined) east to Jerusalem and from there to Bethlehem, down into Egypt and finally to Nazareth. This town was in Galilee, the district where so much of the ministry of Jesus was to take place.

Unlike Mark, Matthew follows the account of the baptism of Jesus with the story of his temptation[14], in which his Messianic vocation was put to the test. In the story too the use by him of the Old Testament and its misuse by Satan figure prominently. After all, much of the controversy in which Jesus was to become involved centred in the question of the right interpretation of the Old Testament. Perhaps there is a hint here that its misuse emanated from Satan.

Soon comes the great Sermon on the Mount in chapters 5 to 7. No doubt many Jews at the time Matthew was writing would have suspected that Christians did not really take the Old Testament Law seriously. What this sermon shows so clearly is that in one respect at least Jesus took it more seriously than anybody else had ever done. He showed its demands to be extremely far-reaching and inward, for it dealt not only with conduct but with the heart and so with the character from which conduct arises. Among other themes, the sermon has much to say about hypocrisy and in it Jesus encourages direct, simple-hearted prayer. It ends with an emphasis on the vital importance of building life on his teaching.

The amazement of the crowds is recorded by Matthew. What amazed them was not simply the teaching itself but the authority with which Jesus taught, for, unlike the teachers of the law, he did not depend on the authority of earlier rabbis (7:28,29). The Jews of New Testament times were born into a culture where the teacher was highly regarded. This is not surprising as their religion and their culture can neither be separated nor understood apart, and a book, the Old Testament, was in fact the basis of their whole way of life. As the Gospel goes on, we begin to realise that its author has given us much more of the teaching of Jesus than Mark, much of it cast in the form of the parable. This form was culturally familiar as it was often employed by the rabbis, the religious teachers of that era.

On the assumption that the Gospel was written by the apostle Matthew, its author was a tax-collector (9:9). This sort of work calls for gifts of organisation and a 'pigeon-hole' mind, especially in those working for such able organisers as the Romans. We can well imagine that they would require financial information to be well presented. We expect then to find the Gospel material well ordered, and we are not disappointed. In fact, Jesus' teaching is largely to be found in five special sections, each concluding with some such phrase as 'when Jesus had finished saying these things' (7:28; 11:1; 13:53; 19:1; 26:1). One of these teaching sections (chapter 13), consists entirely of parables, all of them focusing on the theme of the kingdom of heaven, God's reign.

Just as in Mark's Gospel, the centre of interest here is never simply in the teaching of Jesus but rather in his person. Notice, for instance, three places in chapter 12 where Matthew shows Jesus claiming successively that he is greater than the Sabbath (v. 8), than Jonah (v. 41) and Solomon (v. 42). After reading this chapter, the Jewish reader might well ask who this is that claims to be greater than one of the most revered of God's institutions, one of his prophets and the most magnificent of all the kings of David's divinely instituted and divinely supported line? What is so staggering in the teaching of Jesus about himself is not any one particular claim, although many of these are stupendous in their implications but the combination of them – one person with so many great roles to fulfil!

Because there is so much teaching and many an additional event recorded, this Gospel is half as long again as Mark, but even so it can be read through in less than two hours. Chapters 26 and 27 present the closing events of his life in fuller form than in any of the other Gospels and form the basis for Bach's great St. Matthew Passion.

As we have seen, Matthew wrote for Jews. Like all the early Christians, however, he belonged to a church which had burst the confines of Judaism, and was going out in eager mission to the whole world. So his Gospel ends with the great commission of Christ to eleven Jews to take the good news to every nation.

The Gospel of Luke

Luke, himself a Gentile (that is, a non-Jew)[15] and a member of Paul's evangelistic team[16], appears to have written especially for his fellow-Greeks. His Gospel begins with a formal introduction in classical style which would make the Greek reader realise he had opened a book that aimed to give serious treatment to a serious theme. This would condition him to read with attention, just as the genealogical reference at the start of Matthew would attract the attention of a Jew and, as we shall see, the Prologue to the Gospel of John would interest religious Jew and philosophical Greek alike.

After the first five verses, though, there comes a great stylistic change, the greatest to be found in the New Testament. Luke now enables his readers to enter imaginatively into the fascinating biblical world and to get the feel of it, for there is almost an Old Testament atmosphere about his presentation of the family circle of Jesus. There are strong resemblances particularly to the opening chapters of 1 Samuel, and the poetic utterances of praise Luke records would not be out of place in the Book of Psalms. Luke gives us information not only about the circumstances of the birth of Jesus, complementing Matthew's account, but also of the birth of his predecessor, John the Baptist. At the start of chapter 2 the wider world, dominated by Rome, is glimpsed as the backcloth to the nativity scenes. It comes even more fully into view at the opening of the third chapter.

The Greeks were fascinated by *homo sapiens*. It was a Greek, Protagoras, who said, 'Man is the measure of all things.' Here then is a man indeed, fulfilling all the ideals not simply of the Greeks, but even, far more demandingly, of God himself (3:22; 9:35). When in chapter 3 Luke gives the family tree of Jesus, he does not link him just with David, the father of the Messiah's tribe in Judah, and Abraham, the father of the Jewish race, as Matthew had done, but with Adam, the first human being. In this way he gave Jesus a strong human, and, indeed, universal significance.

The Gospels are not really quite like modern biographies. Their purpose is to tell the good news of Jesus, not to record all the main events of his life, although obviously everything about him would fascinate both writers and readers. Mark gives only the last three and a half years of that life, with a third of his material devoted to his final week. In this way we 'get the message' that his sufferings, death and resurrection are of supreme importance for the good news. Luke too concentrates on the climax of the story. Nevertheless he is more like a biographer than any of the other evangelists. For instance, no other Gospel writer tells us about the childhood of Jesus, with the evidence he showed in one revealing incident that he was conscious of a special relationship with God (2:41-52). Luke also is alone in telling us that Jesus was thirty when his ministry started (3:23).

Another human touch is to be found in the frequent references to prayer (3:21; 5:16; 6:12, etc.). Only a human being prays, and his or her prayer is in itself a confession of dependence. So the humanity of Jesus was not play-acting but a life of real dependence on God.

He was, however, as Luke shows, far more than a man, even a most exceptional man. At his birth, the angel told the shepherds that he was 'Christ the Lord' (2:11). Luke uses this term 'Lord'[17]over and over again in his narrative in application to this man. When used by the Greeks in forms of address to a person, it simply indicates recognition of a higher status without necessarily indicating how high that was, although the context will often show that. When used in the narrative framework of the Gospel, however, it showed the estimate and attitude of the writer, not just of the recorded speakers. Its use by Greek-speaking Jews was highly significant, for they employed it[18] to translate Yahweh, the awesome personal name of God. It is therefore Luke's application of it to Jesus in the narrative framework of his Gospel (in 7:13; 10:1, etc.) which is so significant, for, although a Greek, his mind was steeped in the Old Testament. The implication of this use of it is quite clear. This man was none other than the great God who had revealed himself to his people throughout Old Testament history.

If he was so great, his significance for human beings could not be confined to the people of Israel. Luke was the companion of Paul on some of his missionary travels in Gentile lands and so it is not surprising that we are made aware of the interest of Jesus in non-Jews (4:24-30; 7:1-5, etc.) and especially in the half-breed Samaritans, so disliked by the Jews (10:33ff.; 17:16).

All the Gospels show us the compassion of Jesus. In Mark, for instance, his miracles are so often acts of compassion as well as of power (e.g. Mark 1:41; 6:34; 8:2). Although the actual word occurs less frequently in Luke than in Matthew or Mark, the fact is just as eloquently presented and he shows the great care of Jesus for people without high status in the world of his day, such as women (8:2,3; 7:36-50; 23:27-29) and children (10:21; 18:15-17; 19:41-44). The poor find significant mention (e.g. 4:18; 6:20; 14:13), and he highlights the warnings of Jesus about the dangers of riches (6: 24,25; 8:14; 12:13-21, 33, etc.). Yet it is Luke who tells of the conversion of Zaccheus (19:1-9), who, although very wealthy, would have been despised by the people as a tax-collector who worked for the Romans.

Luke was a doctor and it is noticeable that he often gives more specific information about the diseases healed by Jesus than do the other Gospel-writers, For instance, he says not merely that a certain man was a leper but that he was 'covered with leprosy' (5:12) and later that a man was 'suffering from dropsy' (14:2).

Many of the parables recorded by Luke alone are highly memorable, such as the Good Samaritan (10:25-37) and the Prodigal Son (15:11-32). The concentration on the teaching given by Jesus is not quite so marked as it is in Matthew but is considerably more than in Mark.

The name 'Jerusalem' occurs with some frequency in this Gospel, and particularly in what is known as the 'Travel Document' (9:51-19:28), in which Jesus constantly has his face towards that city. Luke uses the name as frequently as the other three evangelists combined, and in this way focuses our attention on this city as the

great place of destiny for Jesus (e.g. in 9:31, 51; 13:34; 18:31),
and also for the Jews as determined by their attitude to him (13:34;
21:20-24).

As in all the Gospels, disproportionate space is given to the last
week of the life of Jesus, and the account of the resurrection appearances includes the walk to Emmaus (24:13-35), described even
by the sceptic, Renan, as the world's most beautiful story.

The Gospel of John

John's Gospel is a literary marvel. Its vocabulary is so small and
its style so simple that quite a newcomer to the study of Greek
finds to his delight that he can make some sense of it. But its simple language enshrines the deepest of truths. Those who have read
C. S. Lewis' Narnia books as children and enjoyed them greatly as
stories have sometimes returned later to discover much deeper
meaning in them. The Gospel of John is like that – although more,
much more so – and it is not fiction!

This book presents us with the same Jesus as the other three,
but its approach is different in some ways. What then are the differences between the Synoptic Gospels and John?

John does not select for his record some events which certainly
appear to be important in other Gospels. For instance he omits the
birth, baptism, transfiguration, institution of the Lord's Supper and
the agony in Gethsemane, all dealt with quite fully in Matthew
and Luke. On the other hand, he includes much material not found
elsewhere, such as important teaching recorded in chapters 13 to
16, given by Jesus to his disciples just prior to his death.

There are virtually no parables, if we choose to call the Good
Shepherd and the Vine in chapters 10 and 15 'allegories'. This is
certainly an appropriate term for them, for more of the details are
interpreted spiritually by Jesus than is the case with most of the
parables.

Also there are fewer miracles, although this fact is offset by the
great importance attached to the ones John does record, This shows
how strongly Christological this Gospel is, for John treats the miracles of Jesus, not simply as wonders, but as 'signs' of his divine
Sonship (2:11; 20:30,31)

The titles we have found in the other Gospels are all here, for 'Christ', 'Son of Man', 'Son of God' and many another may be discovered in the first chapter, as well as later in the book. In a book in which we are constantly aware of the universal significance of Jesus, it is important to note that the Jewish Messianic theme finds place in its first chapter (1:41-49) and also, in a Samaritan context, in chapter 4 (4: 25,26), while the Son of Man title occurs quite frequently and runs through much of the Gospel (1:51; 3:13,14; 5:27; 6:27, 53, 62; 8:28; 12:33,34; 13:31).

The term 'Son of God' is used in all the Gospels. This term plus passages where God is referred to as the Father and Jesus as the Son, with the clear implication that the relationship between them is unique, are extremely frequent in the Gospel of John. It is very significant however that there is a passage in the Synoptics (Matthew 11:27, with its parallel in Luke 10:22) where its unique content is spelt out for us. Incidentally the view that the terms 'Son of God' and 'Son' have a different origin and history, canvassed by some scholars, is most unlikely.[19]

There can be no doubt that the Jews did not see the use of this term by Jesus simply as an alternative for 'Messiah'. In using it he stressed the intimacy he had with the Father, an intimacy which pre-dated his coming into the world (17:5). The theme merits close and detailed study, but a glance at any of several chapters in John (5, 8, 10, 14 or 17) will open a doorway into eternity and the very nature of God. On one occasion, Jesus declared that he was one with the Father in power, which implies that his nature was divine in the fullest sense of that word, for only God can have omnipotence (10:22-33).

We found in Mark, chapters 2 and 3, that Jesus was often in controversy with the religious leaders of the Jews, and this is a marked feature of the Gospel of John. So often these debates turn on the question as to who he is and what his prerogatives as Son of God are. Especially significant is the series of 'I am' sayings where Jesus uses the great 'I am' affirmation of God in Exodus 3:14. No wonder this produced such strong reactions from his Jewish listeners.[20]

So perhaps the main difference between John and the Synoptics lies in the profound theme of the divine Sonship of Jesus. It is not that this theme is absent from them, for it is not, but rather that it is developed at greater length and with its implications drawn out more fully than in them.

This is why John is sometimes referred to as the 'theological gospel', although the term is not altogether appropriate if restricted to this book, for, as scholars have increasingly realised, all the Gospels, even simple Mark[21], contain much more theology than was appreciated at one time.

John's Gospel, like the other three, ends with a cross and an empty tomb. In this Gospel just as much as in the others we are sure the man we are seeing is real flesh and blood like ourselves, for he is tired (4:6), is deeply moved, even to tears (11:33, 35, 38), and is gripped by an awful thirst in the midst of Calvary's agonies (19:28).

John has in fact whetted the appetite of his reader by his great prologue (1:1-18). The first chapter contains many familiar titles for Jesus, but here is an unfamiliar one. He is the Word – the Logos of God. The reader may be a Jew to whom the Word of the Lord is God creating (cf. Gen. 1 and Ps. 33) and revealing, or he may be a Gentile who is used to the philosopher's use of this term to designate the real, inner, divine meaning of things. Both would expect to find in this book the disclosure of ultimate truth. They are brought up through its chapters to the cross where they see 'truth ... on the scaffold', and then to the upper room where, with Thomas, they fall at the feet of the crucified yet living Christ and cry in faith, 'My Lord and my God!' (20:28). This Gospel challenges all of us to a like response of faith.

References
1. Based on Greek and meaning 'those that see together'.
2. Questions concerning the authorship and destination of each of the Gospels and other matters of background are dealt with (succinctly) in the articles on each Gospel in *The Illustrated Bible Dictionary,* Leicester, IVP, 1980, (popularly) in Donald .Bridge, *Why Four Gospels?*, Christian Focus, and (in detail) in Donald Guthrie, *New Testament Introduction*, Leicester, IVP, 1990, Chapters 1-6.
3. See Donald Guthrie, *New Testament Introduction,* Chapter 5, for full discussion of the Synoptic Problem.

4. There is a brief but helpful comment on this in Ralph P. Martin, *Mark, Evangelist and Theologian*, Exeter, Paternoster, 1972, p. 27, and a fuller note in C.E.B. Cranfield, *The Gospel of Mark* (Cambridge Greek Testament Commentary), Cambridge, CUP, 1963, *ad loc.*

5. C.H. Dodd, *According to the Scriptures*, London, Nisbet, 1952. The significance of this fact will be explored more fully in chapter 6.

6. cf. Isaiah 11:1ff. and in addition 42:1ff. and 61:1ff., both of which, although not specifically kingly references, are also applied to Jesus in the New Testament, e.g. in Matthew 12:18-21 and Luke 4:18,19.

7. The picture of the righteous peaceful rule of the future King in Isaiah 11:1-9 includes the animals, wild as well as domestic, at peace with each other and with humanity.

8. As indicated in 3:22,23, for in the Gospels evil spirits and demons are alternative designations.

9. 3:6. See the articles, 'Herod' and 'Herodians' by F.F. Bruce and J.W. Meiklejohn in J.D. Douglas, N. Hillyer (eds.), *IBD*, Vol. II, *ad loc.*

10. It has sometimes been held that Jesus was not referring to himself but to some other figure when using this phrase, but this would render many passages (e.g. Matt. 20:18) quite nonsensical. Also it has been suggested it meant little more than 'I' but this too is difficult to hold in view of the way the language and thought of Daniel 7:13,14 colours some of the sayings, especially the very important utterance in Mark 14:62.

11. There is a helpful note on the connection of Mark 9:1 to the Transfiguration narrative in C.E.B. Cranfield, *ad loc.*

12. See Hosea 9:10.

13. See Guthrie, *op. cit.* pp. 89-93.

14. For a detailed study of this, based on the Greek text, see B. Gerhardsson, *The Testing of God's Son (Matt. 4:1-11): an analysis of an early Christian midrash* (trans. J. Toy), Lund, Gleerup, 1966.

15. A clear inference from Colossians 4:11,14.

16. Passages in the Acts of the Apostles where Luke, the author, uses the first person plural, the so-called 'we-passages' are usually reckoned to reflect the presence of Luke at the events recorded.

17. Greek *kurios*.

18. For instance in the Septuagint (LXX), the main Greek rendering of the Old.Testament into Greek, employed in the Jewish synagogues in Greek-speaking lands.

19. See I.H. Marshall, *op. cit.*, p. 114.

20. See especially John 8:57-59.

21. This is well demonstrated in Martin, *op. cit.*, Chapters 4 and 5.

Chapter 2

THE HISTORICAL ISSUE

What the issue is

The Gospels are documents which raise some questions of great importance for the thoughtful reader, and these need to be addressed.

The reader may find himself or herself asking what kind of claims the Gospel writers are making for their documents. Are they claiming to be writing historical truth or theological truth or both? In other words, are they telling us that certain events happened or rather that certain ideas matter? Or is this a false posing of alternatives?

Let us note first of all that they certainly give every appearance of reckoning their documents to be records of real historical events. When Luke in his Gospel introduced the story of the birth of Jesus, he set him in his historical and geographical context (Luke 2:1-4).[1] It could be argued of course that Luke was a well educated man familiar with the wider world, and that he might be expected to have something of an historical interest. Yet, despite the amazing claims Christians make for Christ, not just Luke but each of the four Gospel writers simply narrates a sequence of events and conversation in an almost matter-of-fact style.

We note, for instance, the astounding simplicity of the words, 'they crucified him' (Mark 15:25; Luke 23:33; John 19:18), and 'when they had crucified him' (Matt. 27:35). What historical novelist could have resisted the temptation to make much of this simple yet dreadful fact?

Not only so, but despite their simple directness of style the Gospel writers clearly believed they were narrating the most important events ever to have happened in the world. The opening of Luke's third chapter is particularly significant from this point of view: He says, 'In the fifteenth year of the reign of Tiberius Caesar – when Pontius Pilate was governor of Judea, Herod tetrarch of Galilee, his brother Philip tetrarch of the region of Iturea and Traconitis, and Lysanias tetrarch of Abilene – during the high priesthood of Annas and Caiaphas, the word of God came to John son of Zechariah in the desert.'

In this passage Luke gathers together an impressive list of significant names. He begins with the emperor, the most important political figure in the known world, and then goes on to name the main secular officials in the area. Next comes Annas, who had been high priest and who was still regarded by the Jews as such, with great influence behind the scenes. Finally there was Caiaphas, his son-in-law, whom the Romans had installed as current high priest.

What is so striking, though, is that Luke mentions these eminent people only to draw attention away from them all to a tiny scrap of desert in a remote province of the great Roman empire. The activities of John the Baptist mattered more than all that these others were doing, because he was the herald of the Christ. They simply represented the stage setting for the action of really vital importance, but it needs to be specially noted that the setting is itself historical and so we can assume that for Luke the events which have that background are themselves historical.

Although the Gospels are of quite special importance to us, there is history elsewhere in the New Testament. Acts gives us the story of the first generation of church history. Significantly it was written by Luke, who, as we have seen, seems to have been particularly sensitive to the historical background of the life of Jesus. Just as some of the Old Testament books provide us with valuable historical information to enable us to understand the prophets better, so the Acts of the Apostles shows us the planting of several of the churches to which the Epistles were written.

The Epistles contain many reminders that they emerged from that history and were written to real groups and individuals with their own place in the story. For instance, in the Epistles to the Corinthians and to the Galatians, Paul makes quite a number of comments related to the establishment and growth of the churches to which they were written.[2]

The Book of the Revelation certainly shows an historical

interest. It has, of course, been variously interpreted, but it is clear enough that in it events on earth are looked at from the standpoint of heaven. It presents an awesome picture of the Lord Jesus Christ enthroned as supreme over the world's history and destiny. The book of destiny which is given to him (Rev. 5:1-7) contains many historical judgements, which come into view as its seals are opened.

If the evangelists, the Gospel writers, are claiming to be writing historical truth, can this claim be substantiated? Can we be sure that Jesus really was as they portray him and that the events they record in connection with him actually happened? Are all four equally reliable or even equally unreliable, and how can we know anyway?

These are important questions, and they have often been asked and answers to them sought and given. Sometimes however, beginning in the nineteenth century but increasingly in the twentieth century, the whole value of the search for authentic facts about Jesus has been doubted. Some have said that it is the theology, not the history, that matters, and that forms the main content of Christian preaching. Some have gone further still, asserting that at the end of the day Christianity is to be thought of essentially as an experience, something subjective which may be very precious and even life-transforming but which needs neither theological nor historical justification or support.

This last idea, in fact, has quite an appeal to many people as the twentieth century moves towards its close because it fits the cultural mood of our time in so many ways. People of our day, whether religious or otherwise, are preoccupied with personal experience. Surely though what matters is not whether an idea is culturally relevant but whether it is right!

How then do biblical history, Christian theology and my experience of Jesus relate to each other? Before we can answer this question properly of course we have to consider the nature of each of the three. We must start by exploring the character of history in general and of biblical history in particular and the whole issue of the relationship between history and theology and Christian experience. Some of these questions will occupy us in this chapter and others in chapters 4 and 15. So not until the end of this book will we be in a position to give full answers. Perhaps that will make it worth your while to read on!

The nature of history

The term 'history' is commonly used in two senses. It is used of the past facts themselves and it is also used of the historian's record and interpretation of those facts. Sometimes the unwieldy word 'historiography' is employed for the second in order to distinguish it from the first. It is with this second sense of the word that we are chiefly concerned, because, as we have already seen, the Gospels give every appearance of claiming to be records of historical facts.

Herodotus the Greek, who lived almost five hundred years before Christ, is often referred to as the father of history. The appropriateness of the title is open to question, for, on any arguable dating of the Old Testament books, some of the historical narratives of the Old Testament were written before his time. Herodotus wrote the story of the wars between Persia and Greece. It has become evident that these accounts were not completely accurate factually and that Herodotus knew they were not, for he sometimes recorded contradictory accounts of the same event. He was less concerned to check his sources than to write attractively. The major events however probably did happen much as he records them, but we can see in his works some elements of the later historical novel as well as authentic historical facts. We cannot however fault Herodotus too much as far as his approach is concerned, for he lacked models to follow.

Thucydides, who followed him, was much nearer to the historian as that term is normally understood. In him we find a concern for factual accuracy, an interest in the reliability of sources, and so on. Even he sometimes 'improved' the story by putting into the mouths of some of the characters speeches of the kind he would have expected them to say but could not be sure they actually did say. Despite this, however, his work is recognisably history as normally understood in modern times.

Thucydides certainly had considerable influence on later historians and it became their goal to produce accounts of the period in which they were interested which were as true to what actually happened as they could make them. This goal was pursued for many centuries, but in modern times important philosophical developments have taken place which have affected quite considerably the way historians look at their task.

Epistemology is that branch of philosophy which considers questions of knowledge and certainty. The epistemological views of Immanuel Kant (1724-1804) have had an immense influence on subsequent thought. Kant made a distinction between phenomena and noumena, between things as they appear to be and things as they really are. We live in a phenomenal world and Kant maintained that human knowledge cannot, with certainty, get behind phenomena to grasp noumena. We have to take the world, as it appears to us, on trust. We may ask ultimate questions and give speculative answers but we cannot make affirmations about noumena that can be conclusively proved.

Kant's point of view deeply influenced the subsequent history of thought in virtually every realm of human study, and humbler claims began to be made for results obtained in various disciplines. Eventually the general scepticism about certainty which his thought fostered affected the study of history, and historians came to the conclusion that absolute certainty about the past was unattainable.[3] They noted, for instance, that they had to use documents from the past in their search for the facts. Could they rely absolutely on the accuracy of their contents? All of them were written by fallible human beings and these were subject not only to the kind of factual inaccuracy from which none of us can completely escape, but also to the interpreting bias of the writers themselves.

An historian cannot escape the necessity for interpretation. For one thing, he must make a selection from the material that is available to him and that is itself a process of interpretation. In fact, the element of selection occurs already in the sources he uses. For instance, no historian could possibly write about everything that happened in connection with the Battle of Waterloo. He would not go to the trouble of telling us what Napoleon ate that day – unless, of course, he had reason for believing that he had severe indigestion and that this affected his tactical judgement in the conduct of the battle!

So then every historian is bound to select, but selection implies a point of view. If I make a selection of facts about a past event, what I write will not only tell you something about that event; it will also tell you something about me and what I consider to be important. This is why a history of the twentieth century by three writers, one a communist, one a fascist, and one who is neither, would be anything but identical, and the third is just as likely to have a bias of some kind as the first and the second.

The fact is, as Kant recognised, that we need to be fully aware of the role of the interpreting subject as well as of the interpreted object in all our discussion of knowledge in every realm, and that includes history.

It is only recently, with the emergence of what has come to be known as 'Post-Modernism'[4] that the 'Kantian captivity' of modern thought has shown signs of losing something of its grip. It is not so much because it has been answered intellectually, but rather that interest for 'Post-Moderns' has moved away from questions of intellectual certainty to those of personal experience and self-development.

The Post-Modern philosophy of Structuralism and movements that have developed from it or reacted against it have had had considerable influence in recent decades. Structuralists are interested in literature and in the way we communicate through it. The Deconstructionists,[5] whose views arose partly out of and partly in reaction against Structuralism, maintain that we should not think of reading as engaging with the meaning the writer intended but rather as wholly concerned with what I, the reader, make of what has been written. It means, in a sense, that an author who has written only one book has, in actuality, written books without number, for every reader will have a personal understanding of what he or she reads. It is sometimes said that no two members of a congregation hear the same sermon, for each interprets it in terms of his or her own experience. The Deconstructionist applies this same principle to literature.

Another factor has entered into the matter in modern times, and that is the tendency, especially among young people, to doubt the value of history. We cannot be certain of what actually happened in the past. So what? Does it really matter? Henry Ford is supposed to have said, 'History is bunk!' There are many today who would agree with him.

A major reason for this attitude would seem to be that those who take it suspect that history may be used as a means of bolstering tradition or the unthinking nationalism known as Jingoism. This rejection of history is regrettable. Certainly we may have to jettison much that has come down to us from the past, but there is also much of real value. After all, wisdom did not begin in the latter part of the twentieth century.

Many men and women who chose a career in politics often prepare for this by the study of law or else of philosophy and economics. Sir Winston Churchill however reckoned that it was most of all the study of history which was vital for a politician. There is of course some truth in the somewhat cynical comment that the most important thing we learn from history is that we learn nothing from history. On the other hand, it has been said with equal truth that the nation that has not learned from its history may have to repeat it.

As we shall see, history is even more important for theology than it is for politics.

The nature of Old Testament history as the literary heritage of the Gospel writers

No Christian who has thought about his or her faith at all can be satisfied with a total rejection of history. 'Christ died for our sins' is not simply a theological statement. It is also an historical one. Even Rudolf Bultmann, who in his day was described as 'the most radical critic alive', and who doubted the historicity of so much in the Gospels, held to the essential historicity of the crucifixion.

As we need to ask questions about the nature of biblical history, it will be best for us not to concentrate simply on the Gospels but to take in also the historical material in the Old Testament. After all, the Gospel writers knew this well and it is reasonable to expect that it will have influenced the way they went about their own task.

The historical writers of the Old Testament certainly give no indication that they were seeking to do anything other than record and interpret what actually happened. They were not historical novelists and their minds were certainly not possessed by Kantian or Deconstructionist ideas. They recorded what they believed to be actual past events and they gave them a theological interpretation. For instance, the writer of the Books of Kings gives an appraisal of the reigns of the various kings and in each case the verdict is theologically based, for it is concerned with their religious outlook and practice and the religious encouragement, for good or ill, that they gave their subjects.[6]

The material in the Old Testament which is historical in form is very extensive. It includes Genesis, much of Exodus to Deuteronomy and all the books from Joshua to Esther. Not only so, but many of the psalms (e.g. Pss. 105, 106 and 136) make copious reference to historical events. The prophets all pronounce God's word in relation to the history of their own period, and they make a fair amount of reference to earlier events. This means that, with the exception of the Wisdom literature (chiefly Job, Proverbs and Ecclesiastes plus some psalms), every book of the Old Testament shows a strong historical interest.

This in itself must be significant. It means that the writers of these books shared a common conviction that the story of their nation was important, and not only so but that God had a distinct interest in and involvement in that story. This theological element, however, causes some readers to ask whether or not this can be reckoned truly historical writing. What can we say to this?

We saw earlier that the character of an historical document depended on the outlook of the writer. It is of course generally recognised that there is a distinction, for instance, between political, social and economic history. For a very long time political history almost dominated the whole field of historical research and writing, but this situation has altered considerably. There ought then to be more readiness to recognise religious and theological history as valid forms of historical writing.

To explore this a little, we will consider the allegation sometimes made that the author of the Books of Kings shows lack of historical judgement in giving far more space to the reign of Ahab[7] than to

that of his father Omri.[8] Omri was so important internationally
that for some time after his death the Assyrians referred to Israel
as Omri Land, and his reign completely overshadowed that of his
son. It is said that this biblical writer obviously had little historical
sense of proportion. This is not however true, for he was writing a
religious and not a political history, and the religious events of
Ahab's reign, particularly the struggle between his consort Jezebel
and her Baalism on the one hand, and Elijah, the prophet of the
Lord, on the other, were much more important than those of Omri's
reign when viewed from the standpoint of religion.

Are a religious history and a theological history identical? No,
for although they are related there is an important distinction
between them. A religious history gives an account of the development of the religious life of a people. Inevitably it will make judgements concerning the relative importance of events but it will not
necessarily pronounce judgements of value on the actual religious
ideas and practices it records. Theological history, however, is
somewhat different for it will make theological judgements.

The theology is in the mind of the historian himself and it
informs his valuations. Because the writers of the Old Testament
historical books record facts about the religion of the people who
appear in them, these books may be described as religious history,
but they are more, for the writers themselves have a theology and
they estimate, they praise or blame, on the basis of that theology.
They believe that the God of Israel is the true God and that all
other so-called gods are false, so that it is wrong to worship or
promote the worship of them.

Is such a history likely to be at all reliable in its record of events?
There is no compelling reason why it should not be, especially as
the Old Testament historians were worshippers of the One who
revealed himself as the God of truth and as a Hater of lies.

The historical material in the Old Testament comes across to
us as sober in tone. Certainly it records miracles, and it is well-
known that various nations have attributed miracles to those in
their past whom they reckoned great. A careful survey of the
miraculous element in the Old Testament is, however, most
reassuring. For one thing, miracles are not scattered liberally

throughout the books or attributed to all the major figures of the past. Only in the stories of Moses, of Elijah and Elisha, and of Daniel and his friends do they occur with any frequency. It is particularly noteworthy that they are completely absent from the story of Abraham, who was greatly esteemed by later generations as the founder of the Jewish race.

There is other strong evidence of the integrity of the Old Testament historians. An observer of the current scene in Western Europe and America may well be troubled by the tendency of the media to idealise heroes and vilify villains and so to produce stereotypes. For instance, a man who has committed a notorious crime is unlikely to have some act of personal benevolence mentioned in the press. Inevitably the image that readers gain both of the 'goodies' and the 'baddies' is bound to be something of a caricature.

How different is the Old Testament! A list of the more important and respected figures in the history will certainly give great prominence to Abraham, Jacob, Moses, David, Solomon and Hezekiah, yet the historians record serious failure on the part of each of these. There is certainly no attempt at idealisation. The Book of Genesis, which underlines the covenant promises of God to Abraham, Isaac and Jacob to such an extent that 'the God of Abraham, Isaac and Jacob' became an important title of Israel's God, actually gives a little more space to Joseph than to any of those three and his name does not occur in that divine title. Arguably too he is the finest person in the book in terms of his character. On the other side, it is clear that Manasseh was one of the worst, possibly even the worst, of all the kings of Judah, and yet his ultimate repentance is fully recognised in 2 Chronicles.[9]

What makes this even more significant is the nature of the God worshipped by the people of the Old Testament, including the historians themselves. The religion of the Old Testament is ethical monotheism. Its God cared deeply about morality because his own nature was morally perfect. This means that the character of God's people mattered a great deal to him. Yet not only the people at large but even their religious heroes are shown 'warts and all'. This means that the theological interpretation to be found in the books actually becomes historically reassuring rather than the opposite, for it interprets the story from the standpoint of the God of truth who hates lies with all his being and assures his people that every lie will be punished.

Every historian has to have sources and this is no less true of the Old Testament historians. Some of them make explicit reference to them.[10] This implies that the original readers could actually check the books against these sources. This means that these Old Testament historians go beyond some modern ones in the provision they make for the reader when they write for the popular market.

All this does not, of course, guarantee the historical infallibility of the Old Testament books, but it does at least mean that they ought to be considered worthy of serious consideration as reliable historical documents.

We should not give the impression that these books are without problems for us. For instance, there are some difficulties which arise from the apparently large numbers to be found in the Books of Chronicles, but good reasonable explanations, supportive of the reliability of the author, have been persuasively advanced.[11] If there were no problems at all, might this not itself be a cause for concern? A judge, confronted with evidence taken from several witnesses and which fits together just too easily, may begin to suspect that it has been manufactured.

The nature of the Gospel history

This Old Testament history was the literary heritage of the men who wrote the New Testament, including the four Gospel writers. Here too we find the same 'ring of truth' as in the Old Testament.

On any understanding of the course of early church history, Peter is an important figure, and the apostles as a group were the respected leaders of the early church. Yet the Gospels give us anything but an idealised picture of these, and most of all of Peter. In fact, the Gospel which spells out the faults of Peter more fully than any of the others is Mark and there is good reason for believing that this Gospel was written on the basis of material actually provided by Peter himself. The evidence of Papias, an early Christian writer, is of importance in this matter, although his view is supported by evidence internal to the Gospel![12]

This highlights the absolute perfection of Christ's character in a particularly striking way. The faults of Abraham, of Moses, David and Peter are all evident in the material that has come down to us, but where are the faults of Jesus? There are none.[13] Instead there is a picture of a man of the purest holiness and yet at the same time amazing outgoing compassion. We are more inclined to take this seriously when we see this witness of the Gospels against the background of hero failure which is so clearly presented both in them and in the Old Testament.

All four Gospels make compelling reading. They were read by great numbers of Christians for hundreds of years before they were seriously questioned as to their historical veracity. Now this is remarkable, for they are not carbon copies of each other. Matthew and Luke both give much more detail from the teaching of Jesus than does Mark, and, in many cases, not the same details, while John does not even mention some important events which occur in the other three but gives much distinctive material not found in the others. Yet countless Christians, and in fact the church of Christ as such, have accepted them all as authentic.

The historical reliability of the Gospels has however been questioned quite radically in modern times. This questioning goes back to the eighteenth century intellectual movement known as the Enlightenment, which gave great importance to reason. According to Enlightenment thinkers and those who were affected by them, every idea, every theory, every doctrine, must be submitted to rational tests, and, if it fails these, is to be rejected.

David Strauss (1808-1874), whose historical scepticism was somewhat anticipated in the previous century by the deist Hermann Reimarus (1694-1768), applied the principles of the Enlightenment and also the philosophical concepts of Hegel to the life of Jesus as recorded in the Gospels. His book, *The Life of Jesus, Critically Examined*, published in two parts in 1835 and in 1836,[14] caused something of a stir. In it he dismissed the Gospels as practically worthless. His main reason for this judgement was that in them historical fact and unhistorical myth are hopelessly intermingled, although he did admit that there is some historical basis to the overall framework of the life of Jesus recorded in them.

How much direct influence Strauss had on biblical scholars is debatable, but many who assumed there was some truth in the outlook he had promoted, began to seek for a solid historical basis for a life of Jesus. They scrutinised the Gospel records in a search for reliable material. This 'quest for the historical Jesus' [15] produced a flood of books on the life of Jesus which showed no sign of abating until the twentieth century was well under way. Few of these 'lives' were based on full acceptance of the gospel facts but they varied in the extent to which they expressed doubt or reservations about them. It has been remarked of New Testament scholars of this period that 'by their lives of Jesus you shall know them'!

Are the views of Strauss dead now? Rudolf Bultmann, whose work on the Gospels had a major effect and who began to publish it just after the First World War,[16] held, just as thoroughly as Strauss, the mythical character of much of the material in the Gospels. Even though he differed from the earlier writer in having a more positive outlook on the value of this material, he nevertheless dubbed it mythological rather than historical. Although Bultmann is now dead, his influence is not.

In some ways the Bultmann school might appear to be the Strauss school seeking a more acceptable face, although, to do it justice, it shows an interest in finding a basis for Christian preaching and experience that Strauss would have regarded as valueless. It is important to note though that many of Bultmann's most able pupils reacted eventually against his extreme historical scepticism. Ernst Kasemann, in a lecture given in 1953 at Marburg University in the presence of many of Bultmann's former pupils, argued the need for a stronger historical basis for faith.[17] This began what came to be known as 'the new quest for the historical Jesus'.[18]

The Post-Bultmannians have proceeded slowly and cautiously in their reconstruction of the history of Jesus of Nazareth. There is still a widespread tendency to regard much in the Gospels as due to the faith of the church that Jesus had triumphed over death, whatever the actual grounds for that faith were. This faith, it is often maintained, was read back into their perception of the life and teaching of Jesus and so coloured the Gospel presentation, making it very difficult to know what really happened.

George R. Beasley-Murray has protested against this. He says:

> The distinction between pre- and post-Easter traditions of sayings of Jesus is the primary issue of historical criticism in the quest for recovering the authentic proclamation of Jesus. In practice, of course, that depends on one's choice of criteria of authenticity. Experience has shown that that is a highly subjective decision, leading to some extraordinary variations in reconstructions of the historical Jesus .... How often one has heard a saying of Jesus in the Gospels dismissed without adequate reason, or simply because it 'suits' the post-resurrection situation of the early Christians! It seems to be assumed that the disciples' experiences of the presence of the risen Lord were bound to transform their recollection of the teaching of Jesus in the direction of changing its content. On the contrary, is it not altogether more likely that those experiences threw a flood of light on that teaching, so that what before was mystifying now became crystal clear? And would that not apply above all to utterances of Jesus concerning the nature of his mission from God?[19]

He is surely right.

With the rise of what is known as Redaction Criticism, a further factor beyond the general faith of the early church has been posited, the outlook of the particular redactor or editor who actually put the material together in any one Gospel, each of whom was thought to have given the material his own special slant.

Now we may of course recognise an element of truth in this. The Gospels were not written with exactly the same readers in view. A modern preacher will alter his emphasis and his selection of material somewhat from one audience to another because of his knowledge of that audience, while all the time seeking to remain true to the basic facts of the gospel.

If however such a modern preacher is biblically orientated and a person of integrity, he will react with horror and denial to the accusation that he is doing violence to the material. Many of us know of churches where the message is proclaimed in a way that is culturally sensitive and relevant with no loss or distortion of the biblical content. Can we not expect the same to be true of the Gospel writers? David Wells is surely right when he says, 'If the presence of faith in the early Christian writers was to tilt the scales in any direction, it would seem more likely that it would move them toward truthfulness than toward fabrication, given the high morality of that faith.'[20]

Now there is no doubt that some readers will be happy to accept the historicity of the Synoptic Gospels, at least in general terms, while feeling more uneasy about the Gospel of John. It is not just the fact that important Synoptic facts are missing and that there is so much material peculiar to this Gospel. This can be explained if the author in fact knew the other Gospels and felt there was no need to repeat much of what they contained. It is more the fact that theological themes, and especially Christological ones, appear to dominate this Gospel to a much greater extent and, perhaps most of all, that his divine Sonship so dominates the teaching of Jesus recorded there.

It is not possible to deal with this issue in any detail here.[21] It should be asked though if we accept the right of each Gospel writer to make his own distinctive selection of authentic material from the life and teaching of Jesus? Surely we cannot deny any of them this! We then go on to recall that the title 'Son of God' occurs in all the Gospels and also the fact that the use Jesus made of it was unique. From these facts, it would seem natural that a Gospel should be written in which this title, so exalted and so important for understanding our Lord's view of himself, should be given considerable prominence.

Recently, a group of researchers and writers known as the Jesus Seminar, founded in 1985, has achieved notoriety, especially in the USA, because of media attention and reports on their findings and especially because of their joint production, *The Five Gospels: What Did Jesus Really Say?*, published in 1993.[22] The work focuses on the teaching attributed to Jesus in the canonical Gospels plus the apocryphal *Gospel of Thomas*. It is evident, not only that their work is informed by a considerable amount of historical scepticism, but also that they regard this apocryphal Gospel as quite the equal of the canonical Gospels and in certain ways as much superior to them.

Known earlier only from a few fragments, *The Gospel of Thomas* in its complete form was discovered and then translated and published in 1959. It is however extremely unlikely that it is a first century document. Ben Witherington III says of it: 'We must remember where the *Gospel of Thomas* was found – at Nag Hammadi in Egypt, along with a very eclectic set of ancient documents. If one can judge a document by some of the company it keeps, there is little encouragement to see *Thomas* as providing access to the early Jesus tradition or as giving us many clues about the authentic Jesus tradition.'[23] Although some of the Jesus Seminar members date it around AD 30-60, it has to be said that there is no firm evidence for any date before the middle of the second century. Many of the alleged sayings of Jesus in it clearly reflect the influence of the second century Gnostic heresies while others certainly look as if they have been influenced by the canonical Gospels.

The Five Gospels prints the text of the four canonical Gospels and the *Gospel of Thomas* with colour-coding indicating varying degrees of probability in relation to the authenticity of the sayings of Jesus, from red for certainty through pink and grey to black for those most unlikely to be authentic. Only 18% of the sayings are marked red and, most amazingly, these include only one from the Gospel of Mark, that is Mark 12:17. The coding given to any particular saying was decided by a system of voting within the Seminar.

What is noticeable is that the Seminar is dominated by researchers of a very radical type and that their anti-supernaturalist and sceptical approach to early Christianity means that anything savouring, for instance, of genuine prophecy by Jesus about the future is ruled out automatically. This is a kind of obscurantism which is not open to anything which does not fit a naturalistic world-view.

A symposium critical of the Seminar and entitled *Jesus under Fire*[24] has been published, and this includes a devastating critique of the Seminar's methodology by Craig L. Blomberg. It is strongly recommended for reading on this topic.

A further feature of recent study of the Gospels has been a great interest in the first century Galilean background to Jesus. This is being pursued by a variety of scholars, from the strongly sceptical to the strongly conservative. This includes some Jewish writers, including Geza Vermes, who, although now a Jew by religion as well as race, started life as a Roman Catholic.[25] This is a development to be welcomed, but a number of quite different pictures of Jesus are being given, often through a concentration on certain features of the Gospel presentation to the neglect or discounting of others. It is important always that the methodology of those who are pursuing this quest should be critically estimated.[26]

It needs to be said that scholars of the reductionist type are not the only people working in the field. In fact, a great deal of scholarship now exists which vindicates the essential historical accuracy of the Gospel records. Although these fundamental documents of the Christian faith are 'Gospels', and so are really a kind of preaching, they contain a great deal of evidence to support their general historical trustworthiness. A book like this cannot give a detailed survey of this big field, but it is easily accessible.[27]

Particularly since the Second World War, this movement has grown at an increasing rate and needs now to be taken much more into account than it has been. For instance, the television series shown some years ago and entitled *Jesus: the Verdict* proceeded on the quite erroneous assumption that the findings of the sceptical school were almost beyond challenge, which is certainly not the case.

Some readers of this book may, however, be asking whether belief in the historical truth of the Gospels has to wait on the findings of research? If so, how was such belief possible during periods when historical scepticism had great influence and was most plausible?

The answer to this is of real importance. Evidence for the accuracy and trustworthiness of the Gospels is certainly of value. It may clear the ground for faith; it may also help to strengthen faith which already exists; it does not however create faith. The New Testament teaches that it is the Holy Spirit whose work brings men and women to faith in Jesus.[28] What research and the arguments of apologists can and does do, however, is to show that such a faith is not in fact unreasonable.

The Jesus of history and the Christ of faith

For about a century and a half there has been a great deal of debate about the relationship between Jesus as he really was and what the Christian church believes him to be.

If we approach the Gospels with the Kantian philosophy in mind (and many people operate with this kind of philosophy who have never even heard of Kant) then we will doubt the possibility of real certainty. If we are Deconstructionists we will say that it does not even matter. What does matter, they say, is not what Jesus was like but what my reading of the Gospels does to me.

Are the Gospels, with their historical emphasis, really all that important for Christian faith? They certainly are, if we believe it to be important that our faith should be authentically apostolic. Of course, there have been many over the years who have held views of Jesus which have paid scant attention to what the Gospels, or indeed the New Testament as a whole, teaches. Jesus has been viewed as a spiritualist medium or a kind of Buddhist Bodhissatva, on the one hand, or as a mere moral teacher on the other. Paul showed great concern for the preaching of a truly authentic Jesus. He wrote, with a touch of irony, to the Corinthians, 'I am afraid that just as Eve was deceived by the serpent's cunning, your minds may somehow be led astray from your sincere and pure devotion to Christ. For if someone comes to you and preaches a Jesus other than the Jesus we preached .... you put up with it easily enough' (2 Cor. 11:3,4).

In reality, it is almost impossible to exaggerate the importance of the Gospels. Many Christians tend to concentrate on the Epistles without giving enough attention to the Gospels. It is said that 'Rabbi' John Duncan, a Christian scholar of an earlier generation in Scotland, said towards the end of his life that if he had that life over again he would give much of the time he had spent on the Epistles to deeper study of the Gospels. In fact the historical Jesus who is presented in the Gospels is the necessary basis for the theological teaching to be found in the Epistles.

The Gospels give facts, they record history, they tell us about events, conduct, teaching, miracles, deeds of love, acts of judgement, sayings of wisdom; in short they spell out what kind of person Jesus of Nazareth really was. They appear to have arisen out of a great need for facts amongst the early Christians. The apostles were dying one by one. Soon the church would be bereft of those who had first-hand access to the things that had actually happened in the life and ministry of the Lord Jesus. They needed a permanent record, backed by authentic apostolic witness. This became theirs, and is now ours, as the four Gospels were written.

Over the centuries most Christian people have assumed that the Christ of faith and the Jesus of history are identical, and that the person in whom they have put their trust is the same as the One whose life is recorded in the four Gospels. To give the supreme and indeed the crucial example, they have accepted that the resurrection of Jesus is both theological truth and historical fact. There can be no doubt that this was also the view of those who wrote the Gospels.

Ultimately the acceptance or otherwise of the Gospels as reliable history often turns on the way we view the supernatural element in the way they picture Jesus and his activities as presented in them. This raises questions which will take us well beyond the subject of this chapter but we will address them in Chapter 10.

References
1. He refers to Caesar Augustus and Quirinius, to Syria, Nazareth, Judea and Bethlehem.
2. e.g. 1 Cor. 2:1-5; 15:1-3; Gal. 4: 12-15.
3. W. Dilthey (1833-1911) and R.G. Collingwood (1889-1943) are important figures in this reassessment of the historian's task, and Collingwood, in particular, laid great stress on the subjective aspects of it.
4. There is a useful summary of the characteristics of Post-Modernity by Philip Sampson in P. Sampson, V. Samuel and C. Sugden (eds.), *Faith and Modernity*, Oxford, Regnum Lynx, 1993, pp. 29-57.
5. J. Derrida and M. Foucault are the two most influential Deconstructionists. For an exposition and critique of their positions, see L. Wilkinson, 'Hermeneutics and the Postmodern Reaction against "Truth" ' in E.Dyck (ed.), *The Act of Bible Reading: A Multidisciplinary Approach to Biblical Interpretation*, Carlisle, Paternoster, 1977, Chapter 5. For a fuller consideration, see F. Watson, *Text, Church and World: Biblical Interpretation in Theological Perspective*, Edinburgh, T. and T. Clarke, 1994, especially the chapters in Part 2.
6. e.g. 1 Kings 11:6; 15:1-5, 9-15, 25,26, *et al.*
7. 1 Kings 16:29-22:40.
8. 1 Kings 16:21-28.

9. 2 Chron. 33:10-20.

10. e.g. 1 Kings 11:41, 42; 14: 19,29, 1 Chron. 29:29,30; 2 Chron. 13:22.

11. See J. Barton Payne, 'The Validity of the Numbers in Chronicles' in *Bibliotheca Sacra* 136 (1979), pp. 109-128, 206-220. Also Richard Pratt, 1 and 2 Chronicles (Mentor, 1998).

12. Cranfield, *Mark*, pp. 3-5, sets out the evidence and then, after giving a list of incidents where Peter played a prominent part, he says (p. 11), 'With regard to most narratives of this sort we may with considerable confidence accept the tradition of Mark's dependence on the reminiscences of Peter.' Martin, however, is less sure of the complete reliability of this tradition. See R.P. Martin, *op. cit.*, pp. 80-83.

13. The implications of this will be explored in Chapter 8, where ethical questions will be addressed.

14. English edition (ed. P.C.Hodgson), Philadelphia, Fortress, 1971.

15. The phrase is Albert Schweitzer's and is the English title of his book (New York, Macmillan, 1961), first published in German in 1906.

16. i.e. about the time the original quest for the historical Jesus began to peter out.

17. E. Kasemann, 'The Problem of the Historical Jesus' in *Essays in New Testament Themes,* Philadelphia, Fortress, 1982, pp. 15-47.

18. For the earlier stages of this, see J.M. Robinson, *A New Quest of the Historical Jesus*, London, SCM, 1959. One of its earliest and most important products was Gunther Bornkamm's *Jesus of Nazareth* (trans. I and F. McLuskey with J.M. Robinson), London, Hodder and Stoughton, 1960.

19. George R. Beasley-Murray, 'The Kingdom of God and Christology in the Gospels' in *Jesus of Nazareth: Lord and Christ: Essays on the Historical Jesus and New Testament Christology* (eds. J.B. Green and M. Turner), Carlisle, Paternoster, 1994, pp. 23, 24.

20. David Wells, *The Person of Christ: a Biblical and Historical Analysis of the Incarnation*, London, M.M. and S., 1984, p. 14.

21. For a judicious discussion of it, see D. Guthrie, *op.cit.,* pp. 343-347.

22. R.W. Funk, R.W. Hoover, and the Jesus Seminar, *The Five Gospels: What Did Jesus Really Say?* New York, Macmillan, 1993.

23. Ben Witherington III, *The Jesus Quest: The Third Search for the Jew of Nazareth*, Downers Grove, IVP, 1995, p. 49.

24. M.J. Wilkins and J.P. Moreland (eds.), *Jesus under Fire: Modern Scholarship Reinvents the Historical Jesus*, Grand Rapids, Zondervan, 1995.

25. His latest book on our subject is *The Religion of Jesus the Jew*, Minneapolis, Fortress, 1993.

26. See Ben Witherington III, *op. cit.*, Chapter 1.

27. A good discussion of the whole issue in a popular style may be found in John Drane, *Introducing the New Testament*, Oxford, Lion Publishing, 1986, Chapter 12.

28. See e.g. John 3:3-8; Acts 16:14; 2 Thess. 2:13,14.

Chapter 3

JESUS CHRIST IN THE REST OF THE NEW TESTAMENT

The line between presenting and reflecting on facts is not always an easy one to draw, as anybody called as a witness in a court of law quickly realises. Outline a series of events you have witnessed in the past and your presentation will inevitably be influenced by your reflection on them. This is the case even if it amounts only to selecting some items as important enough to present while omitting others you consider less significant.

As we have seen already, the records of the life of Jesus are called 'Gospels' for the simple reason that they tell the good news about him. What then makes a simple sequence of events good news? It is the way we understand them. So, as we saw in chapter 2, even the Gospels present facts that are given special meaning by their authors. Does this mean they are unreliable? Far from it! A competent and trustworthy historian will always seek to present his data accurately even though he cannot avoid interpreting them and may in fact have every intention of interpretation.

There is, however, another important factor Christians take into account when they read the Gospels. The Christian church has always reckoned it insufficient simply to claim they were written by men of good character who were at the same time good observers and recorders. The Christ of the Gospels calls for total commitment to him as the divine Son of God and it is important therefore that the documents that record that claim should have special authority. Christians believe that God's Spirit worked with those who were in any case reliable witnesses so that their records present his truth and meaning, and not simply their own. This is what biblical inspiration signifies.

Chapter 2 took up the question of the historicity of the Gospels and the element of interpretation in the Gospel accounts of the life of Jesus, but it will be necessary to think about this a little further in our next chapter.

When most of us are thinking about reflection on the historical facts about Jesus, however, it is not only the Gospels that are in our minds, but other New Testament material. We might expect this reflective element to be least evident in the Acts of the Apostles, as this is simply a narrative of the early history of the Christian church. There is one type of material in it, however, where we do find it, for this narrative contains a number of sermons and these not only give biographical facts about him but give meaning to them and to him, for they do not simply instruct the hearers in those facts but they make it clear that the facts are of such a nature that the hearers need to make a major decision about him and about their personal relationship to him. This interpretative element becomes considerable in some of the Epistles and also in the Book of the Revelation.

The witness of Peter to Jesus

In the first ten chapters of the Acts of the Apostles, there are five sermons by Peter. These occur in chapters 2 to 5 and in chapter 10. All of them are quite brief and some are very short indeed, taking up only a few verses in Luke's narrative. Now the reader might well suspect that the sermons would normally be longer than the record of them we have here. Some may well be incomplete, and Luke makes it clear that this is the case as far as the first of them is concerned, when he says, 'With many other words he warned them' (Acts 2:40). It may be too that some of them represent the kernel of the sermons in view or else a summary of their essence.

If the gospel is the good news about Jesus, as Mark says it is (Mark 1:1), then the full preaching of it had to await the completion of the great series of events that centre in Jesus himself. This series commenced with his birth and proceeded through his life, death and resurrection. It was completed in his ascension and in the gift of the Holy Spirit whom he sent into the world from his place in heaven at the right hand of God. All these events form integral elements in the good news that is Jesus himself, and of course all these facts are historical in character. It was on the Day of Pentecost, the very day when the series was completed (Acts 2:33), that this full message was first preached.

The sermon recorded in Acts 10 has a different type of audience from the other four, as it was not Jews but Cornelius, a Roman centurion, and his friends who heard the word of the gospel through Peter on this occasion. His message to them is remarkably like an abbreviated form of the Gospel of Mark, as a comparison of the two will quickly reveal. Note, for instance, that both begin with John the Baptist's ministry and that both emphasise the works of power performed by Jesus, especially his healings.[1]

This should not surprise us if in fact, as the early writer Papias maintained, Mark wrote his Gospel on the basis of Peter's memories of Jesus. Not only so, but the Gospel certainly appears to have been written for Romans and Cornelius was a Roman. It is interesting too to note that this sermon was preached to a centurion, for the confession of Jesus as Son of God by another centurion is recorded towards the end of Mark's Gospel (Mark 15:38,39). This is an important link between the Gospels and the sermons in Acts and it underlines for us the 'good news' quality of the Gospels.

The other recorded sermons of Peter were all preached to Jews, although Luke tells us that at Pentecost there were also proselytes (non-Jewish converts to Judaism) present.

Both at Pentecost and in his preaching to Cornelius and his friends Peter began with the man Jesus. Of course he did! It all began for him when he first met and then responded to the call of a man, a Galilean like himself, and so it is with the man Jesus that he begins his proclamation. Peter believed Jesus to be a wonderful man of God. That is clear in all five sermons. But there are special words and phrases he uses which suggest he knew him to be much more than this.

He declared that Jesus was the Prophet foretold by Moses (Acts 3:22).[2] It is evident from the Gospels that this prophet was eagerly awaited by the Jews at this time and that he was regarded as playing an important part in God's programme for his people.[3] Peter proclaimed too that Jesus was the holy and righteous One, God's servant (Acts 3:13, 26; 4:27, 30).[4]

Now these descriptions of Jesus by Peter, abstracted from other assertions in the sermons, need only mean that Jesus was a very special human messenger of God. It is when Peter asserts that he is both the Saviour and the Judge of men (Acts 5:31; 10:42f.), that we begin to recognise a distinctly divine element in his claims for Jesus. Who can be our ultimate Judge but the God who created us? It is quite clear that Peter believed the eternal destiny of men and women depended on their attitude to this Jesus, for, quoting Psalm 118, he said 'He is "the stone you builders rejected which has become the capstone." Salvation is found in no-one else, for there is no other name under heaven given to men by which we must be saved' (Acts 4:11f.). No wonder he could make this very high claim, for to him Jesus was not only the Christ of God but Lord of all (Acts 2:36; 10:36). This last assertion of course has enormous implications, because it means that Peter believed him to be truly God.

Ever since quite early times, however, some readers of Acts have tried to interpret Peter's statements about Jesus in a way that does not tally with belief in his true deity. They have done this by laying stress on the verbs in statements like 'God has made him both Lord and Christ' (Acts 2:36) and 'God exalted him at his right hand as Leader and Saviour' (Acts 5:31). Such statements have been taken to mean that Jesus was at first simply a human being, but that, as a result of his outstanding obedience to God, he was exalted to a very high place indeed, so that people could apply terms like 'Lord' and 'Saviour' to him and treat him as if he were virtually God.

Such 'adoptionism' rears its head from time to time. The simplest way to answer it is to draw attention to the context of such sayings. It is of course quite serious to comment on a person's words taken out of their context, and has often led to gross misinterpretation and even to unjust accusations.

It is important to remember that the first four of Peter's sermons were addressed to Jews in the very city where Jesus had been crucified, and the first of them only a few weeks after the crucifixion had taken place. Because of this, it was essential that the greatness of the people's sinful involvement in this evil deed should be brought home to them, so that, in facing this sin in repentance, they might be able to experience the greatness of God's grace. For this reason it is not surprising that Peter should stress that God has reversed men's estimate of Jesus, and he employs these verbs and others to make this abundantly clear. 'You crucified ... and killed (him) by the hands of lawless men, but God raised him up.... God has made him both Lord and Christ, this Jesus whom you crucified' (Acts 2:23f., 36). The resurrection and exaltation of Jesus were God's way of vindicating Jesus, not means of giving him a rank he lacked without them.

So then no new status is in view here, but a contrast between human rejection of Jesus on the one hand and God's warm approval and vindication of him by raising him from the dead on the other. In Peter's final recorded sermon, in chapter 10, his audience is different and so his approach is different, and he makes it clear to his Gentile hearers that Jesus is the eternal Lord of all.

There is then no question of any 'adoption' of Jesus into the Godhead. What could such an idea really mean anyway? Would it not betray an altogether unacceptable reduction of the awesome distinction between God the Creator and his human creatures? If God is unique, as undoubtedly he is, how could some other being stop being a mere creature and become divine himself?

When people were converted to Christ, they needed to be taught more about him. After recording Peter's Pentecost sermon and the remarkable response of the people to it, Luke says, 'They devoted themselves to the apostles' teaching' (Acts 2:42). The teaching given on the Day of Pentecost was oral and this would have been true of much of the instruction given in New Testament times, but the New Testament contains many letters and in these further teaching is given.

The oral teaching would have been very general at first, but an examination of the Epistles shows that they related the teaching to local needs which had emerged in the growing churches to which they were written. The various letters therefore bear the marks of the problems and difficulties of the recipients as well as being sources for our understanding of the doctrinal teaching of the early church.

The two letters of Peter[5] do not mention his sermons, except perhaps very generally in 1 Peter 1:12, 25 and 2 Peter 1:16, and yet it is true that they appear to build on the basis laid in them. In his sermons, Peter had spoken of Jesus as a wonderful man of God. We must not forget that, along with the rest of the Twelve, he had lived in close contact with him for over three years and had seen his great beauty of character.

There is a moving meditation on that character in 1 Peter 2:21-25. This passage has special interest because of its fascinating combination of personal experience and Scripture. Peter's personal knowledge of Jesus is its basis and this is clear, but his language is coloured by the phraseology of Isaiah 53, with its picture of God's suffering Servant who 'committed no sin, and no deceit was found in his mouth' (v. 22; cf. Isa. 53:9).

Peter had also declared in his preaching that Jesus has a special place in the relations between God and human beings. This theme too he expounds in his letters. It is through Christ we have faith in God (1 Pet. 1:21), through him our spiritual sacrifices are acceptable to God (1 Pet. 4:11), through him we are saved from sin (2 Pet. 2:20). It is quite evident then that to Peter Jesus is the great Mediator between God and human beings.

In his first letter, Peter goes further still and calls Jesus 'Lord' (1 Pet. 3:15). In his second letter, he does this more extensively, often combining the word with 'Saviour' (2 Pet. 1:1, 8, 11; 2:20; 3:18). The claims implied in these terms are very high indeed. Even 'God' is not too great a word for Peter to apply to him. There is some debate about the intended meaning of the language used in 2 Peter 1:1, but it seems much more likely that the author intends us to understand the Greek expression he uses to mean 'our God and Saviour Jesus Christ' (referring to one person) rather than 'our God and the Saviour Jesus Christ' (referring to two).[6] What an exalted description this is!

The Epistle of James
As James Denney demonstrated many years ago in masterly fashion in his book *Jesus and the Gospel* [7], every New Testament writer held basically the same view of Jesus of Nazareth. Denney acknowledged of course that their terminology varied. Not only so, but there were differences of writing style, and the emphasis given by the various writers presented some diversity. Nevertheless

all of them show Jesus not only as truly human but also as fully divine. To use Denney's favourite and memorable phrase, they all place him 'on the divine side of reality'.

What about a book like the Epistle of James? At first sight it seems to contain little that is relevant to our theme. Examine it more closely, however, and it will be found to have a Christology, a way of understanding the significance of Jesus the Christ, as exalted as any in the New Testament.

The letter is full of echoes of the ethical teaching of Jesus, which James clearly considered authoritative. A good example of this can be seen when James 1:22ff. is compared with Matthew 7:24-27. The essential teaching in these two passages is identical, although it is differently illustrated.

He writes of himself quite simply as the slave of Christ, using the Greek *doulos* which necessarily has connotations of bond service (Jas. 1:1), while he links his Master with God himself, and calls him 'Lord', the very 'Lord of glory' (Jas. 2:1). This would be particularly impressive, of course, if this letter was written by the brother of Jesus, as it is often thought to have been.[8]

His use of this expression may be due to his sense that it was fitting for application to Somebody who was glorified beyond death and through resurrection. It is worth recalling, however, that 'glory' is virtually a description of God himself in some Old Testament passages. So, for instance, when Eli's daughter-in-law commented on the capture of the ark, saying, 'the glory has departed from Israel,' she meant that God had left them, for the ark symbolised the presence of God (e.g. 1 Sam. 4:21f.).

The Teaching of Paul[9]

Saul of Tarsus was completely revolutionised in his life and thought by his encounter with the risen Christ on the Damascus road. This is treated as an event of considerable importance for the church by Luke, for he records it no less than three times in Acts, once in his own narrative of events (Acts 9) and twice in addresses recorded by him from the lips of Saul himself (Acts 22, 26).

Sometimes, especially in 2 Corinthians, Paul writes as if he is re-living that experience as he is penning his letter. In 2 Corinthians

4:6 he makes it clear that the light which shone so brightly that day did not simply illumine his pathway but shone right into his heart. With great boldness, he compares this light with the shining of the new-created light on the first day of creation.[10]

There is a most interesting difference of perspective between Paul and the earlier apostles. This difference of perspective relates to the distinction between what is known as 'Christology from below' and 'Christology from above'.

People like Peter and John thought of Jesus Christ as the wonderful man who had called them from their fishing boats and whom they had followed for more than three years. How wonderful that he should now be seated at the right hand of God and acknowledged as Lord! Their Master was now in heaven, so evidently divine.

Paul's first encounter with him (as far as we know) was as the risen Lord, so that the revelation of Christ to him began at the point it reached for Peter and John only after their three and a half years of discipleship. For Paul therefore the wonder was that this great divine One who had called for and captured his absolute allegiance had once lived a humble life of service on earth. For both Peter and John on the one hand and Paul on the other, Jesus was both man and God, but the perspective was different.

Paul makes use of some great titles and applies them to Jesus. He calls him 'Son of God' (e.g. in Gal 4:4; Rom 1:4; 8:29, 32). It is at first sight surprising that he uses this title rather infrequently, for on average there are only between one and two examples in each of the letters claiming Pauline authorship and in some it does not occur at all. It must be clear to us that to him it is a very exalted expression, and therefore to be used sparingly. It has been pointed out that Paul's writing style always seems to become somewhat elevated in passages where the phrase occurs. An examination of the passage in Romans 8 where it is used twice will certainly show this to be the case there.

Does Paul ever actually call Jesus 'God'? It would not really matter at all if he did not, for there are plenty of ways of indicating deity apart from the use of this word.[11] There are however a few passages where he seems to do so, although in some cases there are translation problems. A good case, however, can be made out for some such translation as that of the NIV with respect to the closing words of Romans 9:5, which it translates, 'who is God over all, for ever praised! Amen.'[12] In Titus 2:13 also Paul certainly appears to be calling Jesus God as well as Saviour, and this too is well brought out in the NIV translation, although, somewhat surprisingly, is not favoured by the AV.[13]

Paul's favourite word for designating Jesus as divine is undoubtedly 'Lord'. He uses it well over two hundred times and in the great majority of cases he applies it to Jesus Christ, although occasionally simply to God as such or to God the Father, usually where his language is influenced by some Old Testament passage. This title undoubtedly had divine meaning for the Jews and, therefore, we can be sure, for the earliest Christians who were themselves Jews.

Especially important in this connection is Paul's great expression *Maranatha*, which he uses in 1 Corinthians 16:22. This is composed of two Aramaic words. These should be rendered either as 'Our Lord comes' (*Maran atha*) or 'Our Lord, come!' (*Marana tha*). Most scholars opt for the second possibility. This is because they think it more likely to have arisen as a cry of the Christians in worship than simply as a doctrinal formulation.[14] The reasoning behind this is not conclusive, although the parallel in Revelation 22:20 adds weight to this conclusion. In actual fact it matters little, as, in either case, Jesus is being called 'Lord'.

Some scholars have argued that Paul's doctrine of the deity of Jesus was taken over from Hellenism, which had, of course, a belief in divine beings in human form. The most famous exposition of this theory was put forward in 1930 by Wilhelm Bousset in his book, *Kyrios Christos*.[15] He maintained that Paul probably absorbed it from the Hellenistic Christian community among whom he worked in Antioch. Now this theory just will not do. The language of the phrase *Maranatha* is Aramaic and this clearly indicates not simply a Jewish but a Palestinian origin for it. Here then we have evidence of the faith that Jesus is Lord as found among Palestinian Jews, who had been reared as strict monotheists. It has been well said that this phrase is the Achilles heel of Bousset's whole theory.

If Paul can use such great terms and apply them to Jesus, it is not surprising that in Colossians 1:15-17 (cf. 1 Cor 8:6), he should go so far as to say that Jesus is the great Creator and Sustainer of the whole universe. This simply develops the logic of the Lordship and divine Sonship of Jesus, and this is true of all the so-called 'higher Christology' of Colossians and the other later Epistles of Paul. He sees Jesus to be Lord over all, for the term, 'firstborn of all creation' he uses in that Colossian passage is reminiscent of the place of special privilege and authority in the family held by the firstborn in Old Testament times.[16] In this passage, Paul refers to 'things in heaven and on earth, visible and invisible' and the series of expressions which follow this show that in Paul's thought even great spiritual beings exist only because of the pre-incarnate activity of Jesus. Not only so, but they all exist for his glory, for, as he says here, everything was created *for* him as well as *by* him.

In Colossians 1:17, Paul's assertion, 'in him all things hold together' presents us with a fact of great philosophical importance. This vast and almost infinitely diverse universe in which we live is only maintained in its ordered being by the constant activity of Christ.

It is not therefore to be wondered at that this same Epistle speaks of him as the incarnation of the very 'fullness of deity' (Col 1:19; 2:9). The term *pleroma* (fullness) here is often thought to have been used by the heretics who were troubling the church at Colosse.[17] Certainly it was later put to heretical use by the Gnostics of the second century, who believed in a series of emanations from God's being, each a little lower in status than the previous one. According to them, Christ was only one of these emanations or 'aeons', and they reckoned that he occupied a comparatively lowly position on the scale. So then, by taking over this term and using it without qualification in application to Jesus, Paul is saying that there is nothing proper to deity that is not to be found in him. Can any claim possibly be greater than that!

Genesis 1–3, the opening chapters of the Bible which are so basic to all that follows, must have come wonderfully alive with new meaning for Paul as a result of his conversion to Christ. Not only did he see God the Creator in terms of Christ, but he believed

Jesus to be the new head of the human race, as Adam was its original head. So he combines in himself both the God who creates and man who is the highest product of his earthly creation. He is the truly representative man, the last Adam. In Romans 5:12ff., in a passage of tightly packed reasoning, Paul shows how Christ's work in dying for us[18] has overcome the evil effects of Adam's sin. In 1 Corinthians 15, his subject is the resurrection of believers, and he shows how, just as through Adam death has come, so through Christ the fullness of resurrection life has become a reality for his people.

It is important to recognise that Paul employs the same language here as he does in his speeches in the Acts of the Apostles. There have been scholars who have seen the speeches in the Acts not as authentically historical but as free creations of the author of that book. Yet there are many links between the sermons and the letters, and these links are not so excessive as to make us suspect the sermons are anything but historically authentic.[19]

Christologically, the record of the Pauline sermon delivered at Athens is important. In this Paul spoke of the two most significant men in all human history (Acts 17:26, 31). Speaking of God he says, 'From one man he made every nation of men.' This would have been unwelcome teaching to the proud Athenians to whom he was speaking, for they believed their ancestors were not like others, but that they sprang fully grown from the soil of Attica. Paul does not actually name Adam in the presence of a Gentile audience, for the name would mean nothing to them, but he refers to him more generally as the first man. He then goes on to speak of Christ as the man through whom God would judge the world with justice and then declared, 'He has given proof of this to all men by raising him from the dead.'

As the last Adam, Jesus is the Image and Glory of God (2 Cor 4:4; Rom 8:28-30), fulfilling therefore in himself all God intended Adam to be, but which, as every reader knew, the first man had failed to be.

We shall need to look very carefully at Philippians 2:5-11 in Chapter 11. In some respects this is the most comprehensive statement about Christ contained in the New Testament. Paul dwells especially on the humiliation which the incarnation involved for

Christ, and on the exaltation to the place of supreme power and authority which followed the deepest point of his humiliation, his shameful death on the Roman gibbet.

The Epistle to the Hebrews

The Letter to the Hebrews is anonymous. It was ascribed to Paul fairly early but not early enough to make us sure it is by him. In fact, weighty objections have been advanced against this ascription, so that it is best to treat it as a separate entity within the New Testament with its own distinctive testimony to Christ. It bears the authentic marks of divine inspiration on its every page.

It is chiefly concerned with Christ's work and with its superiority to the Old Testament order of things in every sphere. The word 'better' keeps on occurring in it.[20] It has often been pointed out, however, that we can never really understand that work unless we grasp the fact that it takes its value from his person. Irenaeus, Athanasius, Luther and Calvin are among a host of theologians who have laid great emphasis on this. The fact that Christ is to be viewed as both human and divine gives his death as the final sacrifice for sins an efficacy it could never have had otherwise. The writer of this Epistle is very fully aware of this and he therefore starts his letter with a great four-verse affirmation of the deity of Jesus.

At the very beginning, he declares that Jesus is the last word of God to men. 'In the past God spoke to our forefathers through the prophets at many times and in various ways, but in these last days he has spoken to us by his Son' (Heb. 1:1,2). This in itself would have major implications for Jews who placed much emphasis on divine revelation and its importance.

In what way then is Jesus God's final word? If the writer had made a simple comparison and contrast between the prophets and Christ, we might have thought it was simply the teaching of Jesus which formed God's final revelation, but he goes on immediately to write of him in such a way as to indicate that the glory of God shines out of his whole person. He declares that he is the exact representation of all that God is in his inmost nature, the Creator and Sustainer of all that exists.

These are simply stupendous claims. If they are true, then, as the hymn-writer has put it, 'the highest place that heaven affords is his by sovereign right'. Not only so, but he also occupies the place of divine power because he has dealt finally with sin. So both in his essential person and in his decisive work we see how fully qualified he is to be regarded as fully divine. It is in the total fact of Christ that God's final word is to be heard. This prepares us for an outstanding exposition of the significance of Christ, and the writer does not disappoint us.

For reasons that relate to the special problems faced by the first readers of his letter, its author proceeds to demonstrate the absolute uniqueness of Jesus over against other spiritual beings, the angels who played such a big part in the earlier and fragmentary revelation given in Old Testament days. He quotes a number of Old Testament passages in support of his thesis. Some of these are conventional messianic passages that would have been accepted as such by the Jews as well as by Christians,[21] although there are others which do not appear to have been identified as belonging to this category.

. There is one quotation however that demands special attention because of its implications. It is the substantial quotation from Psalm 102:25-27 which is found in Hebrews 1:10-12: 'In the beginning, O Lord, you laid the foundations of the earth, and the heavens are the work of your hands. They will perish, but you remain: they will all wear out like a garment. You will roll them up like a robe; like a garment they will be changed. But you remain the same, and your years will never end.' These words come from a psalm which was not identified by the Jews as messianic and which certainly on the surface does not seem so, yet this language, about God and his work of creation, is applied by the writer of Hebrews to Jesus!

This would be remarkable enough in itself, but what is so impressive is the fact that he does this without employing any arguments at all. It must mean that both the writer and his readers believed that if an Old Testament passage referred to God it could be applied to Jesus. Could there be any clearer evidence of a shared belief in the deity of Jesus in New Testament times?

Hebrews chapter 2 presents the complementary truth of the

humanity of Jesus, and the writer shows how important it is that Jesus should have entered fully into the human situation. He is the Saviour of men and he could not do this work at all without full identification with those he came to save. 'He had to be made like his brothers in every way, in order that he might become a merciful and faithful high priest in service to God and that he might make atonement for the sins of the people' (v. 17).

There are other passages in the letter which dwell on the humanity of the Saviour, but none more moving than a short one in chapter 5 (vv. 7-10). The reference to 'loud cries and tears' is a clear allusion to Gethsemane, even though the wording here is not represented in the Gospel accounts. It makes us realise that the prayer-life of Jesus was not play-acting but a real cry for strength from above in the face of the most awful pressure from temptation and suffering. The writer says, 'Although he was a son, he learned obedience from what he suffered and, once made perfect, he became the source of eternal salvation for all who obey him' (5:8-9) What does this mean? It indicates that only as he came this way and learned in testing what obedience really involved that he could come to that perfection of experience which was the human complement of his eternal divine fitness to be our Saviour.

The writer undoubtedly considered the true humanity of Jesus to be of quite special importance, for he gives unusual emphasis to the human name 'Jesus' almost everywhere it occurs. Greek has several ways of giving emphasis and one is to hold back the word or phrase it is desired to stress until an unusually late point in the sentence. This is what the writer here does almost every time he uses the name 'Jesus', although this is not evident in most English translations.

The Teaching of John

The Johannine group of writings makes many important contributions to New Testament Christology. Much has been written about the authorship of these books. A good case can still be made out for the apostle John as the author of them all, but it is aside from our purpose in this volume to deal with the authorship issue. There is in any case quite wide agreement that, whoever wrote them, they emanated from the same circle of Christian believers and so represent a particular theological slant or emphasis. We will assume unity of authorship and call the author 'John'.[22]

The Fourth Gospel is no less a Jewish book than the Gospel of Matthew, even though John emphasises so much the universal relevance of Jesus Christ. Here we see Jews eagerly awaiting the fulfilment of God's promise of a Messiah (John 1:41, 45, 49; cf. 20:30f.). We have already noted that here too, as in the Synoptic Gospels, the terms 'Son of Man' and 'Son of God' are applied to him.

There is no doubt though, that John lays special stress on the relationship of Jesus to God as his unique Son. He is God's 'only-begotten Son' (AV) or 'his one and only Son' (NIV) (1:14, 18; 3:16, 18; cf. 1 John 4:9). This kind of language shows that there is no question of John regarding Christians as equal in status to Christ. An interesting fact that is often overlooked is that this writer never applies the term 'sons of God' to Christians (some English versions are a little misleading in this respect), but always refers to them as 'children of God'. Take these two facts together, and the conviction is inescapable that John held the relationship of Jesus to God to be absolutely unique, without any parallel in other human beings.

Some aspects of the teaching of the Fourth Gospel have been mentioned in Chapter 1 of our book. The other Johannine books also make their contribution to our theme. This literature as a whole relates particularly to the spiritual needs of the church at Ephesus and other churches in the area.[23]

Ephesus was an important centre for the teaching of Greek philosophy. Ever since human beings began to ponder the meaning of the universe and their own place within it, as the Greeks did very extensively, they have been fascinated by a number of great basic questions. What is life? What is truth? What is love? John knows the answer to questions like these. One answer may be given to them all, not in terms of philosophical definition but in terms of God incarnate. God is the source of all values and so when God became incarnate in Christ, life, truth, love and many other abstract ideas came into concrete manifestation, all found in the life and character of this amazing person (1 John 1:1; 4:8-10, 16; 5:11; cf. John 1:4; 5:26ff.; 11:25).

The Book of the Revelation is unique in the New Testament and even in the Johannine group. It consists of a series of visions and it makes very extensive use of imagery and symbolism drawn from the Old Testament. In a key passage in this book, Jesus is presented as the Lamb of God in the midst of the throne of God (Rev. 5:6). This phrase, 'Lamb of God', is applied to him a great many times but in each case we ought to remember this first instance of it in the book, for this is the perspective from which the later occurrences should be viewed. The Lamb has suffered and yet is triumphant. His victory has been achieved at great cost to himself.

John has no doubt as to the true manhood of Jesus, for he appears to him in a vision as 'one like a son of man' (Rev. 1:13). A study of this passage alongside Daniel 7, where this complete phrase first occurs in the Bible, reveals something most striking. The picture of the risen Christ in Revelation 1 combines characteristics of the Son of Man and of the Ancient of Days (God) as these are displayed in that Old Testament chapter! Could John have shown us any more clearly his belief in the unqualified deity of this Jesus?

Coming as it does right at the start of the book, this vision sets the tone for all that is to follow. We are not surprised then to find that each of the letters to the seven churches given in chapters 2 and 3 commences with a series of great titles of the Lord Jesus, some of them with clear overtones of deity. At its end, he calls himself, 'The Alpha and the Omega, the first and the last, the beginning and the end.' Such language has already been applied to God in the book (Rev. 1:8), and in any case would remind the Jewish reader of similar language used of the divine being in the pages of the Old Testament (Isa. 44:6; 48:12). Jesus Christ is Lord and God.

References
1. For a more detailed comparison of the structures see Donald Bridge, *Why Four Gospels*, pp. 52-53.
2. cf. Deuteronomy 18:15-18 and 34:10-12.
3. See especially John 1: 21, 25, where 'the Prophet' must mean 'the well-known Prophet', i.e. the one promised by Moses.
4. It seems likely from Peter's language here that he intended his hearers to understand that Jesus was to be identified with the Suffering Servant of Isaiah 52:13-53:12.

5. We are, of course, assuming the Petrine authorship of both Epistles. This is rejected by many scholars, and 2 Peter, in particular, is often treated as non-Petrine and therefore as pseudonymous. Despite some real difficulties which can be frankly faced this conclusion is not inevitable. For a balanced discussion of the whole question of pseudonymity, see Donald Guthrie, *op. cit.*, Leicester, IVP, 1970, pp. 671-684, and for arguments supporting the Petrine authorship of 2 Peter, see E.A. Blum, '2 Peter' in *EBC*, Vol. 12, pp. 257-261.

6. See E.A. Blum, *op. cit., ad loc.* where he summarises the arguments used in C. Bigg's commentary on the Petrine Epistles and Jude.

7. James Denney, *Jesus and the Gospel: Christianity Justified in the Mind of Christ,* London, Hodder and Stoughton, 1909, pp. 1-104.

8. This view has been the majority one since the early third century but, although it can be well supported, little depends on it for our purposes in this volume. See J.B. Mayor, *The Epistle of St. James,* Grand Rapids, Zondervan, 1954, pp. iii, iv.

9. Here we are assuming that Paul wrote each of the thirteen Epistles in which he appears as the author and also that the speeches attributed to him in Acts are authentic. For support of these positions, see the articles on each Epistle in the *IBD* plus F.F. Bruce, *The Acts of the Apostles* London, Tyndale Press, 1951, pp. 18-21.

10. The NIV's unfortunate omission of anything corresponding to the Greek *idou,* 'behold', before the last clause of 2 Corinthians 5:17 robs the passage of something of its drama, for this word surely expresses Paul's own amazement at what had happened. 'If anyone is in Christ, he is a new creation, the old has gone, (behold) the new has come!' It is just as if, in his imagination, he is standing once again on the Damascus Road.

11. For instance, when divine qualities, such as omnipotence and omniscience, and divine actions, such as creation and judgement, are attributed to him.

12. See the brief discussion of this in E.F. Harrison, 'The Epistle to the Romans' in *EBC*, Vol. 10, *ad loc.*, and a much fuller discussion in Bruce M. Metzger, 'The Punctuation of Romans 9:5' in B. Lindars and S.S. Smalley (eds.), *Christ and Spirit in the New Testament,* Cambridge, CUP, 1973, pp. 95-112.

13. See the brief discussion by D.E. Hiebert in *EBC*, Vol. 11, *ad loc.*

14. See C.T. Craig and J. Short, '1 Corinthians', in *The Interpreter's Bible,* Vol. 10, *ad loc.*

15. W. Bousset, *Kyrios Christos: A history of the belief in Christ from the beginning of Christianity to Irenaeus* (trans J.E. Steely), Nashville, Abington, 1970.

16. See Deuteronomy 21:15-17; cf. also Psalm 89:27, which is particularly significant as background to Colossians 1:15.

17. It is discussed in all major commentaries on the Epistle.

18. This is what 'one act of righteousness' in Romans 5:18 must mean.

19. See note 8 above.

20. Hebrews 1:4; 6:9; 7:7, 19, 22; 8:6; 9:23; 11:35, 40; 12:24.

21. e.g. Psalms 2 and 110.

22. For discussion of the whole issue, see the article on each of the books in *IBD*, and at much greater length in Guthrie, *op. cit.*, Chapters 7, 23 and 25.

23. The connection of the writer of Revelation with the area of the Province of Asia which found its centre at Ephesus is evident from Revelation 1–3. John's connection with Ephesus, although not mentioned in extant literature dating from earlier than the late second century, is mentioned by writers who will have had special access to the facts. Polycrates was bishop of Ephesus, and Irenaeus was a pupil of Polycarp, who was himself a pupil of John.

Chapter 4

THE THEOLOGICAL ISSUE

We have already noted that the New Testament in all its parts presents an interpreted picture of Jesus and that such a picture was inevitable when due consideration is given to the nature of historical writing. We have not yet however addressed issues which arise from the kind of interpretation of him we find there.

Some readers will now raise an objection. They will draw our attention to the fact that the understanding of Jesus which the New Testament writers had was of a highly distinctive kind and they will question whether that type of interpretation is a legitimate exercise in historical writing.

It might be helpful for us to make a comparison. The Emperor Augustus was an important figure (this itself is an historical judgement!) who was an older contemporary of Jesus. Now a number of different kinds of biography might be written with him as their subject. One author might write a military biography, presenting him as a strategist of considerable skill. Another might write a political biography in which he was shown to be a man of great practical wisdom who had learned much from the recent sorry political history of Rome and was determined to devise an administrative structure that would prevent things from going so wrong again. Yet another might be interested in the social history of Rome in his day and so relate him to this. Without doubt these three kinds of biography would all be regarded as legitimate tasks of an historian. Each of them would require a selection of events that took place during his life, but the selection would differ from book to book.

In his day a movement developed which magnified the significance of the emperors so greatly that they were reckoned to be gods and were worshipped as such. This probably started in Egypt, and we can understand why it arose there, because the Egyptians had been used for centuries to worshipping great monarchs as gods. From there it spread eventually throughout the empire. Would it then be legitimate to select material from his life-story to seek to support this view of him? Could an historian properly devote himself to the task of showing, for instance, that his wisdom was too great for him to be merely human?

Why not? Is a theological valuation all that different from a political, a military or a social one? Yes, it must be admitted that it is. Political, military and social biographies all arise from a similar world-view. They assume that the person concerned is a mortal who, if different from other mortals, is so only in degree and not in kind, and so he or she can be estimated by the sort of criteria we apply to other people. The attempt to demonstrate that a human being was really a deity however goes much further. In fact, it presupposes a particular world-view in which the supernatural impinges on the natural.

It is often forgotten though that to exclude the possibility of the supernatural itself also presupposes a world-view, and that this itself is no more completely demonstrable than a supernaturalist view. Remember Kant![1] It is often forgotten too that Kant's philosophy bans us from arriving at any dogmatic view of things-as-they-are and not simply a supernaturalist view. If you are convinced of his philosophy and you apply it right across the board, then you can no more exclude pure naturalism than pure supernaturalism, for both presuppose that you have gained an understanding of the noumenal structure of things.

What we have in the case of Jesus of Nazareth are four books which, although not quite biographies in the normal sense, are like them in that each makes a selection from the life of a particular person. In addition to this, we have other New Testament material which contains an estimate of the significance of Jesus from the pens of various writers. We must now give some thought to this material and the way in which Jesus is interpreted in it.

What we have to do at this stage is not to try writing a biography of Jesus ourselves, but rather to investigate those who have and to consider the outlook of their contemporaries who held similar views of Jesus and who wrote other books of the New Testament. Later on, we will ask whether we have good grounds for holding this view ourselves today.

The Theological Jesus of the New Testament

As we have seen already, the original quest for the historical Jesus was an attempt to find a solid historical core of facts which could be relied on in building up a picture of him from the New Testament. What happened to that quest and how successful was it?

It has to be admitted that it eventually petered out because it came to be realised that it was an attempt to find the unfindable. The theory behind it was something like this: the New Testament contains documents of varying value from the point of view of history. It is obvious that Jesus, as he is presented in the Epistles, the Book of the Revelation and even the sermons recorded in Acts, is seen through theological spectacles. The writers of the Epistles, for instance, treat him as the Object of their faith and devotion as Christians, as he clearly was to those to whom they wrote, so that they can hardly give an objective historical presentation of Jesus as he really was.

So then, those who were pursuing this quest turned to the Gospels. There is one Gospel, they maintained, that is clearly unreliable historically and that is the Gospel of John. It cannot be relied on, for the presentation of Jesus there is just as theological as in the Epistles. The emphasis of it is so much on the fact that he is the Son of God.

What about the Synoptic Gospels then? They are somewhat better, although even in them Jesus speaks occasionally of himself as the Son of God and predicts his resurrection from the dead. It is evident too that the writers of these Gospels believed these claims. Two of them, Matthew and Luke, show their theological outlook very early in the way they tell the story of Jesus, for they say that he was born of a virgin.

That leaves the Gospel of Mark. Perhaps here at last we may find the true historical Jesus!

Because Mark was believed to be the least theological of the Gospels, lives of Jesus were written which employed it as their main basis.[2] Also they usually made a cautious selection of material from Matthew and Luke, but they avoided the Gospel of John like the plague.

But can we find a purely non-supernatural Jesus even in Mark's

Gospel? Here too, as in all the other Gospels, Jesus is recorded as speaking of himself as God's Son and he is no less emphatic about his resurrection than he is elsewhere. Hoskyns and Davey, in their book *The Riddle of the New Testament*,[3] made it clear that the whole New Testament presents us with a supernatural Jesus as Denney's *Jesus and the Gospel* had already done some years earlier.

So then it became clear that the writers who were looking for a non-theological Jesus were trying to find a Jesus who does not exist in the pages of the New Testament. Every New Testament writer and every New Testament book presents him as the Object of the faith and devotion of his people,

Was the quest itself completely impartial anyway? Were those who pursued it free from presuppositions? Of course, none of us can be certain we are completely independent of these, but the presuppositions of many of these writers can be fairly easily discerned when we set them in the thought-world of their day. Many of them seem in fact to have been looking for a Jesus who was simply a great social reformer, very much like the great philanthropists of the nineteenth century, but going beyond them in the depth of his willingness also to share in the poverty of the poor.

Towards the end of the nineteenth century, there were murmurs of dissent to be heard even in the major German university faculties which were the chief centres where this quest was being pursued. Scholars like Martin Kahler and Adolf Schlatter argued for the oneness of the Christ of faith with the Jesus of History.[4]

Then, around the turn of the century, two very able scholars, from what was later to be called 'the history of religions school', Johannes Weiss[5] and Albert Schweitzer[6], showed that the 'Liberal Jesus' these writers were seeking was in fact quite unhistorical. Each of these writers, it was alleged, was looking down through history as if to the bottom of a deep well, and there, in the water at the bottom, he was seeing the reflection of his own face. Could this pursuit claim to be any more objective than the outlook of the New Testament writers themselves? Surely not! Schweitzer's criticism was particularly acute and the quest virtually ended once these criticisms had been thought through.

We come back once again then to the fact of an interpreted

history, an interpretation which is frankly theological. If the quest for the historical Jesus did nothing else, it at least made crystal clear the nature of the documents with which we are dealing in the New Testament. Every one of them is a theological document.

What then could be done? It was at this point that Rudolf Bultmann comes into the story. Bultmann was a Gospels' scholar, but his interest was less in the task of reconstructing a picture of Jesus than studying the Gospels as the written deposit of the oral traditions of the early church about him, traditions which admittedly had considerable theological colouring.

His concern was to investigate the various forms in which that tradition has come down to us in the Gospels. As we have already seen, his conclusions on the question of the historicity of the facts, were highly negative. Other scholars, such as Martin Dibelius, joined him in this enterprise.

Eventually Bultmann went further. He had been deeply influenced by an academic colleague at Marburg University who taught philosophy, Martin Heidegger, and he came to embrace Heidegger's Existentialism as the key to interpreting the New Testament, which he regarded as the first classic text of Existentialism.[7] To him the Gospels, as the whole New Testament, contained a message, an important message, which was of abiding significance for the human race. It was the challenge to adopt a particular attitude to life and death, and, as a consequence, to adopt a particular lifestyle.

Along with his Existentialist interpretation of the New Testament, Bultmann proposed a rigorous programme of demythologisation.

According to him, the whole New Testament can be viewed from two different standpoints. On the one hand, it can be seen as a web of mythological material centring in Jesus. Bultmann maintained that all the great doctrines of the New Testament, such as the incarnation, the sinlessness of Jesus, substitutionary atonement, the resurrection of Jesus, the existence of the Holy Spirit, the doctrine of the Trinity, etc., are essentially mythological. The fact that they came to be held by the early Christians is testimony to the great impact Jesus made on his followers. At the heart of all this material, however, there is a challenge, rather like the kernel of a nut from which the shell has first to be removed before that kernel can be reached and enjoyed.

So, Bultmann proposed, we should not simply discard the mythology as Strauss wanted people to do. It may well be unacceptable to us today with our scientific world-view but it is not therefore worthless, for it contains within itself the challenge of Jesus. So we need to interpret it before discarding it, when we will be left with what he called the kerygma or proclamation, the challenging message of Jesus.

Because the programme of demythologisation proposed by Bultmann was put forward in Germany in 1941, during the Second World War, it did not make an immediate impact on the English-speaking world. As soon as the war was over, however, it began to exercise considerable influence. This impact was still extremely vigorous when John Robinson published his *Honest to God* [8] in 1963, for his book shows the influence of Bultmann and his way of thinking at point after point.

The Relationship of Theology to History

What becomes clear as we consider the thought of Rudolf Bultmann is that his view was a reductionist one in two ways.

First of all, he was an historical reductionist in relation to the story of Jesus. He considered the crucifixion to be a certain fact, for such an event, with all its shocking implications, is something no devoted follower would ever have invented. He reckoned too that his baptism and also his entry into Jerusalem riding on an ass had a high degree of probability as actual historical events. Apart from these items, there is little else on which we can rely.

He was also a theological reductionist. In Bultmann's view of things, all the great theological doctrines of the New Testament are removed and nothing is left but what he calls the kerygma. Now, as the Greek word *kerygma* means 'proclamation' in the sense of the thing proclaimed, the message, this might appear to be reassuring. There is then apparently a message left for the Christian church to proclaim.

But what is that message? It shows little resemblance to the

message preached in the Acts of the Apostles and referred to in the
Epistles. There is a passage in which Bultmann shows clear understanding of the kind of message preached by Paul, but also his
own decisive rejection of that message in the form in which Paul
proclaimed it.

Summarising Paul's message about the cross, he says, 'The Jesus
who was crucified was the pre-existent, incarnate Son of God, and
as such he was without sin. He is the Victim whose blood atones
for our sins. He bears vicariously the sin of the world, and by
enduring the punishment for sin on our behalf he delivers us from
death.' There can be no real doubt as to the accuracy of this
summary. He then goes on, however, to declare, 'This mythological
interpretation is a hotchpotch of sacrificial and juridical analogies
which have ceased to be tenable for us today.'[9]

In Chapter 10, we will see that his own reason for rejecting this
is the acceptance of a particular world-view that excludes the
supernatural fully and decisively.

Bultmann's favourite New Testament passage was Romans 6.
According to him, the Christian message in its essence is to be
found in that chapter. There Paul challenges his readers to reckon
themselves to have died with Christ and with Christ also to have
risen from the dead. Heidegger, Bultmann's philosophical teacher,
had taught that the most important thing in life, what made all the
difference between what he called inauthentic and authentic
existence, was that we should embrace our death before it comes.
This, said Bultmann, was what Jesus did and we are challenged by
Jesus to do the same. If we do this at the instigation of Jesus, then
we will find that, like him, we will rise from the dead and have
newness of life. So then, for the Christian, life out of death becomes
the pattern of his existence.

Now this sounds perfectly fine, but can we accept it? We must
examine it with care. Bultmann says, 'By the word of preaching
men are confronted with the question whether they are willing to
understand themselves as men who are crucified and risen with
Christ.'[10] Again, he says that in preaching, 'Christ's death-and-
resurrection becomes a possibility of existence in regard to which
a decision must be made.'[11]

We are being asked to identify ourselves with Christ in his death and his resurrection. Surely Paul would have approved of this as authentic Christianity! But would he? What we need to realise is that in Bultmann's thought the cross of Christ and his resurrection belong to two entirely different and irreconcilable realms of thought. His cross was historical but his resurrection was mythological. How can I truly identify myself with Christ's death and resurrection when the one is historical and the other is not? If we view both as historical, then we can make good sense of Paul's teaching, but not otherwise. Death-and-resurrection becomes simply 'a sort of formula for existential living'.

Something else needs to be mentioned before we can see Bultmann's view for what it really is. This pattern of existential living which is ostensibly derived by him from Romans 6 is for this world only, for Bultmann regarded the teaching of the New Testament about life after death as just another part of the mythology. To him, death is the end of the road for us all.

What we see so clearly here then is that, for Bultmann, both the history and the theology of the New Testament are reduced almost to vanishing point.

Now Bultmann's influence, although by no means dead, is not as commanding as it once was. Nevertheless a consideration of his viewpoint is valuable, not only because of its continuing influence, but also because it points up certain important issues very clearly.

It enables us to see with crystal clarity that, as far as Jesus is concerned, we may distinguish historical and theological issues but we cannot separate them. Bultmann's introduction of the category of mythology as an instrument of historical criticism was itself a theological judgement, and he himself came to recognise that this was so. What in fact he did was to discard the theological interpretation of Jesus which the New Testament gives and to substitute for it a theology based on a modern philosophy, that of Existentialism. In his theology, death and resurrection, which he saw as its heart, becomes little more than a lifestyle formula. It lacks a full basis in Jesus himself, for according to Bultmann the resurrection never happened in the literal sense although the death was literal.

The truth is that, in the New Testament, as in the Bible as a whole, history and theology are inextricably intertwined. To give an Old Testament example, we may ask what happens if we remove the Exodus from Egypt from the sphere of history so that it is no longer viewed as an actual event? What happens to the Exodus theology? It was in the context of the Exodus as an event that God revealed himself as the Redeemer, the deliverer of his people. But if the Exodus did not happen, redemption is nothing more than an idea. It was not to a mere idea that later Israelites appealed when they prayed to their God as Redeemer. What they were really saying was, 'Lord, you delivered your people once before. Please do it again!'[12] Neither must we forget that it was in the context of the Exodus that God revealed the meaning of his great name, Yahweh, to his people (Exod. 3:11-15; 6:2-3).

The same principles apply in the New Testament. Take away the resurrection as an event, and what happens to the Christian faith? It disintegrates, for, as we will see in Chapter 10, it is the resurrection of Christ that holds everything in that faith together. It is the apologetic heart of the Christian faith. In fact, many Christian apologists hold that, once the resurrection of Christ has been defended as true, there is hardly a need to defend any other aspect of the faith, for all has been made secure.

It is of course true that history alone is not the essence of the faith. The Christian preacher, whether ancient or modern, never preaches simply, 'Christ died', but he always goes on to say 'for our sins'. In other words he adds theological interpretation to historical statement. It is that addition which makes this good news. It is however obvious that the theology cannot be detached from its historical roots. We need to know what in fact Christ did – historically – to deal with our sins.

This matter of the relationship of history and theology has vexed many modern theological writers, even somebody as positive in his outlook on the doctrines of the historic Christian faith as Karl Barth, whose first essay in theology was an attempt to deal with this relationship.

Without embracing Bultmann's historical and theological reductionism, we can of course still ask questions as to what is the minimum basis for true Christian faith. It is not that we want to preach a bare minimum, for there is no value in this, but rather so that we may identify the heart of the message. This issue was tackled by S.G. Craig in his book, *Christianity Rightly So-called*.[13] In this he discusses what is minimum objective and minimum subjective Christianity. His conclusions, useful as they are, need not concern us here, for the important point is that he sees an historical basis and a theological interpretation of that basis as both essential to objective Christianity, the Christian faith as it is preached for the subjective appropriation of the hearers.

Soren Kierkegaard, back in the mid-nineteenth century, had maintained that if a notice appeared in a newspaper saying 'that in such and such a year God showed himself in the humble form of a servant, lived among us, taught, and thereafter died',[14] that would be a sufficient basis for true Christian faith. Now Kierkegaard was reacting against an excessive intellectualising of the Christian faith and to some extent we may sympathise with this, for to embrace Christianity is much more than an intellectual exercise. We have to say, however, that his assertion is most doubtful, for it raises the whole question of authority. Have not some of us learned over the years that, to say the least, we cannot take everything newspapers say as gospel truth? The message needs to come over to us, not simply as history, nor simply as theology, nor even simply as theology grounded in history, but as the Word of God. The most wonderful message will lack the full reliability that faith craves, unless the believer can be certain that it is God who has revealed it and it is not simply human speculation.

So it is the conviction of the Christian that Scripture is God's Word that undergirds both the history and theology of the Christian faith. There is plenty of evidence available for this estimate of Scripture, but such evidence is in fact confirmatory of the conviction wrought in the heart of the believer by God the Holy Spirit. As John Calvin saw particularly clearly, it is the Spirit's great work to convince us inwardly of the truth. He said, for instance, 'As God alone is a sufficient witness of himself in his own word, so also the word will never gain credit in the hearts of men, till it be confirmed by the internal testimony of the Spirit.'[15] This means then that there is a spiritual basis to our acceptance of what God says through these writers about his Son, who was delivered to death for our sins and raised again for our justification.

The United Theological Witness of the New Testament Writers

Some reader who has followed the argument so far, may at this point raise an objection. He or she may well point out that we have been referring frequently to the theological interpretation of Christ in such a way as to take it for granted that the New Testament writers speak with one voice as far as this is concerned. He or she may ask if we have given serious consideration to the possibility that this is not so. Obviously this is an important issue and we must address it. To do so in the detail it deserves would take us well outside the scope of this book, but we need at least to look at the main elements in the issue.

It should be said straightaway that there is obviously some truth in the idea. The Gospels, for instance, are not carbon copies of each other. The Epistle to the Hebrews deals at length with the priesthood of Christ, a concept little touched on elsewhere. Surely we would not have it otherwise! It is this that gives us constantly renewed stimulus as we turn from one New Testament book to another. Yet most of us discern, beneath the fascinating variety, the deepest unity on the great central truths of the Christian faith in general and of Christology in particular. Their Christologies may have a measure of variety but this exists within an over-arching unity.

The question of a variety which amounts to disunity has been raised in our own day by a number of writers. John Robinson, in an essay, 'The Earliest Christology of all?'[16] presented a study of the sermons attributed to Peter in the Acts of the Apostles, and sees several different Christological positions represented in them. Acts 2 he viewed as adoptionist, an interpretation against which we have already argued.[17]

Robinson did not however consider this to be the earliest type of Christology. This was to be found rather in Acts 3:20, 21, and in his view these verses teach that Jesus is only the Christ-elect until his second advent. We need also to quote verse 19 to get the complete thought, and the verses read, 'Repent, then, and turn to God, so that your sins may be wiped out, that times of refreshing may come from the Lord, and that he may send the Christ, who has been appointed for you – even Jesus. He must remain in heaven until the time comes for God to restore everything, as he promised long ago through his holy prophets.'

Robinson's position can, however, only be maintained if this sermon is torn apart, for verse 18 reads: 'But this is how God fulfilled what he had foretold through all the prophets, saying that his Christ would suffer.' Not only is Jesus here clearly designated as the Christ in respect to his sufferings, but there is a reference to prophecy here just as there is in the later verses.

The issue has been taken up by a number of modern writers. John Knox[18], for instance, holds, like Robinson, that there are different Christologies in the New Testament and that they cannot be reconciled with each other. Colin Gunton has shown that, in fact, Knox's whole approach is governed by his assumption that it is impossible to hold to both the divinity and the humanity of Jesus at the same time, and that, once this possibility is granted, his arguments lose their weight.[19]

One of the most influential of modern Christological studies in English is *Christology in the Making* by James Dunn.[20] He too sees a variety of Christologies in the New Testament and holds that the full confession of the deity of Jesus is not found until the great Prologue to the Fourth Gospel. His position is distinctly more moderate than that of Robinson or Knox but, as he has said in a more recent article, he believes there was some kind of 'unfolding', 'the recognition of what had always been true of Jesus and only awaited the eye of faith to see with increasing clarity.'[21] Now unfolding is certainly not an inappropriate term if it refers simply to the fact that the implications of the deity of Jesus are brought out more and more fully in later parts of the New Testament or even in later writings of the same apostle.[22] It is quite another matter, however, to see the affirmation of the deity of Jesus as itself belonging to the latest stage of the New Testament literature.

There are problems even in Dunn's position, as a number of writers have argued. One of the most effective answers, in an article

which does not actually mention Dunn, is given by Richard
France.[23] Among other evidence, he refers to the antiquity of the
Aramaic formula *Maranatha* (1 Cor. 16:22), which we have
already discussed[24] and also to a whole series of passages in which
in Paul's letters 'the same divine function is credited sometimes to
God and sometimes to Jesus', including Col. 1:16,17 (cf. Rom.
11:36), 2 Cor. 5:10 (cf. Rom. 14:10-12), Col. 1:13 (cf. Col. 4:11)
and many other passages.[25]

We should note that there are various titles and descriptions of
Jesus which appear, either in similar form or transmuted in some
way, in a variety of New Testament books, thus providing points
of unity which bind the material together.[26]

The most obvious but, at the same time, one of the most
overlooked, is his simple human name 'Jesus'. Even the most
exalted appellations are still titles of the man Jesus, so that his
manhood is taken for granted by every New Testament writer.
This name occurs in every New Testament book, with the exception
of 3 John, which is much too short for the omission to be of any
significance.

He is also 'Christ'. This term also occurs virtually everywhere,
although perhaps less in the Gospels than we might have expected.
It is true that, particularly in Paul's Epistles, it appears at times to
have lost its etymological significance as simply meaning 'Messiah'
and to have become a virtual name and so to be more identifying
than descriptive.[27] This is however no denial of its meaning but
simply means that we need to recognise that the Messiahship of
Jesus had become such an accepted fact among the early Christians
that it could now be taken for granted and did not require constant
demonstration.

Then there is the term 'Son of Man'. This occurs in all four
Gospels, and, as we have seen already, its main Old Testament
background can be found in Daniel 7:13,14.[28] Whenever it is used
along with language which suggests an Old Testament passage it
is almost always this. This is invariably the case in the Gospels
and also in Revelation 1:13, where the reference to Jesus as an
obviously heavenly being and as Someone like a son of man is
strikingly reminiscent of that Old Testament passage.

It occurs also in Acts 7:56 where, as in Daniel 7, the one referred to is a heavenly being, for Stephen sees him through the opened heavens. The only other place where it occurs in the New Testament is in Hebrews 2:6 in a quotation from Psalm 8. Here the term does not relate directly to Jesus, but the writer argues that there is a notable application of that part of the psalm to him. There seems little doubt that his choice of this passage will have been guided, at least in part, by the use of the term by Jesus himself.

It is true that Paul does not use it, but he does write of Jesus as the Last Adam. This term could well be his equivalent of the phrase employed by his Master, and, because of his interest in the comparison and contrast of Adam and Christ, it would actually suit his purpose better.

The term 'Son of God' is used in all the Gospels, extensively in the Johannine literature, more sparingly in the Epistles of Paul and in some very significant contexts in the Epistle to the Hebrews. It also occurs twice in references to Paul's preaching in Acts and in a reference to the Mount of Transfiguration experience in 2 Peter 1:17. Too much stress should not be placed on its absence from James, Jude and 1 Peter, all comparatively short books. In any case, 1 Peter uses the term 'God and Father of our Lord Jesus Christ' (1 Pet. 1:3), which implies a special filial relationship of Christ to God.

What is striking is the manner in which it is employed. In the Synoptic Gospels it often occurs in passages of major importance where it is clearly regarded as a great title, in connection with events such as the baptism and transfiguration of Jesus. In Paul, as we have seen, there is often a heightening of his writing style where it is present.

It is of special interest to study its employment in the Epistle to the Hebrews, for here every passage in which it is used implies its greatness. There is Hebrews 1:2, where there is not only comparison but also implied contrast with the prophets. Then, when applied to him as our High Priest, this is in passages which indicate respectively either his greatness or the continuing nature of his priesthood (Heb. 4:14; 7:3, 28). It also occurs in the two most solemn warning passages in the book, implying that it is very serious indeed to reject such a person (Heb. 6:6; 10:29).

Any particular writer is allowed special emphases and, given the greatness of this expression, it is not surprising that there is one New Testament writer who majors in it, as we see in the Gospel of John and the Johannine letters. This is particularly understandable in view of the fact that the Gospel of John is, in any case, the most concentratedly Christological book the New Testament contains.

As we have already seen, 'Lord' is employed with great frequency in Paul's letters. This is in tune with his perspective on the person of Jesus and his recognition of his Lordship on the Damascus Road. It is therefore not surprising to find Luke using it, not only in the sermons in Acts, but also in the narrative sections of his Gospel, for he was a companion of Paul. Why is it then that in the other three Gospels it does not appear in the narrative framework until after the resurrection?

A clue to this is probably to be found in the way it and 'Son of God' are employed in the Gospel of John, where 'Lord' is used sparingly but 'Son of God' (or 'Son') very frequently. The two terms may be regarded as alternative ways of expressing the deity of Jesus, but with somewhat different emphases. 'Son of God' focuses on his relationship with the Father, while 'Lord' his position as supreme Governor of creation and of the human race. The latter therefore is particularly appropriate of the risen and exalted Christ, and it is in this connection that John uses it, while the use of the former indicates that although he stepped down during the days of his flesh from his position at God's right hand, his essentially divine status continued unaltered.

There are of course many other designations and descriptions of Jesus to be found in the New Testament, some of them distinctive to particular writers. The outstanding example of a distinctive title is perhaps 'High Priest' as employed in the Epistle to the Hebrews. Our purpose at the moment is not, however, to focus on the distinctives but rather on the common features of the different strands of New Testament Christology.

The Christology of Jesus

One question that keeps on being asked concerns the faithfulness of the New Testament writers to the thought and claims of Jesus himself.[29] Did they follow him or did they in fact make claims for him that he never made for himself? The latter position has been held by many modern scholars, but it faces, among others, a major historical difficulty. Martin Hengel puts this well when he says:

> The basic question of New Testament Christology is: How did it come about that in the short space of twenty years the crucified Galilean Jew, Jesus of Nazareth, was elevated by his followers to a dignity which left every form of pagan-polytheistic apotheosis far behind? Pre-existence, Mediator of Creation and the revelation of his identity with the One God: this exceeds the possibilities of deification in a polytheistic pantheon.[30]

Of course, the simplest answer is that the New Testament Christology simply spells out the implications of the claims Jesus made for himself. This raises again, of course, the question of the historicity of the Gospel documents. This emphasises then the intimate connection between historical and theological questions in Christology.

We could, of course, go through all the main titles of Jesus used in the New Testament and ask if they are true to the teaching of Jesus about himself, but it is not necessary to do so. That he saw himself as a man is too obvious to need demonstration. The crucial question is whether he taught his deity, and here the important titles are 'Son of God', 'Lord' and 'God'. We will therefore concentrate attention on these.

The Gospels show us Jesus using the term Aramaic term *abba* in his Gethsemane prayer ('father')[31] J. Jeremias has shown that this term, which was a familiar one used in the family, not unlike our English 'dear father' or even 'daddy', cannot be paralleled in address to God from Jewish sources and that it must testify to a sense of unique relationship to God, the kind that his special use of the terms 'Son' and 'Father' in any case suggests.[32]

As far as 'Son of God' is concerned, the closing verses of Mark 13 are of great importance. Jesus is speaking about the coming of the Son of Man and he says, 'At that time men will see the Son of Man coming in clouds with great power and glory' (v. 26). This is strongly reminiscent of the key Old Testament passage in Daniel 7:13,14, so that it is not simply a use of the term 'Son of Man' but one that echoes the one Old Testament passage where it is clearly used of a heavenly being.

Then a few verses later he makes a major affirmation about his teaching. 'Heaven and earth will pass away, but my words will never pass away.' As far as the Synoptic Gospels are concerned, this is the strongest assertion he makes about the truth and authority of his own teaching. He then goes in the next verse to say, 'No-one knows about that day or hour, not even the angels in heaven, nor the Son, but only the Father.'

It is important that these two verses should be taken together and interpreted in relation to each other, and it is singularly unfortunate that so many English translations, including the NIV, separate these two verses by the paragraphing structure they adopt. Verse 32, taken by itself, might be used, although without any real warrant, to imply that Jesus did not claim infallibility for his teaching, but, in the light of verse 31, this cannot be maintained. Any teacher who confessed to ignorance on one point would be astounded if somebody was to use that confession to accuse him of giving erroneous teaching. This would be very bad logic.

Then we need to note that, in verse 32 itself, there is a really clear implication of his words, and that is that he had either an intrinsic status or else a depth of knowledge (or both) which placed him not only above human beings but also above the angels.

Nevertheless, when we have said all that, it is still true that this verse has proved difficult for many Christians down the years. How significant then that in it Jesus uses the crucial term 'Son', and, in fact 'Father' and 'Son' together, in the way he so often did in the Gospel of John to suggest the uniqueness of Each in relation to the Other!

What we have to ask is whether any Christian would ever have invented such a saying and only one answer to that is really possible. It is inconceivable. Therefore we must conclude that Jesus did actually use the term 'Son of God' of himself and in such a way as to point up the uniqueness of his relationship with the Father.[33]

The saying does not appear in either Matthew or Luke, but they do record his words, 'All things have been committed to me by my Father. No-one knows the Son except the Father, and no-one knows the Father except the Son and those to whom the Son chooses to reveal him' (Matt. 11:27; cf. Luke 10:22). Because this saying seems so much like the kind of language Jesus uses in the Gospel of John it has been termed 'a bolt from the Johannine blue'. We should note though that it has very strong authority in the manuscripts, so much so that both in Matthew and Luke the text is dubbed 'certain' in the United Bible Societies Greek text of the Gospels. Incidentally, this is true for Mark 13:32 also.

So then it seems clear that Jesus called himself 'Son of God' and, if we take account of this Matthean/Lucan passage, we can assume that he understood the term in the high sense it has in the Gospel of John.

What about 'Lord'? Two other Marcan passages are important here. Early in the Gospel, Jesus is recorded as saying, 'the Son of Man is Lord of the Sabbath' (Mark 2:28; cf. Matt. 12:8; Luke 6:5). Who was it that instituted the sabbath? It was God. Surely only God could claim lordship over it! Then, in a context where the authority of Jesus has constantly been in focus, the Day of Questions, he ends the day by underlining the fact that in Psalm 100 David calls him 'Lord', so calling into question the idea that he was simply David's son (Mark 12:35-37; cf. Matt. 22:41-46; Luke 20:41-44).

If we accept the integrity of the Gospel writers, it is not easy to turn aside these passages in their testimony to Jesus' view of himself.

But, it may be asked, did not Jesus by implication deny his deity on one occasion? To a questioner who addressed him as 'Good teacher', Jesus responded, 'Why do you call me good? ... No-one is good – except God' (Mark 10:17-18; cf. Luke 18:18-19). It seems most likely that Jesus was telling the man not to use important words without due thought. Moreover, if we take his teaching in the Gospel of John seriously, it is clear that he was fully aware of his own goodness (John 4:34; 5:30; 6:38). The ethical implications of these passages will be considered in Chapter 9.

It is difficult therefore to avoid the conclusion that the claims made for Jesus by the New Testament writers are fully in accordance with his view of himself.

The faith-creating and faith-developing function of the New Testament

We have been thinking about the historical basis and the theological super-structure which we have in the New Testament, and have seen that the two are most intimately related to each other. They are distinguishable and yet inseparable.

What then is the function of this material? Important, indeed unique, as it is, it is nevertheless a means to an end, a divinely-given means to a divinely-determined end. That end is well expressed in two of the Johannine writings. As we have already seen, the Gospel of John gives a clear statement as to its purpose: 'Jesus did many other miraculous signs in the presence of his disciples, which are not recorded in this book. But these are written that you may believe that Jesus is the Christ, the Son of God, and that by believing you may have life in his name' (John 20:30,31). The First Epistle of John also gives a statement of purpose: 'I write these things to you who believe in the name of the Son of God so that you may know that you have eternal life' (1 John 5:13).

Here then we see that the purpose of this literature, and this appears to be true of the New Testament as a whole, is to elicit and to strengthen faith; faith, that is, in Jesus as the Son of God, faith in Jesus as theologically interpreted. Faith grows as it feeds on facts, not on feelings nor on fancies. Faith is greedy for facts; it has an insatiable appetite for them.

The early preachers preached Christ, and this is true of every truly Christian preacher since New Testament times, but 'Christ' is a mere word without content unless there is a communication concerning who he was and is, what he has done and what he can be to those who hear the preaching. So often, the New Testament writers refer to specific facts about Jesus as the content of faith. For example, Paul writes of the need to 'confess with your mouth,

"Jesus is Lord," and believe in your heart that God raised him from the dead' (Rom 10:9). John says, 'If anyone acknowledges that Jesus is the Son of God, God lives in him and he in God' (1 John 4:15).

This kind of statement is of frequent occurrence. It does not of course mean that faith is merely intellectual belief, but it does mean that living faith in Christ has some real doctrinal content. 'Jesus' is the name of an historical person, while 'Lord' and 'Son of God' are theological estimates of that person.

A study of the New Testament as a whole reveals that there is one basic gospel which forms the background to it all.[34] There have been attempts to disprove this, but the case against it is not easy to make out. Paul really sums up this gospel in 1 Corinthians 15:3f. when he says: 'For I delivered to you as of first importance what I also received, that Christ died for our sins in accordance with the scriptures, that he was buried, that he was raised on the third day in accordance with the scriptures.'

The Gospels are rightly so called because in fact they reflect this gospel and fill out its details. They have an important role in the communication of these essential facts about Jesus as the Son of God and Lord of all, and they give faith more historical and theological 'body'. They tell us who the Christ was, and they spend much of their space preparing us for his death and resurrection and recording the events themselves.

Also in the Gospels we find Christ calling people to faith. It was after the disciples had been with him for some time and had observed his life and listened to his teaching that they confessed him to be the Christ (Matt. 16:13ff.). It was through their actual contact with the facts that the divine revelation came. These primary Christian documents still do that kind of work today when people approach them with a willingness to learn and an openness to receive truth through them.

The Acts of the Apostles is a book of vital importance. It is the only historical record we have of the first generation of the church's life. It is therefore highly informative and interesting. It is however more than that. Luke's two volumes are intimately related to each other. There are all sorts of points of contact between them, and fascinating and spiritually profitable comparisons between the life of Christ and the life of the church can be made from a study of the two taken together. Incidentally, he records one saying of Jesus which is not found in the Gospels, not even in his own: 'It is more blessed to give than to receive' (Acts 20:35).

As he opens his second volume, Luke gives Theophilus a brief reminder of the contents of Volume One. In it he had dealt with 'all that Jesus began to do and teach'. That word 'began', coupled with many a reference later in his second book, makes us aware of the fact that Acts should be thought of as the record of what Jesus continued to do and teach – from his throne in heaven and through the Holy Spirit. It was the exalted Christ who gave the Holy Spirit (Acts 2:33), and it was in the name of Jesus that the church did what she did (Acts 3:6, 16; 4:30, et al.). At various points the risen Christ appeared as a reminder that he was at work (Acts 7:55; 9:3ff.; 9:10ff., et al.). So the book encourages faith in Christ, in the contemporary Christ, the Christ of faith who is also the Jesus of history. Churches as well as individual Christians need to grow in faith, and the Acts of the Apostles is a major means of grace for local churches.

The Epistles are certainly well designed to strengthen faith. They take the historical basis of the faith for granted and they interpret the historical, crucified and exalted Jesus in a wide variety of ways. Each letter has its characteristic emphasis, its function in showing us something further of him. His example of godly and innocent suffering is given to us in 1 Peter, the deep meaning of his death and resurrection is brought out in Romans, his exaltation is the subject of much teaching in Ephesians, his supremacy over every kind of being in Colossians, his superiority to everything provided in the Old Testament order in Hebrews, and so on. For a full understanding of the many-sidedness (and yet essential simplicity) of the Christian gospel, which reflects the fullness of Christ himself, we need to read every book of the New Testament. We cannot afford to neglect even the shortest of them if we would know him in fullest measure.

In his first letter to the Corinthians, Paul makes some comments which are best understood as references given to the teaching given by Christ during his earthly ministry (1 Cor. 7:10, 11; 11:23). There is much evidence that the whole ethical tradition in the New Testament Epistles is based on teaching recorded as from him in the pages of the Gospels.[35]

The book of Revelation is unique in the New Testament. There are a number of passages (e.g. Mark 13) and even books (e.g. 1 and 2 Thessalonians) which have much to say about Jesus' second advent. Here, however, is the one long book which has his return as its main subject. We might well say that even this book is historically orientated, provided we can use a phrase like 'future history' without contradiction. Eschatology is really history extended into the future.

The book professes to deal with facts which, although not part of history when they were written, were, the writer was convinced, as sure to happen as if they already existed. But there are two important ways in which it is very much anchored in past history. First, it is written to seven churches in the Roman province of Asia, actual local churches set up during the kind of evangelistic enterprises of which Acts tells us. Secondly, its main theme is the activity in judgement of the Lord Jesus Christ from the throne in heaven, and the term used over and over again to describe him is 'the Lamb'. Now this phrase, symbolic as it undoubtedly is, nevertheless points us to history. It is a sacrificial term. The New Testament uses this kind of language about the cross, so that 'the Lamb' is the crucified Christ, who also rose from the grave. We have the evidence of the Gospels to underline these historical facts for us.

References
1. See p. 34.
2. Although one of the most famous of these attempts, *Jesus of Nazara*, by K.T. Keim (1825-78) relied more on Matthew than on Mark.
3. Sir E.C. Hoskyns and F.N. Davey, *The Riddle of the New Testament*, London, Faber and Faber, 1931.
4. See P. Stuhlmacher, *Jesus of Nazareth – Christ of Faith* (trans. S.S. Schatsmann, Peabody, Hendrickson, 1993, pp. 1-3.
5. J. Weiss, *Jesus' Proclamation of the Kingdom of God*, ET, Philadelphia, Fortress, 1971, first published in German in 1892.
6. See p. 49, n. 15 above.

7. J. McQuarrie, *An Existentialist Theology,* London, SCM., 1955, is a major study of Bultmann's theology by a writer who is partly positive and partly negative in his assessment of him and who particularly considers the influence of Heidegger on his thought.

8. J.A.T. Robinson, *Honest to God,* London, SCM, 1963.

9. Rudolf Bultmann, 'New Testament and Mythology' in *Kerygma and Myth,* London, SPCK, 1954, p. 35.

10. *op. cit.* p.42.

11. Rudolf Bultmann, *Theology of the New Testament,* Vol. l, London, SCM, 1952, p. 302.

12. See especially Isaiah 51:9-11.

13. S.G. Craig, *Christianity Rightly So Called,* London, Tyndale Press, 1947.

14. Quoted in H.R. Mackintosh, *Types of Modern Theology: Schleiermacher to Barth,* London, Nisbet, 1937, p. 243.

15. John Calvin, *Institutes of the Christian Religion,* I, vii, iv.

16. J.A.T. Robinson, 'The Most Primitive Christology of all?' *Journal of Theological Studies* 7 (1956), pp. 177-189.

17. See p.53 above.

18. John Knox, *The Humanity and Divinity of Jesus: A Study of Pattern in Christology,* Cambridge, CUP, 1967.

19. Colin E. Gunton, *Yesterday and Today: A Study of Continuities in Christology,* London, Darton, Longman and Todd, 1983.

20. J.D.G. Dunn, *Christology in the Making: An Inquiry into the Origins of the Doctrine of the Incarnation,* London, SCM, 1980.

21. J.D.G. Dunn, *The Making of Christology - Evolution or Unfolding?* in J.B. Green and M. Turner (eds.), *Jesus of Nazareth, Lord and Christ,* p. 437.

22. This is the view persuasively argued for Paul's Epistles in Alexander B. Bruce, *St. Paul's Conception of Christianity,* Edinburgh, T. and T. Clark, 1894.

23. R.T. France, 'The Worship of Jesus: A Neglected Factor in Christological Debate?' in H.H. Rowdon (ed.), *Christ the Lord: Studies in Christology presented to Donald Guthrie,* Leicester, IVP, 1982, pp. 17-36. See also the criticisms of Dunn's position in an article by John F. Balchin, 'Paul, Wisdom and Christ' in the same volume, pp. 204-219.

24. See p. 66, n.15 above.

25. *op. cit.* pp. 31,32.

26. Good brief discussions of the terms 'Son of Man', 'Christ', 'Lord' and 'Son of God' are to be found in I.H. Marshall, *op. cit.*

27. This kind of phenomenon is also found in Buddhism, where 'Buddha', originally meaning 'the enlightened one' is often used as a simple designation of the man Gautama Siddartha, to whom Buddhists apply this description.

28. See two articles in the symposium edited by H.H. Rowdon and referred to in n. 23 above. These are 'The Background to the Son of Man Sayings' by

F.F. Bruce (pp. 50-70) and 'Is Daniel's "Son of Man" Messianic?' by R.D. Rowe (pp. 97-114).

29. See I.H. Marshall, *op. cit.*, Chapter 3.

30. M. Hengel, *Studies in Early Christology*, E.T., Edinburgh, T. and T. Clark, 1995, pp.383-384.

31. Mark 14:36 and Matthean and Lucan parallels; cf. Paul's use of it in Romans 8:15; Galatians 4:6.

32. J. Jeremias, London, SCM, 1967, pp. 11-65.

33. Arguments have been advanced against this line of reasoning on the assumption that the words, 'nor the Son, but only the Father' may have been added later to counter the arrogance of apocalyptic teachers prepared to assert a definite date, but of course this cannot be proved. See the discussion in I.H. Marshall, *op. cit.,* p.116.

34. See C.H. Dodd, *The Apostolic Preaching and its Developments*, London, Hodder and Stoughton, 1951.

35. See A.M. Hunter, *Paul and his Predecessors,* 2nd Edn., London, SCM., 1961, especially Chapter 5 and pp. 126-128.

Chapter 5

JESUS CHRIST IN THE OLD TESTAMENT

The Gospel of Luke tells us that the risen Lord Jesus Christ met two of his disciples on the road from Jerusalem to Emmaus. They did not at first know him, but on the way, 'beginning with Moses and all the Prophets, he explained to them what was said in all the Scriptures concerning himself' (Luke 24:27).

Later the same day, he did virtually the same for the whole group of his disciples, saying:

> This is what I told you while I was still with you. Everything must be fulfilled that is written about me in the Law of Moses, the Prophets and the Psalms. Then he opened their minds so that they could understand the Scriptures. He told them, This is what is written: The Christ will suffer and rise from the dead on the third day, and repentance and forgiveness of sins will be preached in his name to all nations, beginning at Jerusalem (Luke 24:44-47).

As we read the New Testament it becomes clear that his 'fulfilment' of the Old Testament was one of the most basic convictions shared by its writers, whatever differences there may be in the way this fulfilment is expressed in what they write. In our next chapter we will need to investigate what precisely lies behind this shared conviction. It is however quite clear that the writers, inheriting a great body of literature they believed given by God, saw in that literature various figures, some historical, some prophetic and some both, who had in some sense their counterpart in Jesus Christ and that in him they found perfect form. We will look at the most important of these one by one.

The prophet

The prophet occupies a very important place in the Old Testament. It is not easy to say when prophecy began. Some tend to think of it as starting with Elijah, or even Amos, but with little real justification. Peter evidently saw Samuel as an important figure in its early history, for he declared, 'All the prophets from Samuel on, as many as have spoken, have foretold these days' (Acts 3:24). Within the Old Testament itself, the writer of Psalm 105 clearly believed that the patriarchs were in some sense prophets of God (v. 15). Even Noah is presented in 2 Peter 2:5 as 'a preacher of righteousness'.

A prophet was the mouthpiece of God, and so, in view of the fact that he is shown as the one to whom and through whom the Law was given, it is not surprising to find that in Deuteronomy Moses is regarded as the supreme prophet. In chapter 18 of that book the use of soothsayers, diviners and others who claimed special knowledge of and power over the unseen world is condemned. They were certainly very common in the Near East. Then comes a passage in which Moses promises that the Lord would raise up for the people a prophet such as he. This is followed by a condemnation of false prophecy.

In one sense we may see the fulfilment of this promise in the long line of prophets to be found within the history of the nation of Israel, but Deuteronomy itself suggests that this is not the whole story. In its closing chapter the death of Moses is recorded. When this chapter was written we do not really know, but the writer was sure that the promise of chapter 18 had not been perfectly fulfilled by his day. Here are the closing lines of Deuteronomy : 'Since then, no prophet has risen in Israel like Moses, whom the LORD knew face to face, who did all those miraculous signs and wonders the LORD sent him to do in Egypt – to Pharaoh and to all his officials and to his whole land. For no-one has ever shown the mighty power or performed the awesome deeds that Moses did in the sight of all Israel.'

The common people among whom the ministry of Jesus was performed certainly regarded him as a prophet and this identification endured throughout his ministry. Matthew records that the crowds coming up the Jericho road to Jerusalem with him on Palm Sunday declared, 'This is Jesus, the prophet from Nazareth in Galilee' (Matt. 21:11).

The New Testament writers go further than this however in

their claims for a prophetic role and ministry by Jesus. If we take the Gospel of John seriously, it is clear that there was a lively expectation of the fulfilment of the Deuteronomic promise at the time of Jesus. The priests and Levites asked John the Baptist, 'Are you the prophet?' (John 1:21). The feeding of the five thousand by Jesus brought an immediate reaction from the crowd. 'When the people saw the sign which he had done, they said, "This is indeed the prophet who is to come into the world!" ' (John 6:14). This thought may have been stimulated in them by the miracle for, they would think, here was the new Moses giving new manna from heaven (cf. John 6:30-35).

It is interesting to compare the close of Deuteronomy 34 and that of John 20. The latter may well have been the close of a first edition of the Gospel, as chapter 21 is a kind of appendix, although we have no real reason for thinking it was not by the same hand.[1] Here the Gospel writer says, 'Jesus did many other miraculous signs in the presence of his disciples' (John 20:30). Whether he intended any comparison with the close of Deuteronomy, it is impossible to say, but the fact that they are both concluding comments may well be significant. The likelihood of it is increased when we note that there is a clear literary allusion to Genesis 1:1 in John 1:1, so that prior to the adding of its appendix the Gospel may have begun and ended with literary allusions to the start and finish of the Pentateuch.

Just as many of the Old Testament prophets declared God's word by act as well as deed, so we find acted prophecies too in the ministry of Jesus. The fig tree was an Old Testament emblem of Israel, as in Hosea 10:4, but he not only told a parable about the judgement of God on Israel in terms of the cursing of a fig tree (Luke 13:6-9) but cursed an actual tree (Mark 11:12-14, 20-21).

Although some of them did perform prophetic actions, it was chiefly in their words that the Old Testament prophets made known the truth of God. No doubt qualities of godliness in them provided some illustrations of the truth they proclaimed, although it is clear that there were very occasional exceptions. Balaam and Hosea represent two extremes here. Balaam had been hired by Balak and so was most reluctant to speak in blessing on Israel, but God used him to do so despite his unwillingness, as the story told of him in Numbers 22 to 24 makes clear (cf. Deut. 23:4,5). The nature of his character becomes evident when we are told that he gave advice to the women of Midian which was intended to subvert Israel morally (Num. 31:16). On the other hand, Hosea was prepared, for God's sake, to show love to a wife who had shown herself utterly unfaithful to him (Hosea 1–3).

The New Testament preaching included the assertion that Jesus fulfils the Deuteronomic prophecy (Acts 3:22-24). In one respect, however, he went far beyond any prophetic ministry to be found in the Old Testament and this is most strikingly indicated in the same Gospel, the Gospel of John.

In the case of Jesus lip and life were completely in harmony, so much so that John could write of him as the Word of God made flesh (John 1:1-18). Here the revelation of God comes in the total event of Christ, not simply in his verbal utterances. This is perhaps given special emphasis by the fact that this estimate of Jesus comes right at the beginning of the Gospel of John, as though to indicate that everything recorded after that was a record of divine revelation through Jesus.

This is what the writer to the Hebrews means when he says that God has now spoken in a Son (Heb. 1:1f.). Hebrews 1 contains no specific reference to the teaching given by Jesus but concentrates on his person and his activities in creation and redemption. It is in the full fact of Christ that God is heard and seen. 1 Peter 1:10-12 attributes the revelation that came to and through the Old Testament prophets as the product of 'the Spirit of Christ in them'.

The priest
The prophet represented God to the people, while the priest represented the people to God. These two functions have been well described as descending and ascending mediation respectively. Many of an earlier generation of Old Testament critics used to think of prophets and priests as standing in opposition to each other and virtually representing two entirely different approaches to religion. This polarising is now largely a thing of the past although it is still, quite rightly, recognised that the prophets were critical

of the externalism in relation to religious ritual which possessed the minds of so many Israelites.[2]

The book of Genesis shows the head of the family acting as its priest, building altars and offering sacrifices and the same kind of picture emerges in the first chapter of the Book of Job. There is in Genesis no sign of a developed system of worship with a priestly caste in control of it such as we get in the other books of the Pentateuch.

Under the Mosaic legal system, however, the tribe of Levi was set apart for duties connected with Israel's place of worship, and within this tribe the clan of Aaron was selected for priestly functions. At the apex of the whole system stood the high priest. Basically the same system obtained once the temple had been built. Some critics have represented the record of the tabernacle and its regulations as a re-writing of history, so that the later system, instituted, it is alleged, well after the temple was built, was read back into earlier times. This need not detain us now, and many of the arguments formerly used against its historicity are now considered invalid.[3]

One day in the year, the Day of Atonement, was set apart in the legislation (Lev. 16) as a very special one in the life of the people. On this day, the high priest was to act as the representative of the whole nation. Only on this day could the most sacred part of the tabernacle (or, later, the temple) be entered, and then by him alone. He could not enter it, even on that day, without the blood of sacrifice. Bringing with him sacrificial blood, he pushed aside the great curtain that shut off the Holy of Holies from the remainder of the tabernacle (or temple), and entered it on behalf of the whole people.

The priests of Israel were very concerned to preserve their genealogies, for they needed to be able to demonstrate their pedigrees in order to be able to function as priests at all. Pedigree was important for the kings as well, for they needed to be of the tribe of Judah and also descendants of David. In this way, the powers of the king and the priest were for ever separated within the normative Old Testament structure.

It would therefore seem impossible for Jesus to be a priest, because he was a member of the tribe of Judah. He needed to be of Judaean blood if he was to fulfil the functions of king. Yet one New Testament writer fastens on an interesting exception to the rule within the Old Testament itself and argues for the true high-priesthood of Jesus on the basis of it. The writer to the Hebrews points his readers to Melchizedek as an important precedent for such a union of the kingly and priestly offices (Heb. 5:6, 10; 6:20-7:19).

Melchizedek simply appears in Genesis 14 without any introduction, and the writer to the Hebrews says of him that he was 'without father or mother, without genealogy, without beginning of days or end of life' (Heb. 7:3). All these phrases are intended to stress his uniqueness in the record, as a man without any stated family connections. He occurs of course in the pre-Mosaic history, centuries before the institution of the Levitical priesthood, and yet he was clearly recognised by Abraham, a man of God and the most eminent ancestor of the nation, as a true priest. Here then, the writer to the Hebrews is saying, is good biblical precedent for a non-Aaronic priest.

This writer could in fact make out a very strong case. The only other Old Testament reference to Melchizedek is in Psalm 110, a psalm apparently recognised by the Jews as Messianic.[4] He quotes from it several times in different parts of his book, but the Melchizedek theme dominates chapter 7. In this psalm, the psalmist writes, 'You are a priest for ever after the order of Melchizedek.' This means that the significance of the historical Melchizedek had not been missed by the psalmist himself, so that his recognition of the priesthood of the Messiah pre-dated that of the author of Hebrews.

By combining his comments on Genesis 14 and Psalm 110 as he does in chapter 7, the writer is saying that both history and prediction support the validity of the priesthood of Jesus.

What then are the functions of this great High Priest? Although his standing as a priest depends for its vindication on the comparison with Melchizedek, his functions are of course those of the normal Levitical priests, so that he is the people's Representative, offering sacrifice on their behalf and interceding for them. His uniqueness as the Son of God, however, gives his work added dimensions of very great importance, for the sacrifice he offers is in fact the sacrifice of himself. This never needs repetition and it is the basis of an intercessory ministry which, because of his abiding life, is eternal, for he lives for ever in the very presence of God.

The king

Deuteronomy looks forward to the prophet like Moses. It also anticipates the establishment of a monarchy and provides a constitution for the king (Deut. 17:14-20). This constitution is not, as in modern western monarchies, imposed from below, but rather it is imposed from above: it is God-given.

The constitution is very specific in its terms. It emphasises that the king must be chosen by God and must be an Israelite. The prohibition of the multiplication of horses means that he should not regard military might as the foundation of his kingdom, for the horse was the animal employed in warfare. He must not take many wives lest they seduce him from pure devotion to the Lord. It would of course be assumed that, as a royal person, some at least of his marriages would be motivated by a desire for alliances with other lands and so they would be with pagan foreigners. He should not accumulate great wealth, for he was to be a humble man of God. This is emphasised when it is said that he is to be a diligent student of God's law and not arrogantly reckon himself above it and so better than the common people over whom he ruled.

Did any monarch fulfil this ideal? Not perfectly, but David with all his faults approximated more nearly to it than most. He therefore became a kind of standard for kingship in the Old Testament. The Books of Kings constantly evaluate the reign of a king of Judah in terms of his conformity or lack of conformity to the example of David (1 Kgs. 11:38; 15:3, 11 *et al.*). In fact, after Saul the Benjamite, Judah's tribe (Gen. 49:10) and David's family (2 Sam. 7) provide the continuing line of valid monarchs up to the division of the kingdom for the people as a whole, and after it for the southern kingdom which the Old Testament simply calls Judah.

2 Samuel 7 is a foundational chapter for the hope of a continuing line of kings, and of course the messianic hope is built on this. It is

clear that Solomon is specifically in view in some parts of this chapter, for he was the offspring of David and built the house of God. He is called 'son of David' with great frequency in the Old Testament. If however the record of his life and reign is compared with Deuteronomy 17, it will be clearly seen that he fell short of this ideal most strikingly. In fact this is so striking that it must have been evident both to those who wrote and to those who read the Books of Kings and so may well have itself fostered the messianic hope. So the Old Testament contains within itself evidence that the promise of a great 'son of David' was not fulfilled in Solomon and that the people needed to look beyond him for its fulfilment.

Christian interpreters of the psalms have often discerned in some of them, those which focus on a king like Psalms 2, 45 and 72, language which would be extravagant if applied to any of the monarchs of Israel or Judah but which would fit perfectly what the New Testament says of Christ. The New Testament confirms this general approach by the way it quotes from them in application to him.[5]

This approach to the psalms has been greatly strengthened by recent research in which the Book of Psalms has been seen, not simply as a collection of discrete items (which, at one level it certainly is), but as a book, with a deliberately structured order, reflecting the messianic hope.[6] By New Testament times the book was seen as a five-volume work, perhaps after a pattern set by the Pentateuch, and one of the chief elements binding it together appears to have been the messianic theme. Many of the psalms will of course be very ancient, and there is a more positive attitude now to claims of Davidic authorship for some of them than there was at one time, but their place in an ordered structure, of course, invested them with new significance.

In Books 1 and 2 the historical King David is under attack, but is maintained as a result of God's assurance, given to him in Psalm 2. Psalm 72 sees this promise passed on to David's son, Solomon.[7] Book 3 has many Problem Psalms, that is psalms in which the writer faces problems, of which 73, 77 and 89 are notable examples. It is clear, especially from Psalm 89 which closes this book, that the Davidic kingship is under attack and perhaps is already in eclipse, suggesting that this book may have been compiled during the Exile. Books 4 and 5 strengthen faith with their emphasis on the kingship of God himself and the assurance that his kingdom purposes would be fulfilled in a universal reign. The kingly theme continues in psalms like 110[8] and 132, the second of which promises the coming of a Davidic monarch in the future. It certainly looks as if it was the hope of a Messiah that determined the structure of this book.

Isaiah fills in a great deal of detail for us (Isa. 7:10-18; 9:6f; 11:1-10 and 32:1-8), and other prophets too have much to contribute. The number of passages relevant to the theme is so vast that we cannot survey it adequately in the space available. The picture that emerges is one that must have been most attractive to the Jewish reader. The throne had been occupied by such a wide variety of men, all of them imperfect and some extremely wicked and oppressive. Isaiah had himself known five kings, as he almost certainly died in the reign of Manasseh. With what delight must he have received the revelation of a king who would reign supreme but whose reign would be a blessing not only to his own nation but to the whole world, including even the animal kingdom (Isaiah 11), and who would be absolutely just in all his dealings with his subjects!

The Lord's servant
The book of Isaiah provides us also with another very important line of preparation for the coming of Christ. Biblical scholars have long recognised that certain passages in it can be taken together and that they form a series dealing with the theme of God's Servant. They are known as the Servant Songs.[9] These are Isaiah 42:1-9; 49:1-13; 50:4-9 and 52:13-53:12.[10] Also we note that Isaiah 61:1-4 was applied by our Lord to himself in Luke 4:17-20 and that Isaiah 63:1-6 has some links of language with it.[11]

Prophets, priests and kings were all servants of God, and the nation of Israel herself was called to be his servant. At first, we are not sure whether the servant that appears here is to be thought of as an individual or whether he is a personification of Israel or some group, perhaps the godly remnant, within the nation. As however we move from one Servant Song to another, we become increasingly aware of the fact that the language, however applicable in part to a group, seems to be contemplating an individual, whose dedication to God's service is complete and who suffers greatly in fulfilling God's design for his life.

In some ways he seems to sum up in himself elements of the three great offices of prophet, priest and king. Like a prophet he speaks for God (Isa. 49:1; 61:1ff.), like a priest he is engaged in the offering of sacrifice (Isa.53:10), like a king he wins victories and divides spoil (Isa. 53:12) and is exalted to a place of great authority (Isa. 52:13).

The Jews were themselves uncertain whether a group or an individual was intended in the Songs. Those who thought in terms of an individual were themselves quite unsure as to his identity. In fact, many of the godly characters of the later part of Old Testament history and also of the inter-testamental period were suggested at one time or another. It cannot be said that modern biblical scholarship has reached any greater consensus.[12] What concerns us, however, is how the Songs are interpreted within the Bible itself.

There is an interesting passage in Jeremiah 11 where in verse 19 the prophet says of himself, 'I was like a gentle lamb led to the slaughter' (cf. Isa. 53:7), and this may suggest that he saw his mission and perhaps his sufferings as modelled on, or as partaking of some of the characteristics of the Suffering Servant depicted in this passage.[13] This may have provided a precedent for Paul's application of one of the Songs to the mission of Barnabas and himself to the Gentiles.[14]

For all his faithful service to the Lord and his suffering as a result of that faithfulness, however, there is language in these Songs that goes far beyond Jeremiah. The New Testament writers of course apply the Servant Songs to Christ, and there is evidence within his own teaching that he believed himself called to fulfil the destiny depicted in these passages. See, for example, the quotations from Isaiah 53:12 in Luke 22:37.[15]

The righteous man

The story of Israel embraces the lives and activities of a great number of men and women. Among them are characters of true godliness. Not one is perfect, but men like Abraham, Joshua, Moses, David and many another show clearly their love for God and their desire to serve him and to bring glory to his name through their service. In chapter 11 of his book, the writer to the Hebrews was able to present a considerable selection of Old Testament people of true faith, some of them named and some unnamed, who were to encourage the faith of those to whom he was writing. Interestingly, this line appears to go on beyond the end of the Old Testament period itself,[16] so that, even if there was no valid revelation during the period between the Testaments, there was still true faith and godly character resulting from it.

For the Christian all godly character points, even though it does so imperfectly, to the perfect character of Christ. This is true for Christian character, which can of course be judged in the light of the perfect character now fully revealed in him, but it is also true of the men of the old order as worshippers of the same God. When we read their story in the full light of the New Testament, we can see much in them that reminds us of Christ. In a way, even their sins point to him, because they show by their imperfections the need for the coming of him who is perfect.

This Old Testament literature not only presents us with many an insight into the characters of these imperfectly godly men but it does something more. It presents us with ideals of godliness.

Take Psalm 1, for example. This may have been written specially to open the Psalter, although we cannot be sure of this. It shows us piety and ungodliness in stark contrast, and of course depicts the godly life in ideal terms. Such an ideal stood upon the pages of Holy Scripture for the rest of Old Testament history and throughout the inter-testamental period. It no doubt furnished a challenge and a stimulus to godliness – but it was never perfectly exemplified. Then Jesus came, and the ideal took flesh.

The same is true of Psalm 40, although this in fact depicts a godly but not perfect person.[17] The writer to the Hebrews clearly saw it to be an apt use of Scripture to apply the words of Psalm

40:6-8 to Christ in Hebrews 10:5-7, because they state godly
aspirations and a readiness to do God's will.

The son of man

A few passages of Scripture have been given names which have
become standard designations in scholarly or theological circles.
One of these is Genesis 3:15, which has been known for centuries
as the Protevangelium, a Latin word meaning 'the first gospel'.
This fastens on the element of promise contained in what, strictly
speaking, is a curse on the serpent. It is the promise that he will be
overcome by a human being, the 'seed of the woman'.[18] Here then
is a God-given hope that the effects of sin would be undone, by
God's initiative, from within the human race.

Paul is sometimes criticised when, in Galatians 3:15,16, he
places a lot of emphasis on the singular form of the word 'seed'
employed in the promises to Abraham recorded in Genesis 12:7,
etc. This is held to be unconvincing reasoning because of the fact
that, as in English, the singular for 'seed' can be used in Hebrew
in a collective as well as a truly singular sense. This is in fact a
misunderstanding of the situation, for Paul's point is undergirded,
in a study of the Old Testament itself, by the constant recognition
that God would send a specific person to fulfil this developing
promise, for there was of course a continuous genealogical line
from the seed of the woman through the seed of Abraham, of Isaac,
of Jacob and of David.

An expression often used as a synonym for 'man' is 'son of
man'. 'What is man that you are mindful of him, and the son of
man that you care for him?' (Ps. 8:4; cf. Num. 23:19). A study of
the historical development of biblical words and phrases is
fascinating, for a word that begins quite simply will often come to
its ultimate meaning filled to the brim with profound truth. This
may happen even within the limits of one biblical book. Isaiah
contains several striking examples of this.[19] In the case of this phrase
developments in its significance took place within the Old
Testament before it came to its supreme use in the New Testament
in application to Jesus.

A development beyond its basic sense occurs when it is used

by God when he is addressing Ezekiel. It is used so frequently in this prophet's book that it can be found almost by opening the prophecy at random. Why? Probably because, as we see in Chapter 1, God is revealed to this prophet in all his majesty and holiness, and the use of this phrase, suggesting as it does the human frailty of the recipient of the revelation, may be intended to underline the divine greatness still more. The prophet is, to borrow Paul's phrase (2 Cor. 4:7), simply a jar of clay when seen in contrast to such a great person.

Having been used to address one prophet, however, we discover that it is used in this way again, this time in Daniel 8:17. This reveals then that it is coming to have something of a technical sense, and now seems to be a natural phrase to use of a prophet, and perhaps could be employed of other servants of God.

Psalm 80 appears to represent a further step. Here Israel is depicted in the figure of a vine. In verse 15 the people are described collectively as 'this vine, the root your right hand has planted'. In verse 17 the figure changes. Now the psalmist cries out, 'Let your hand rest on the man at your right hand, the son of man you have raised up for yourself.' Another synonym for man? Yes, but much more. The man, or son of man, here would seem on the face of it to be Israel.

The rabbis however had a most interesting interpretation of this verse. The Targums are Aramaic paraphrases of Old Testament passages and they reflect rabbinic theology. The Targum on these words, translates 'son of man' as 'king messiah'. Perhaps then, as the rabbis thought, verse 17 does not simply apply to Israel but to the king who summed up the nation in himself. Even if their interpretation is incorrect, it at least shows that the title could be applied to a king as well as to a prophet.

All this prepares us for the supreme passage, Daniel 7. Daniel is given a vision of four great beasts rising up from the sea one after the other. Then there is a judgement scene presided over by the 'one that was ancient of days', who is of course Almighty God. The beasts are judged, but then, apparently in a separate but related vision (Dan. 7:13ff.), the prophet sees 'one like a son of man' who came, not from the sea but with the clouds of heaven, and who received a kingdom which was universal and, unlike the kingdoms of the beasts, eternal.

Who is this 'son of man'? It seems clear that the four beasts symbolise both four kings (v. 17) and also the kingdoms they rule and represent (v. 23). Although the language of verses 13 and 14 is applied in verses 18 and 22 specifically to a group, 'the saints of the Most High', the analogy of the beasts would suggest that the son of man too is an individual and not simply a group. In this case he is a king, in fact because his reign is both universal and eternal, the greatest of all kings, but he is not viewed simply in himself but as the head of a community.

The 'son of man' in Daniel 7 fascinated some non-biblical Jewish writers, like the man who composed a document called 'The Similitudes of Enoch', but our chief interest in it lies in the fact that Jesus applied it to himself. It was in fact the self-designation which as we have seen, is found on his lips most frequently in the Synoptic Gospels and it occurs too in the Fourth Gospel. So it suggests real humanity, but also kingship and even heavenly origin.

The son of God

The phrase 'son of God' does not occur with great frequency in the Old Testament. We find it being used of angels, but always in the plural (Job 1:6; 2:1; 38:7). Its use in Genesis 6:2 may also be a reference to angelic beings, in this case fallen ones, although the interpretation of this passage has been much disputed.[20] The fact that it is never applied to them in its singular form justifies an otherwise puzzling statement from the writer to the Hebrews (Heb. 1:5). Sonship and likeness are ideas which belong very much to each other in Hebrew thought, and so the angels may be called 'sons of God' because they are like him in being spiritual beings.

More important for our purposes is its use in application to Israel. In Exodus 4:22f. God appeals to Pharaoh as one father to another: 'Let my son go that he may serve me; if you refuse to let him go, behold, I will slay your first-born son.' God takes up this people Israel, adopts them (cf. Rom. 9:4), and lavishes on them all the love and care a father gives his son – and more, because he is

God and not man. So, at the beginning of a moving chapter, Hosea pictures God as the tender father holding out his arms to the little son as he makes his first attempts at walking (Hos. 11:1).

As the term 'son' had been used with reference to the nation as a whole we are not surprised to find it applied to its people in its plural form, although such instances are rare (Deut. 14:1; Isa. 1:2). Just as in the case of the angels, however, there is no example of the use of it in the singular to designate an individual, with one important exception.

This exception is the king. He is called 'son of God' in three passages. 2 Samuel 7:14 is the basic one, because both Psalm 2:7 and Psalm 89:27 assume the certainty of the promises recorded in that chapter. 2 Samuel 7:14 and Psalm 2:7 are each quoted or alluded to in the pages of the New Testament. Moreover it seems likely that Psalm 89:27 lies behind an expression like 'firstborn of all creation' in Colossians 1:15. See also Revelation 3:14. An examination of 2 Samuel 7 shows us the justification for this application to Christ, for it is the promise of a continuing dynastic line and yet at the same time there is an individualising of the language which makes it especially appropriate when applied to a particular person.

How could the term be used of the historical kings of the Old Testament? Probably because the king summed up the chosen nation in himself, but also because he foreshadowed the great King of the future.

It is true that in certain forms of ancient Near Eastern paganism the term, 'son of God' was a virtual synonym for 'king', but it was not really this in the Old Testament, as the rarity of its occurrence shows us. It is a term of relationship rather than one of office, and seems to have been used because of the special care God would give to the king as the leader of his chosen and deeply cared-for people. This relationship was of course seen in all its fullness, indeed in a unique form, when Jesus of Nazareth came into our world as the Son of God. The implications of its use by him and of him are many, but one of these is that it eminently fitted him for the kingly office *par excellence*.

The Angel of the Lord

A strange phenomenon appears in the Old Testament from time to time, especially in its narrative portions, in references to a supernatural being known as the Angel of Yahweh. In many of these passages he speaks as if he is God and yet the language used also suggests that he is distinct from him.

Hagar, Sarah's maid and the mother of Ishmael, was found by the Angel of the Lord beside a spring of water in the wilderness. He spoke to her, not in the name of God but as if he were God. The story comes to its conclusion with the words, 'She gave this name to the LORD who spoke to her, "You are the God who sees me"; for she said, "I have now seen the One who sees me" ' (Gen. 16:13). His appearances may also be studied in passages like Genesis 22, Exodus 3 and 14, Judges 13 and Zechariah 3. Genesis 18 and 19 are also illuminating. Here, although three men came to Abraham he spoke to one only. It is said, without explanation, that the Lord spoke to him, that the men left for Sodom but Abraham still stood before the Lord (Gen. 18:22), and finally that two (not three) angels arrived in Sodom (Gen. 19:1).

It is likely that the writer of the Book of Joshua saw this angel in the person who confronted Joshua as the captain of the Lord's host, as the same kind of phenomena appear in that passage (Josh. 5:13-6:2), and also that the person who wrestled with Jacob was this angel (Gen. 32:24-30; cf. Gen. 48:15f.). Hosea's comment on the latter incident is illuminating. Genesis 32 refers to the wrestler as 'a man', but Hosea, writing of Jacob, says, 'as a man he struggled with God. He struggled with the angel and overcame him; he wept and begged for his favour. He found him at Bethel and talked with him there - the LORD God Almighty, the LORD is his name of renown!' (Hos. 12:3-5) Here the identification between God and the angel is close and yet there is still distinction.

It will come therefore as no surprise then to find that the appearances of this Angel have been seen by many Christian theologians over the centuries as pre-incarnate manifestations of Christ. It is also no surprise to find that this identification has been seriously questioned by many modern Old Testament scholars. There are two chief theories put forward by such scholars to account for the Old Testament evidence.

The first view is that this angel was a demoted deity, originating within pre-Yahwistic paganism.[21] Now there are serious difficulties with this view. Given the implacable opposition the Old Testament shows to all forms of paganism, it is difficult to see how its writers could turn such an enemy into a friend, and moreover one intimately associated with the true God, the God of Israel.

Alternatively, it has also been suggested that the language of the kind of passages we are considering is an application of the principle of representation, in which the representative is regarded virtually as an extension of the personality of the one he represents, so that he can speak as if he is that person. This is more plausible, but still has difficulties as an explanation. In Judges 13, Manoah and his wife have an encounter with the angel of Yahweh. At the close of this encounter, the angel of Yahweh ascended in the altar flame, and, of course, fire is a symbol of deity. The two humans fell on their faces and, the writer says, 'Manoah realised that it was the angel of the LORD. "We are doomed to die!" he said to his wife. "We have seen God." ' The language here seems too strong to be interpreted in terms of representation.

It is, of course, one thing to say that this Angel is a divine person, but something more specific to assert that he is none other than a pre-incarnate manifestation of Christ. Can we take this further step? On general grounds, many theologians have concluded that we can. If Jesus Christ is divine and is the great Revealer of God, then we might expect to see his activity within the pages of the Old Testament as well as the New. If he is not Christ, then who can he possibly be? Viewing the matter from a Christian standpoint, we might suggest that this Angel could be the Spirit of God, but evidence for this is completely lacking, for there is no instance in either Testament of the Spirit of God appearing either in human or in angelic form.

Can we find any grounds for such an identification with Christ within the Old Testament itself? We could establish the matter if we could find clear links between the Angel of the Lord and messianic prophecy, that is prophecy which finds its focus in a man of the future and which we see fulfilled in Christ. There are three such possible links. The name of the Angel of the Lord is 'wonderful' (Judg. 13:18, RSV) and so also is the name of the messianic King (Isa. 9:6). Moreover, the Hebrew word employed here is normally used in reference to deity. If Malachi 3:1-4 speaks of the Messiah, and if 'the messenger of the covenant' in verse 1 stands in apposition to 'the LORD of hosts', then we have additional evidence. Finally Micah 5:2, which identifies Bethlehem as the birthplace of the messianic King, also indicates that he had a life long before he was born there, and perhaps, that he had some involvement in ancient history.

It should be said, of course, that such pre-incarnate manifestations anticipate but are not real parallels to the incarnation. The latter was a unique fact because only in Jesus of Nazareth did God actually come in a real human life from the womb to the tomb – and, of course, after the tomb!

References
1. See e.g. M.C.Tenney, 'Gospel of John' in *EBC*, Vol. 9, p. 197. He points out that every complete manuscript of this Gospel contains it.
2. See the following passages: Isa. 1:10-17; 29:13; Jer. 7:21-26; Hos. 6:6; Amos 5:21-27; cf. Ps. 50:7-15.
3. See David W. Gooding, 'Tabernacle' in *IBD,* Vol. III, pp. 1506-1511.
4. This is evident from the way it is used by Jesus during the Day of Questions (Mark 12:35-37).
5. See e.g. Acts 4:25,26; Heb. 1:5, 8,9.
6. See G.H. Wilson, *The Editing of the Hebrew Psalter,* Sheffield, Sheffield Academic Press, 1985; J.C. McCann Jr. (ed.), *The Shape and Shaping of the Psalter*, Sheffield Academic Press, 1993; D.C. Mitchell, *The Message of the Psalter: An Eschatological Programme in the Book of Psalms*, Sheffield Academic Press, 1997. The theory has been criticised by N. Whybray, *Reading the Psalms as a Book*, Sheffield Academic Press, 1996.
7. See the heading of this psalm.
8. See our discussion of this psalm on p. 85 above.
9. 'Servant Songs' is a long-standing description of this group of passages and is still largely employed, although it is not altogether appropriate.
10. Accepted by virtually all scholars except that there is some difference of opinion as to the length of the first two.
11. J.A. Motyer sees Isa. 61:1-3 and 63:1-3 as two parts of a sequence of four Songs, which he calls 'Songs of the Anointed Conqueror' and which were, like the Servant Songs, fulfilled in Christ. See J.A. Motyer, *The Prophecy of Isaiah,* Leicester, IVP, 1993, pp. 489-490.

12. All the main interpretations, Jewish and modern, are outlined and discussed in C.R. North, *The Suffering Servant in Deutero-Isaiah*, Oxford, OUP, 1956.

13. Of course, much depends here on the relative dating of Jeremiah and of Isaiah 53.

14. Quoting Isa. 49:6 in Acts 13:46-47. See also the description of the man of God in 2 Tim. 2:24-26 when compared with Isa. 42:1-3.

15. There has been some debate in modern times, initiated by M.D. Hooker in *Jesus and the Servant*, London, SCM., 1959, as to whether the extent of the New Testament's use of the Servant Songs has been exaggerated in the past and whether Jesus actually identified himself with the Servant, or simply saw himself fulfilling an Old Testament servant ideal. Hooker's views have been countered, among others, by R.T. France, *Jesus and the Old Testament*, London, IVP, 1971, pp. 110-132.

16. See verses 36-38.

17. Verse 12 shows his awareness that he was not sinless.

18. The Messianic interpretation of this passage and its place in Genesis, interpreted as a thoroughly Messianic book, is strongly defended by T.D. Alexander, 'Messianic Ideology in the Book of Genesis' in P.E. Satterthwaite, R.S. Hess and G.J. Wenham, *The Lord's Anointed: Interpretation of Old Testament Messianic Texts*, Carlisle, Paternoster, 1995, pp. 19-39.

19. I have tried to indicate some of these in the Introduction to my Commentary on Isaiah in *EBC*, Vol. 6, pp.16-19.

20. See J.H. Sailhamer, 'Genesis', in *EBC,* Vol. 2, *ad loc.*

21. See A.R. Johnson, *The One and the Many in the Israelite conception of God*, Cardiff, University of Wales Press, 1961.

Chapter 6

THE HERMENEUTICAL ISSUE

Our study of the application of the Old Testament to Christ raises a number of important questions of a hermeneutical nature.

Hermeneutics is the study of principles of interpretation and, although mostly applied to biblical and other literary studies, it can also have wider application. Scientists, for example, are also concerned with a very broad type of hermeneutics, for they seek to interpret some aspect of the natural universe.

Hermeneutical questions are very much to the fore these days. Shifts in scholarly interest are often due to movement in the general philosophical world, and this is certainly a main reason for the current interest in hermeneutics.

Modern hermeneutical theory

Philosophers today are very interested in the principles behind the way human beings understand things. There is interest, for instance, in the thought-processes which lie behind scientific and artistic creation. A scientist may be studying some phenomena in physics or biology, or whatever his chosen field may be, and he may find that the theories of earlier scientists do not fit these phenomena. He wrestles both with the phenomena and with these theories, and then, in a moment of insight, he sees some new way of viewing not only the phenomena but the whole field of knowledge to which they belong. He may propose some quite new theory which will fit the facts. This will mean then that the 'model' of the universe he has in his mind will change somewhat and perhaps quite radically. The insight that came to Copernicus concerning the nature of the solar system and which eventually completely replaced the Ptolemaic model is perhaps the best-known example of this.

Thomas Kuhn was interested in this feature of science and he called such changes 'paradigm shifts'. The term has been taken up especially by the social scientists who have seen clearly that such shifts do occur from time to time in their particular areas of study. Arthur Koestler[1] was interested in links between what have been called 'the two cultures', the arts and the sciences, and he argued persuasively that these two major disciplines have more in common than most people think. They are united in the fact that the flash of insight is a moment of great importance in both scientific and artistic creation.

Michael Polanyi has examined the nature of the fundamental convictions or faiths human beings have and how they affect the way they think about everything.[2]

Somewhat in line with this, Herman Dooyeweerd, the great Dutch Christian philosopher, has given much attention to what he calls 'the religious root', which is the deepest conviction a man or woman has and which influences all their thinking and their actions.[3]

Kuhn, Koestler, Polanyi and Dooyeweerd are by no means identical in their outlook on many things, but they are at one in seeing how important a person's really basic concepts and convictions are. Of course these convictions may change, as, for instance, when somebody is converted to Christ from atheism or from Buddhism or from a life completely dedicated to amassing money. Such a radical experience sets in motion a more or less total reorientation of a person's outlook and life-style.

Those who belong to the school of thought known as Structuralism have taken a related and yet somewhat different line of approach. They have emphasised the deep structures that lie beneath the surface of literature. They point to the fact that all thinking reflects the way our minds are patterned, so that all human thought inevitably observes these fundamental structures. For instance, when we become aware of something new in our environment, our minds start to ask questions about its origins and its causes. So 'every effect must have a cause' is a basic structure of the human mind. So, although people may differ in their deep convictions, there are basic patterns common to all.

Noam Chomsky was fascinated by the way children pick up, with such apparent ease, the language of their parents and their peers and he came to the conclusion that we are all biologically programmed for language learning, that the minds of all of us contain innate logical structures and that these are the key to language learning.[4] The Structuralists have stressed also the sociological factors which have helped to determine our mental structures. As John Riches, summing up this outlook, says, 'It is not just individual readers but readers in community that interpret texts.'[5]

Obviously such theories were bound to have some influence on biblical studies and they undoubtedly have. There has probably never been so much interest as there is now in the literary characteristics of the books of the Bible. Paul Ricoeur has written in a stimulating fashion on the application of such thinking to our understanding of Holy Scripture, and his work is a good antidote to the more extreme forms of this type of thinking, for he stresses the importance of a reverent and teachable approach to the text.[6]

Structuralism has however given way, at least in part, to what is known as Deconstructionism and it is here that this type of thinking really went to extremes. This movement has arisen partly out of Structuralism and partly in reaction to it. It lays stress on the inevitable relativism of all knowledge and so has a deep element of scepticism in it. For Derrida and other Deconstructionists my interpretation of reality at this present time depends not simply on the way my thinking has been shaped by a multitude of factors but also by the fact that this shaping is still going on. My interpretation is constantly changing, for it is affected by my moods, my circumstances, and the way I am being moulded and changed throughout my life.

This leads to an extreme form of subjectivism, in which there is no embarrassment whatever in setting aside a search for an objective meaning. Once again Riches summarises this outlook well in saying, 'Certain texts, at least, like works of art, cease to be the property of the author once they have been published. It is for the public to make of them what they will.'[7] Deconstructionism is the product of a wider movement known as Post-Modernism, which rejects the whole idea of objective truth.[8] If carried through rigorously, this approach would sweep away at once the vast labours of commentators down the centuries, or, at least, would deem these simply the personal opinions of the commentators which individual readers are free either to accept or reject in their search for the meaning of the text for themselves.

This approach is, of course, open to strong criticism, for it is self-contradictory. If all statements are purely subjective and relative, then this applies as much to the statements of the Deconstructionists as it does to any other statements, and so logically there is no reason whatever why we should accept them!

Despite this, however, there is undoubtedly some measure of truth in Deconstructionism. It is a reminder to the Christian of his or her fallibility and fallenness. Our search for truth tends to be undermined by presuppositions which come from the various educative factors that arise from our social environment, and by our changeableness, our profound ignorance of so many things and by our unwillingness to accept the truth if it is unpalatable. The fact that we often fail to find absolute truth does not, however, mean that it does not exist. It is vitally important that Christians do not give up altogether the notion of absolute truth. Jesus said 'I am .... the Truth' (John 14:6).

While rightly reminding ourselves of our fallibility and fallenness, we should at the same time recognise that the Holy Spirit can bring us, through the Scriptures, into a true if incomplete understanding of God and of our relationship with him. This is itself a basic conviction of the faith of Christians, and moreover is neither entirely subjective nor relative for it is held by Christians generally and not simply by one or a few individual Christians.

The history of biblical hermeneutics

In this chapter we are not concerned so much with the way *we* interpret the Scriptures, but rather the way the New Testament writers interpret the Old Testament, although of course we may learn much from them that will help us in our own reading of both Testaments.

It is important to enquire if their methods of interpretation are legitimate or whether in fact they distort the older literature in the process of interpreting it, especially, of course, when they seek to prove from it that Jesus is the Christ and to show what kind of Christ he is.

Before we do this, it will be helpful to trace in outline the way the Bible has been interpreted since the close of the New Testament canon, so that we can put more recent studies into an historical context. It would have been interesting also to consider Rabbinic and other interpretations of the Old Testament, but this would take us too far afield.

Biblical interpretation in the second and third centuries after Christ exhibited two somewhat different tendencies, one towards literalism and the other towards spiritualisation. Eventually these came to be represented in two important theological schools which produced contrasting theologians during the fourth and fifth centuries.

The Antiochene School adopted a rigorously literal approach. Philosophically it was under the influence of Aristotle, who is really in some ways the common sense philosopher or the plain man's philosopher. The Alexandrian School, on the other hand, was somewhat under the influence of Plato and it favoured a degree of spiritualisation and allegorisation. This school tended to see deeper meanings lying beneath the surface of the biblical text. We will see later that the differing emphases of these two schools affected the history of Christology itself.

Although the Antiochene tradition had its later supporters, there is no doubt that the Alexandrian emphasis became dominant during the Middle Ages, when the concept of the fourfold use of Scripture came to the fore. These four uses or levels of understanding were the literal, the allegorical, the anagogical and the tropological uses. Theologians often stressed the allegorical interpretation, especially when they were dealing with the Old Testament, but also they were interested in the anagogical, which involves spiritualisation. The tropological was the moral application.

The Reformers reacted strongly against this 'sensus plenior', this tendency to seek deeper meanings beneath the surface of the text. The reason for this is that they considered it had been unhelpful theologically, and had often meant that the plain meaning of the text could be evaded by appealing to some other sense. To them this plain sense was of over-riding importance and they regarded attempts to side-step it in this way as sophisticated expressions of the way the human mind has been affected by sin.

The Reformers saw that Scripture was addressed to the plain man, who would read it with the normal principles of grammar in mind, although of course it was important to seek the guidance of the Holy Spirit. In their emphasis on literal meaning they had strong support from scholars like Erasmus, who were as much influenced by Renaissance humanism as they were by the Reformation. Incidentally, the term 'humanism' did not have the anti-religious connotations it so often carries today, but simply referred to those who were interested in the group of subjects known collectively as the humanities.

In the field of hermeneutics, we might describe the Reformation as the triumph of Antioch over Alexandria. This does not mean that the Reformers always agreed with the Antiochenes theologically. It is possible to approve somebody's method without necessarily endorsing his conclusions. The Reformers wrote of the one meaning of Scripture, the meaning intended by the writer, although of course they recognised that the text may take on added significance when seen in the light of other parts of Scripture.

A couple of centuries after the Reformers the rationalists of the Enlightenment came on the scene. Their handling of Scripture was deeply affected by their rejection of the supernatural, and so they had an inbuilt bias against any understanding of an Old Testament passage in which the supernatural played a part, as, for instance, in predictive prophecy. Some of this thinking, usually in milder forms, came to influence the various schools of Liberal Christian writers, who showed something of an unease in their handling of the supernatural elements in the Bible. Major differences of approach in Liberal writers were usually due to the influence on them of the shifting philosophical scene.[9]

It came to be increasingly held that the New Testament writers were arbitrary in their handling of the Old Testament. It was alleged that this was largely due to their need to justify Christianity when talking to Jews. Jews and Christians both held to the authority of the Old Testament, so that discussions between them invariably turned on its interpretation. So, it was said, Christians went through the Old Testament looking for material that reminded them in some way of Christ, and simply applied it to him quite arbitrarily in their writings. These interpretations became somewhat standardised so that several writers might well employ the same Old Testament passage. Rendel Harris compiled two volumes of 'Testimonies', consisting of Old Testament passages which he saw reflected in the New Testament either by direct quotation or by allusion. Sometimes it was thought that this was simply a standard oral tradition although Harris himself held that these collections of interpretations were also given literary form.[10]

After the Second World War, the discovery of the Dead Sea Scrolls began to affect hermeneutics. It led especially to an interest in the method known as Midrash Pesher. In using this method, the Qumran sectaries who produced these scrolls would quote Old Testament passages, adapting the wording of these passages to fit their own situation, so that Scripture and interpretation became interwoven with each other. Such a method, which might seem dishonest to the modern reader, seems to have been accepted then as quite justifiable. Presumably the reader would normally be well acquainted with the passage in its original uninterpreted form and so could see exactly what was happening. Modern quotation conventions did not then apply and should not be employed by us as tests of validity.[11]

C.H. Dodd did valuable work in the area of the New Testament use of the Old Testament, the results of which were crystallised and popularised in his short but seminal work, *According to the Scriptures*.[12] In this he showed that the use of the Old Testament in the New Testament books was not arbitrary and that the Old Testament context was normally kept very much in mind. It might even have been the case that those for whom the New Testament books were originally written were intended to look up each Old Testament passage and read it in its context. Finally Dodd maintained that in all probability this method of understanding the Old Testament was learned by the New Testament writers from Christ himself.

Following this there was a spate of works dealing with some important New Testament passages which make copious use of the Old Testament. Writers such as B.Gerhardsson,[13] B. Gartner,[14]

J.H. Elliott[15] and E. Lovestam[16] wrote impressively detailed studies of particular New Testament passages which interpret the Old Testament. In such studies Dodd's thesis was explored and vindicated in terms of these specific passages.

Then came Structuralism. It was a new hermeneutical approach to all forms of literature. This approach was new in the sense that it showed little interest in the historical background of the authors of literature, but focused attention exclusively on the text. This has led to a renewed concentration among many biblical scholars on the text itself and its literary qualities rather than on matters of background.

Post-Structuralism and notably that form of it known as Deconstructionism, as we have already seen, went further still and interest in the reader completely took over from interest in the writer. What mattered was not what the writer intended but what the reader understood. Any attempt to find the objective meaning of the text was rejected. The text means whatever it means for me, and, furthermore, for me now. It may mean something different to me at a later reading.

The Post-Structuralists are still very much with us, but it would be a serious mistake to think they are the only workers in the field of interpretation, particularly biblical interpretation. Good work of a totally different kind is being done, work which still takes objective truth seriously. There are scholars, for instance, who are seeking to show that the New Testament writers do not violate the sense of the Old Testament. The recent symposium, *The Lord's Anointed* [17] makes an important contribution. In this volume, a number of Old Testament specialists demonstrate that various Old Testament books have a major interest in the coming of a Davidic Messiah.

In addition we might refer again to recent work on the Psalms by G.H. Wilson[18] and others[19] in which the Davidic Kingdom and the Davidic Messiah are seen to be major themes of the Book of Psalms. This group of scholars maintain that the Psalter was given a canonical shape, prior to the coming of Christ, which was determined by theological considerations, and which was intended to rebuild faith, after the trauma of the Exile, and particularly to foster the expectation of the coming Messiah.

Despite the current philosophical climate, we will assume that Scripture does have objective meaning, and that there is point therefore in seeking to show that the New Testament writers do not mishandle the Old Testament but that they interpret it in a way which is consistent with its intended meaning.

The Importance of the Messianic Theme in the Old Testament

The Rabbis of New Testament times, most of whom belonged to the party of the Pharisees, had their own conception as to what was central in the Old Testament. The traditional Christian view of the Pharisees is that their emphasis was chiefly on the Mosaic Law. Certainly a straight-forward reading of the New Testament with its comments on the Pharisees and lawyers who are closely associated with them there would seem to support this.[20] It has however been more recently challenged by E. P. Sanders, who has been followed by many other scholars. Sanders holds that Pharisaic Rabbinism was less legalistic than might appear from the pages of the Gospels, and that its chief emphasis was on the covenant of God with Israel. This would mean that, simply in this respect, the Pharisaic emphasis would be in line both with the theology of the Westminster Confession of Faith of the Westminster divines and also the view of Old Testament Theology promoted in Walter Eichrodt's pioneering work on this subject.[21]

We may have to make a distinction between the major Pharisaic theologians, who would be centred in Jerusalem (later in Jabneh) and in Babylon, and the local practitioners in places like the towns and villages of Galilee where so much of our Lord's ministry took place. There can be little doubt, if we take the Gospels seriously, that the latter were very legalistic. We should realise, of course, that an emphasis on covenant can become legalistic if its main concern is with a covenant that has law at its heart.

This does not mean that Rabbinism had no interest in the Messiah. It would probably be accurate to say that for the Rabbis Messianism was important but less central than the Law.

We should not forget the place of the Sadducees in the religious life of the people of Israel in New Testament times. They were an important party who were the core of the priesthood, and the chief priests (the high priest and his family and close friends and colleagues) were the controlling group among them. There can be little doubt that they were not so deeply motivated by religion as the Pharisees. Their main religious interest was in the temple and its ritual calendar. They certainly had little interest in Messianism for it was not in keeping with their general preoccupation with the benefits of religion within the present life. Not only so, but there was always a suggestion of sedition about it, and they were eager not to antagonise their Roman overlords.

In a remarkable address recorded in Acts 7, Stephen took on both the Pharisees and Sadducees, and suffered martyrdom as a result. He accused the Pharisees, who were so preoccupied with the Law, of failure to keep it, and he accused the Sadducees of settling down with the solid, immovable temple when in fact the centre of God's purpose had now moved on to Christ. The implication is that both groups had missed the main point, and that they should have recognised Jesus when he came to be God's Messiah.

There are passages in the New Testament where there appears to be a deliberate exaltation of Jesus as the Christ in contrast to the Law. It seems to be the case in the Prologue to the Gospel of John, and may also be so in the Beatitudes, so that, for example, 'Blessed are the poor in spirit, for theirs is the kingdom of heaven' (Matt. 5:3) was probably intended to be understood to mean, 'Blessed are the poor in spirit, for the kingdom of heaven belongs, not to the legalists but to them.'

Can the centrality of Messianism be conclusively demonstrated from the pages of the Old Testament itself? The authors of *The Lord's Anointed* have certainly made out a good case for the importance of a messianic motif in quite a number of the Old Testament books. No doubt others will be stimulated to work also at the remaining books. Ultimately, of course, we look to the authority of Jesus himself on the matter and there can be no doubt that this was his view.

Different Kinds of New Testament use of the Old Testament
It is important to recognise that there is considerable variety. The basic assumption of it all is that the Old Testament finds its fulfilment in Jesus as the Christ, but within this there is much difference of approach.

We will now look at the various ways in which the Old Testament is handled.

There is *Promise*, perhaps a better term than prediction, because we may predict what we do not cause and prediction may take the form of threat as well as promise. The promises were made by God, often through the agency of a prophet.

Because these promises were made by God either directly or through agents, the coming of Christ is presented in the New Testament as the supreme example of the trustworthiness of God, so that we are encouraged to make a wholehearted commitment to his final Word, Christ himself. For instance, in 2 Corinthians 1:18-20, after affirming that God is faithful, Paul goes on to say, 'For the Son of God, Jesus Christ, who was preached among you by me and Silas and Timothy, was not "Yes" and "No", but in him it has always been "Yes". For no matter how many promises God has made, they are "Yes" in Christ. And so through him the "Amen" is spoken by us to the glory of God.'

It is worth noting that Jesus is the supreme but not the only example of God's faithfulness. In an unusual work, *The Old Testament of the Old Testament*,[22] R.W.L. Moberly deals with the Book of Genesis and shows how many of its promises were fulfilled within the later Old Testament, especially of course in the Exodus from Egypt and the entry into Canaan. God gave Abraham great promises. He said that he would make a great nation of his seed and give him a land in which this nation would live (Gen. 12:1ff., *et al.*). He kept these promises. Isaac's descendants did become a great nation and they were given the land of promise.

Many of the promises of God in Old Testament days may appear at times to be like a number of streams flowing independently. As we saw in the last chapter, the people of Israel were encouraged to look forward to a number of great figures. The New Testament proclaims that in one person all these figures are united, and so this justifies Paul's statement that Christ is God's 'Yes' to all the promises he has made.

The Old Testament looks beyond itself to a future day when God will reveal himself in some new and special way and this will mean the final establishment of his great purposes both for Israel and for the world as a whole.

Ezekiel, for example, declared the judgement of God on the shepherds (the kings and other leaders) of Israel. God then promises, 'Behold, I, I myself will search for my sheep, and will seek them out' (Ezek. 34:11). The Lord Jesus fulfilled this. He and the New Testament writers often use shepherd language about him (e.g. in John 10 and 1 Peter 2:25; 5:4); and he also said, 'The Son of Man came to seek and to save the lost' (Luke 19:10). If this is an allusion to Ezekiel 34, as it may well be, then we see in Jesus the God of the Old Testament revealing himself in his seeking and saving action.

He is also God's great man of the future, for, as we have seen in Chapter 5, there are many passages in Old Testament books which look forward to a great king, a perfect prophet, an eternal priest, and which find their fulfilment in Jesus. Perhaps even more basic are the prophecies of a special seed in whom great purposes of God would find their fulfilment. These promises start with the Protevangelium in Genesis 3:15 and find repetition and expansion in later parts of Genesis. [23]

In terms of kingship, we find, for instance, in Isaiah 8, a prophecy of the coming of a Child with most exalted names who would sit on the Throne of Judah. Micah, Isaiah's contemporary, who also prophesied in Judah as Isaiah did, wrote of him that he would be born in Bethlehem (Mic. 5:2). Here then is both prediction and promise.

The great passage in Deuteronomy 18:15-18 partakes mainly of the characteristics of a promise but also has qualities of a threat as well, for there is a warning of judgement on the person who does not listen to the words of that prophet.

The Son of Man of Daniel 7 is also clearly promissory and predictive. Along with the references to Enoch in Genesis 5, it gave rise to a whole corpus of literature, outside the canon of

Scripture, purporting to fill out these predictions in more detail.[24]

Can we vindicate the way the New Testament writers view the Old Testament as promise and prediction? If we rule out supernatural prophecy as impossible, then of course we cannot, but there is an arbitrariness about such an attitude which needs to be challenged. Much depends on whether we thoroughly accept the biblical doctrine of God and the scriptural record of his supernatural acts. This is of crucial importance and will be considered in a later chapter.

In addition to promise, there is also *typology*. In this there is a comparison between some Old Testament person, office, institution or event and Jesus Christ, so that this item in the Old Testament foreshadowed him in some way or ways. Often this involves some degree of spiritualisation, although not always. For instance, he was quite literally a prophet, but he was not literally a tabernacle, although he was foreshadowed by both.

Typology is extremely extensive and is closely related to promise and prediction.[25] The New Testament writers use terms like 'prophet', 'priest' and 'king' of him. These terms suggest pictures. They come from the Old Testament, because there we have legislation and other information which enables us to see the kind of functions these men were called by God to perform. The Old Testament is therefore important because it gives 'body' to many of the terms used by the New Testament in connection with Christ.

We need to remember though that terms like 'prophet', 'priest' and 'king' are meaningful for some other cultures too. For instance, all kinds of conceptions of kingship have existed. Sometimes a king has been an absolute monarch with the arbitrary power of life and death over his subjects, while at others he has been a constitutional monarch whose powers are severely circumscribed, and who may even have less real power than his chief minister. To find the exact meaning of 'king' as applied to Christ we must study the Old Testament background. We need not only to look at the actual historical kings for it is even more important to consider the regulations for their appointment and their relationships and their functions. We could easily misunderstand such terms without relating them to this Old Testament context.

Incidentally, this is even more important with terms like 'Son of God', 'Lord' and 'Saviour', which were being employed in the Graeco-Roman world in New Testament times. We must understand them in terms of the Jewish background of belief in one holy God and not the Graeco-Roman world with its polytheism and its frequent failure to link religion and morality.

So this Old Testament background gives very full intellectual content to the great words and phrases applied to Jesus Christ in the pages of the New Testament. Faith is essentially trust in a person, but it cannot exist unless we have an idea as to who that person is and what he is like. The more we learn of him, so the richer faith becomes on its mental side, and the greater its formative influence on our lives can be.

It is very interesting to find that the Old Testament itself contains typology, as, for instance, when there are references to a new Exodus. In Isaiah 51:9-11, for instance, the prophet's language clearly suggests that he was looking to God to effect a new Exodus, this time, of course, not from Egypt but from Babylon. This means that the method, as a method, could be thoroughly vindicated in discussion with an orthodox Jew because it could be shown to have Old Testament precedent.

Akin to typology is the way godly people in the Old Testament prefigured something of Christ's character in their own. Of course, he alone is perfect, but just as Christians may portray Christ in so far as, by his grace, they live to his glory, so did those who lived in Old Testament days.

In addition to promise and typology, there is what we might call *terminological seedbed*. There are some words which are important for the New Testament's understanding of Jesus, which have an Old Testament background that does not exactly fit into the category of typology, chiefly because they are too abstract to be classified in this way. Typology by its various nature is concrete.

To give some examples, we find that New Testament terms like 'wisdom' (e.g. 1 Cor.1:24) and 'word' (e.g. John 1:1, 14) need a literary setting to give them fullness of meaning, and that the Old Testament (in these cases passages like Proverbs 8 and Psalm

33) provides this. Again this is important and vital, lest we should misinterpret such words. For instance, if we were to understand 'wisdom' in the context of Greek philosophy or think of 'word' as it was employed in Stoicism or Hermeticism we would certainly misinterpret each.[26]

Also there are terms like 'life' and 'light' and 'truth'. These words are used much in the Johannine literature, and in each case it is made clear that they are no longer to be thought of simply as abstractions, but that they found incarnate form in Jesus Christ. It is important also to say that, although abstracts, they are not to be interpreted philosophically but rather in terms of their use in the Old Testament, which was of course the Scripture of those who wrote the New Testament books. We need to remember that such language comes into the New Testament from the Old by way of the Septuagint, the great Greek version of the Old Testament which was widely used in the synagogues of the Dispersion, heavily laden with Old Testament meaning. So this gives still more clarity to what the New Testament writers claim for Christ and what he claimed for himself. In the Old Testament, such terms are found particularly, but not exclusively, in the psalms.

Because so many of these terms in their Old Testament setting apply to God, their application in the New Testament to Christ is very significant indeed. This in itself suggests that the New Testament writers were convinced of his deity.

Both typology and the use of the Old Testament as a terminological seedbed really require no justification, for a great deal of literature does this kind of thing. For instance, G.K. Chesterton wrote a book called *The Napoleon of Notting Hill*, and the application of the name 'Napoleon' to the leading character in it was based on their possession of some similar qualities. So then typology is really a literary device, although the theological status of typology in Scripture is due to the conviction the correspondences between the Old Testament types and Christ as the great Antitype were divinely intended.

Next comes *verbal adaptation*, where New Testament concepts are simply clothed with Old Testament phraseology. This is not therefore an attempt to prove anything, but simply the use of a familiar medium to clothe something that is less familiar to the readers.

When this happens, however, there is often a special fitness in that the two are related in some way or other. For example, in Deuteronomy 30:8-16, it is said that God's law is accessible to the people of Israel, so that they have no excuse for their disobedience to it. In Romans 10:5-10, Paul applies this language to the gospel, for he knew that the gospel was just as accessible as the law, for he and many others had been preaching it to the Jews. So, although he is not seeking to prove a point, there is real appropriateness in what he does, because law and gospel come from the same God.

John 1:1-18 and Matthew 5:1-12 are other passages where Jewish readers would have been reminded of what the Old Testament and the rabbis taught about the Law, and would see these passages as deliberately comparing and contrasting Christ and the gospel with it.

Then there is *verbal assonance*. This would not perhaps seem very significant to a modern Western reader, but it should be remembered that the Hebrew people have always been fond of word- play and that, in fact, this may be found in significant contexts within the Old Testament itself.

An interesting New Testament example of this may be found in Matthew 2:23. The term 'Nazarene', although of course meaning an inhabitant of Nazareth, might well remind Jews of the Hebrew word *nezer* (branch), which, through its use in the Old Testament[27] became a synonym for 'Messiah'. Matthew's point therefore would appear to be that it was eminently fitting that Jesus should be brought up in a place with such a name.

Now this would probably commend itself to a Jew, for something very similar occurs in Micah 1:10-16. In that passage the prophet selects a number of place-names in Judah and indicates that God will bring on each a punishment that exactly matched the name of the town.

It might be asked whether it really matters that Jesus Christ came as the fulfilment of the Old Testament, as the climax of a long historical story. Does it matter that he was born into the nation of Israel, and that people like Abraham, Jacob, Moses, David and many another belonged to that story?

Yes, it does indeed, and for a number of important reasons.

The Old Testament presents a lot of really basic truth about God, truth its writers believed was given by him to his people. It was in the course of the history of the people of Israel that they were taught this truth. They learned through his dealings with Abraham and Moses that he was a God who makes and keeps covenants. They learned through the events of the Exodus that he is a God of mercy and judgement. They learned through his dealings with them in the land over many years that he is a God of great patience and long-suffering.

All these lessons, and countless others, were stamped on their minds and hearts in relation to historical events, as these events were interpreted to them by the men of God he sent to do that very thing. All these truths, and the history upon which they are based, are important, because it was that God, and no other, who, according to the New Testament, became man in the Lord Jesus Christ.

Variation in Use of the Old Testament among the New Testament writers

As we have seen, the New Testament writers are at one in seeing Jesus Christ in the Old Testament and also in applying it to him in certain standard ways, such as promise and Fulfilment, type and Antitype. There is, however, no wooden uniformity in the way they do this.

For instance, in the Epistle to the Hebrews, typology is extremely common, but particularly characteristic of this writer is his strongly theological use of the Book of Psalms. Simon Kistemaker[28] has argued persuasively that the main theological argument of the writer is carried by the way he expounds four psalms (Psalms 8, 95, 110 and 40) and applies them to Christ. The psalms are, of course, frequently quoted and alluded to in the New Testament, just as we would expect, as the Psalter is the longest book in the Old Testament, but the way this writer uses them is unique.

Then there is the Book of the Revelation. Whereas the other New Testament books tend to employ various formulae of quotation, such as 'It is written' or 'What does the Scripture say?'

or 'that it might be fulfilled' this kind of language does not appear in this book. Instead, this book is simply saturated with Old Testament allusions and symbols. A reader familiar with the Old Testament would find, in reading Revelation, that he or she could hardly read more than two or three verses anywhere in it without being reminded of something in the Old Testament.

It is important to realise that many passages which seem to be arbitrary in their use of the Old Testament are in fact theologically motivated. This is markedly true of the Gospel of Matthew, the New Testament book which has perhaps been the most criticised from this point of view. This Gospel is characterised by the frequency with which the quotation formula 'that it might be fulfilled' is employed in it. An examination of Matthew's use of it reveals that, in fact, he worked with a very flexible concept of fulfilment. He employs virtually all the devices we have outlined above as characteristic of the New Testament writers in relating Christ to the Old Testament, and to him each of them involves 'fulfilment'. So fulfilment for him seemed to suggest not simply that a prediction had come to pass on the plane of history but rather the much wider idea that there was a meaningful correspondence of some sort between some Old Testament passage or passages and Christ.

These are simply examples of the individuality, within a general unity, of the New Testament writers in their use of Old Testament material. This is surely one reason why the New Testament constantly feeds the Christian's faith in Christ and yet does so by a marvellously varied and balanced diet.

References
1. A Koestler, *The Act of Creation*, London, Picador, 1989.
2. See the references to Polanyi's work (and also to Thomas Kuhn) in L. Newbigin, *The Gospel in a Pluralist Society*, London, SPCK, 1989, especially in Chapters 3 and 4, and also T.F. Torrance (ed.), *Belief in Science and in Christian Life: The Relevance of Michael Polanyi's Thought for Christian Faith and Life*, Edinburgh, Handsel Press, 1980.
3. His views on this are set out in his major work, *A New Critique of Theoretical Thought* (4 vols. trans. by D.H. Freeman, etc)., H.J. Paris, Amsterdam, 1953-1958. See also the article on him by William Young in P.E. Hughes (ed.), *Creative Minds in Contemporary Theology*, Grand Rapids, Eerdmans, 1966, pp. 270-305.

4. A straight-forward introduction to Chomsky's thought may be found in J. Lyons, *Chomsky,* London, Fontana/Collins, 1970.

5. J.K. Riches, *A Century of New Testament Study*, Cambridge, Lutterworth, 1993, p. 223.

6. See, e.g. Paul Ricoeur, *Essays on Biblical Interpretation*, Philadelphia, Fortress, 1980. Some of the essays in Elmer Dyck (ed.), *The Act of Bible Reading: A Multidisciplinary Approach to Biblical Interpretation, Carlisle,* Paternoster, 1996, relate the Christian's reading of Scripture both positively and negatively to modern literary theory. See also P.E. Satterthwaite and D.F. Wright, *A Pathway into the Holy Scripture*, Grand Rapids, Eerdmans, 1994.

7. J.K. Riches, *op. cit.* , pp. 223-224.

8. For an exposition and criticism of Post-Modernism and of Deconstructionism, see D.A. Carson, *The Gagging of God*, Leicester, Apollos, 1996, Chapters 2 and 3.

9. See Geoffrey W. Grogan, 'Modern Theology and the Evangelical Faith' in *TSF Bulletin* 49 (Autumn 1967) pp. 1-9. A very detailed treatment may be found in John McQuarrie, *Twentieth Century Religious Thought,* London, SCM., 3rd edn. 1981.

10. J.R. Harris, *Testimonies,* Cambridge, CUP, I (1916), II (1920).

11. See F.F. Bruce, *Biblical Exegesis in the Qumran Texts,* London, IVP, 1960.

12. See p. 29, n. 5.

13. *The Testing of God's Son*, Lund, Gleerup, 1966 (a study of Matt. 4:1-11).

14. *The Areopagus Speech and Natural Revelation,* Lund, Gleerup, 1955 (a study of Acts 17).

15. *The Elect and the Holy: An Exegetical Examination of 1 Peter 2:4-10*, Leiden, Brill, 1966.

16. *Son and Saviour, a study of Acts 13:32-37*, Lund, Gleerup, 1961.

17. P.E. Satterthwaite, R.S. Hess, G.J. Wenham (eds.), *The Lord's Anointed: Interpretation of Old Testament Messianic Texts,* Carlisle, Paternoster 1995.

18. G.H. Wilson, *The Editing of the Hebrew Psalter,* Chico, Scholars Press, 1985.

19. See J.C. McCann Jr. (ed.), *The Shape and Shaping of the Psalter,* Sheffield, Sheffield Academic Press, 1993.

20. e.g. see Matt. 23:2-4,23,24; Mark 2:23-3:6; Luke 11:37-53

21. W. Eichrodt, *Theology of the Old Testament* (in 2 vols.trans. by J. Baker), London, SCM, 6th edn., 1959.

22. R.W.L. Moberly, *The Old Testament of the Old Testament*, Minneapolis, Fortress, 1992.

23. See T.D. Alexander, 'Messianic Ideology in the Book of Genesis' in Satterthwaite, Hess and Wenham, *The Lord's Anointed*, pp. 19-39.

24. For a brief survey of this literature, see the article 'Enoch' in *IBD*, I, p. 458.

25. I have tried to elucidate the relationship between prophecy and typology in an article in the *Scottish Bulletin of Evangelical Theology*, 4:1 (Spring 1986) pp. 5-16.

26. This does not mean of course that the term *logos* (word), used in John 1 may not have been a 'carrot' to encourage the philosophical reader to embark on a study of this Gospel, but simply that the basic significance of the term must be sought in the Old Testament and Jewish background, not in Greek philosophy.

27. e.g. in Isaiah 11:1.

28. Simon Kistemaker, *The Psalm Citations in the Epistle to the Hebrews*, Amsterdam, 1961.

Chapter 7

JESUS CHRIST IN HIS HUMILIATION

What do Christians mean when they say that Jesus Christ came from heaven to earth and what does such language imply? What was involved in such a coming?

Our space age has got used to the idea of a universe 'out there' and to the possibility of exploring it from earth. Is this place 'out there' what the Bible means by 'heaven'? Not really. If it was then there would be point in Yuri Gagarin's reported comment that although his space journey took him beyond earth's orbit, he failed to find God there.

The Jews of the inter-testamental period used to speak about three heavens. Nearest to us is the first, where the birds fly. Next comes the second, where the sun and the moon and the stars are. Last of all is the home of God. The big difference between the first two and the third is that they are visible while it is not. This is the main distinction the New Testament makes. There is a visible and there is an invisible universe and it is this invisible realm to which chiefly the name 'heaven' is given (Col. 1:16).

Of course spatial language is used in the New Testament about heaven and earth, but some such modes of expression are hardly avoidable. In his book, *Honest to God*,[1] John Robinson said that we need to get rid of such language and replace it by talking about the depths rather than the heights. God is not 'out there' but 'in here'. We cannot look at all the implications of this suggestion and the way he sought to link it up with Depth Psychology, but it is subject to at least one weighty criticism. It means that we lose altogether the transcendence of God, the sense that God is to be contrasted with his creation as infinitely great and, because of this, worthy of worship. It is true that Robinson tried to retain the word 'transcendence' but in a very different sense, a sense difficult to understand as anything but a special aspect of his immanence.[2]

The fact is that the spatial language used in the Bible in this connection is metaphorical and this has probably always been clear to most Christians who have thought at all deeply about the matter. Metaphors stand for something, however, and this space language helps to secure for us the truth of God's infinite greatness.

John records the Son of God as saying, 'I am the living bread that came down from heaven' (John 6:51). What did he mean by this, and what does the New Testament teach about his life before he came at Bethlehem?

His Pre-existent Life

He was always with God

The serious fourth century heresy known as Arianism has appeared in different guises in modern times, notably but not exclusively in sects like the Jehovah's Witnesses and the Christadelphians.

The Arians were prepared to say all sorts of high sounding things about Jesus Christ, but they stopped short at the most important point. They were not prepared to say that he was God. The greatest man who had ever lived? – Yes! The greatest being in the created universe? – Yes! God? – No! So, they said, 'there was a time when he was not.' Athanasius was clear sighted enough to see not only that this robbed the Christian faith of its unique distinctiveness but also that it completely undermined the New Testament teaching about salvation through Christ.

John declares, 'In the beginning was the Word, and the Word was with God, and the Word was God. He was with God in the beginning' (John 1:1,2). This great passage really makes four statements about him. The third of them is of supreme importance and we shall look at it later. Notice for the moment, though, that the fourth is a combination of the first two, and so has the effect of emphasising the point John is making.

Our English word 'with' here is a translation of the Greek preposition, *pros*. Common as this word is, it is uncommon in the sense it must have here. Its basic meaning is 'towards', and so John appears to be saying more than simply that Jesus the Word was always with the Father. This use of this word suggests that Jesus was eternally with God in the sense that he was facing towards him, surely intended to picture the fact that they were for ever in fellowship with each other. John goes on at the end of his prologue to speak of Christ as the one who was 'at the Father's side' (John 1:18). This again implies close fellowship.

In the teaching of Jesus recorded in the Gospel of John he often uses language which suggests a kind of wistful 'homesickness' for heaven (John 8:23; 13:3; 14:28; 16:28). It is particularly moving to be able to listen in to his prayer as he addresses the Father shortly before the crucifixion (John 17). This prayer reflects a beautiful intimacy of love and shows an awareness on his part that this relationship existed before the universe came into being, for he says, 'And now, Father, glorify me in your presence with the glory I had with you before the world began ... You loved me before the creation of the world' (John 17:5, 24).

It is not only in the Gospel of John that this kind of teaching occurs. Paul, for instance, when writing to the Corinthians and seeking to stimulate them in their Christian giving, uses – as he so often does – the highest possible illustration: 'For you know the grace of our Lord Jesus Christ, that though he was rich, yet for your sakes he became poor, so that you through his poverty might become rich' (2 Cor. 8:9). When was Christ rich? Certainly not during any period of his earthly life. This expression then can only have meaning if we relate it to his life before he came into the world, his eternal life with God.

He created everything

Modern men and women have a bigger conception of the universe than any have had before in earlier generations. Modern science is still discovering how vast it is, and scientists present statistics to us that baffle the mind and that even the imagination cannot really handle. If we take the teaching of the New Testament seriously, every new discovery will serve only to make us more aware of the supreme greatness of Christ, who created it all.

For this is indeed what the New Testament teaches us about him. John 1:1-18 constitutes the Prologue to the Gospel of John and it is reasonable to assume that the writer intended his readers to bear its teaching in mind throughout their reading of the chapters that follow it. The language of its first verse ('in the beginning ...') appear to be deliberately reminiscent of the opening of Genesis 1. Then in verse 3 comes the statement, 'through him all things were made; without him nothing was made that has been made.'

Paul takes up this theme in two passages. In 1 Corinthians 8:6 he states, 'For us there is but one God, the Father, from whom all things came and for whom we live; and there is but one Lord, Jesus Christ, through whom all things came and through whom we live.' This statement occurs in the course of a polemic against paganism, so that we must give the term 'Lord' its full meaning for those who knew its Old Testament background, its application to the only God who exists.

In Colossians Paul spells this out in more detail when he says, 'by him all things were created, things in heaven and on earth, visible and invisible, whether thrones or powers or rulers or authorities; all things were created by him and for him. He is before all things' (Col. 1:16,17). Paul seems here to be particularly concerned to show that creatorship implies overlordship by his emphasis on the created status of all other authorities. They may exercise power, but they would not even possess it apart from his creative activity.

The first two chapters of the Epistle to the Hebrews are strongly Christological and they lay a basis of teaching about the person of Christ which is built on when the theme of Christ's work is expounded in much of the remainder of the book. Writing of God's speech to us through his Son, the author says, 'through whom he made the universe' (Heb.1:2).

The teaching of the passages we have been considering is simply staggering. They mean that, although he was born as a baby, probably six or seven pounds in weight, nineteen or twenty inches long, yet he is the Creator of everything that exists!

Why do our New Testament writers say not only that the universe was created by him but also through him? It is because they believed in the Father as well as the Son. One of the many things John is suggesting when he uses the term 'Word' of Jesus (John 1:1, 14) is that we should interpret Genesis 1 with its oft repeated 'and God said' in terms of Christ. It was God's Word that created the universe, but that Word is to be thought of not simply as a meaningful sound but as a person. God made everything through his eternal Son.

He sustains everything

Creation is an act or a series of acts. It is of course a manifestation of great power, revealing that the Creator is almighty. Just as wonderful, however, is the power to keep in being what has been created. This too is ascribed to Christ in two of the passages whose teaching about his creative work we have already considered.

After writing of this creative work, Paul goes on to say, 'and in him all things hold together' (Col. 1:17). The scientist and the artist are somewhat closer in their outlook on the universe than they always realise, for both are interested in its order. The scientist marvels as he studies this order and the artist sees beauty in that order. Everything that exists, says Paul, is held together in an ordered structure by the Son of God.

This thought has great philosophical value. It provides the Christian student with a standpoint from which to view ordered structure in his own chosen field of study. All true order comes from his Saviour, who is the Creator and Sustainer of everything.

The writer to the Hebrews takes this thought even further in two ways. He says that Christ sustains all things by his powerful word (Heb. 1:3). This suggests that we are not to think simply in terms of impersonal laws. What we call law in the universe is simply evidence that God is consistent. Everything began with the uttered word of God and it continues in its ordered being on the same basis.

There is a further relevant thought in Hebrews 1. The picture of Atlas in Greek mythology shows us a man carrying the universe on his shoulders. It may seem at first sight that this is parallel to what the Epistle to the Hebrews says of Christ, but in fact it is not. The word *pheron* translated 'sustaining' really implies motion. To some this has suggested a universe in motion which would, of course, harmonise with the modern scientific model of the universe. It is more likely though that it suggests that Christ himself is moving everything forward in accordance with a divine plan.

He rules everything

This takes us further still. When we think of the universe apart from personal beings like men and angels, it is enough to say that Christ upholds and sustains it all by his power. The idea of a kingdom, however, suggests personal beings who are called to submit to his will and to serve his purposes. Paul speaks of Christ as 'the Head over every power and authority' (Col. 2:10), employing terms denoting authority status in the spiritual as well as in the human world. Christ is superior to them all and rightly rules over all.

It is worth remembering that if Jesus is both God and man, he now reigns in virtue of both facts. It is clearly the right of God to rule. If he cannot rule, then who can? We shall see later that the New Testament also relates Christ's right to rule everything and everybody to his true humanity and to his work of redemption.

In the Gospel of John, there is an important change at the close of chapter 12. Up to this point, Jesus is seen working and teaching openly among the Jews. In chapters 13-17 he takes his close disciples aside and concentrates on them. Chapter 12:35-50 brings his ministry among the Jews to a close and John comments on it, partly in the words of Jesus himself, but also, in verses 36b to 43, in his own words. He uses two quotations from the book of Isaiah, the first from chapter 53 and the second from chapter 6. Then he makes this astonishing statement: 'Isaiah said this because he saw his glory and spoke of him' (John 12:41).

It is no surprise to us that John believed Jesus is to be seen in Isaiah 53, because we could find a number of New Testament passages which imply the same thing.[3] What is so startling is the thought that in his great temple vision in Isaiah 6 the prophet saw the glory of Christ. Isaiah 6 is one of the most awe-inspiring encounters between God and a person that the Old Testament records. The seraphim acknowledged the utter holiness of the Lord, the prophet abased himself and confessed his sinfulness and the Lord spoke his word of great authority. He is 'the King, the Lord of hosts' (Isa. 6:5). The implication of John's quotation and his comment on it must be that the Son of God, long before he came to earth and before his exaltation to a kingly throne as man, reigned over everything from heaven as God.

He revealed God

If, as we argued in Chapter 5 on the basis of certain biblical phenomena, the Son of God manifested himself from time to time in the world as the Angel of the Lord prior to his coming at the Incarnation, then here is evidence that he was revealing God in Old Testament times. Does this mean simply that he was one of those who revealed God to people then, or can we go further than this and say that, in some sense, all revelation of God prior even to his special coming in the Incarnation was really revelation through him? If Isaiah 6 is a revelation of him, how many other parts of the Old Testament could be also?

We may get some light on this matter from Peter in his first letter. He writes about the Old Testament prophets (1 Pet. 1:10-12), and says, 'the prophets, who spoke of the grace that was to come to you searched intently and with the greatest care; trying to find out the time and circumstances to which the Spirit of Christ in them was pointing when he predicted the sufferings of Christ and the glories that would follow. It was revealed to them that they were not serving themselves but you, when they spoke of the things that have now been told you by those who have preached the gospel to you by the Holy Spirit sent from heaven. Even angels long to look into these things.'

This passage links together the Word of God in the Old Testament and in the New, and attributes both to the Holy Spirit, whom here he calls 'the Spirit of Christ'. It should not surprise us to find Peter using this term about the New Testament revelation, because he assured his hearers in Acts that the Holy Spirit sent from heaven came from the risen Christ (Acts 2:32f.). This is not however the way he uses the term in this passage. It is most significant that he calls the Spirit of God in his work in the Old Testament prophets by this title. It seems then that the Holy Spirit in his work of imparting divine truth to and through people worked in both testaments as the divine agent of the divine Christ.

If this is the case, then we can now read John 1:1-18 in an even deeper way. Jesus is the Word of God, not only because he brought the fullness of revelation from God when he came in the flesh, but because all true revelation of God, long before the incarnation, was not only revelation *of* him, having him as its great subject, but revelation *through* him. He is the master Revealer who instructs everyone through whom God's truth comes to men and women. It would appear then that the work of the Spirit in both economies was performed by him as the Agent of Christ.

He is God
We have left this point to the end. It hardly needs to be proved now, because all the other major statements we have made so far in this chapter point in this direction. If he created everything, sustains and rules everything and is the one great Revealer, how can we stop short of saying that he is God? No wonder John goes on from the statement 'the Word was with God' to assert 'and the Word was God' (John 1:1)!

Much has been sometimes made of the fact that there is no definite article in the Greek text before the word 'God' here. The omission of this article does not however have the significance that some sects have tried to give it. The use of the definite article in the Greek language is not identical with its use in English. Here it does not and cannot imply that the Word was 'a god', for what could such a statement mean to a Jew (and John was a Jew) but that he was a pagan deity? No, the omission of the article here is a perfectly regular way in Greek to show that 'the Word' and not 'God' is the subject of the clause. It also lays emphasis on the nature of the Word.

What finally confirms that the reductionist interpretation of John 1:1 cannot be correct is shown when the Gospel which opens with this verse comes to its climax in the worship of Jesus by Thomas, when he declares, 'My Lord and my God!' (John 20:28).

What his humiliation means
The word 'humiliation', in its modern English usage, suggests the words and actions that demean and insult a person and that treat him or her with a measure of contempt. This is not precisely what is meant by the word when used in theology. Rather it is employed as a general term for our Lord's voluntarily accepted status during his earthly life and also the conditions which obtained in the course

of that life. Yet the word does approach its modern sense somewhat when we realise that it was because of his human life that he suffered so much.

The reality of his human experience

The coming of the pre-incarnate Word to earth and his assumption of human nature was no play-acting, but an experience of human life just as real as our own. The church of Christ has always accepted this, even if it has sometimes given it less than sufficient emphasis. This fact has theological implications of the very deepest kind and we will be exploring these in some later chapters.

We must also consider what is meant by his virgin birth in a later chapter, where we will see that it is better designated a virgin conception, for in fact his birth was perfectly normal. We will also need to give careful thought later to other questions, such as the nature and extent of his knowledge, and whether we should think in terms of his possessing it eternally or acquiring it through earthly experience.

Meantime we will reflect on some of the conditions that obtained during his earthly life and especially on the cost to him involved in this human experience.

The suffering involved in his human life

Self-giving, especially when it takes a person through a deep valley of sorrow or suffering, is extremely moving for the onlooker. So much in this world is done with an eye for praise or for personal gain that people are very impressed when they see a love that is pouring itself out at real cost to the one who loves. The life of Jesus Christ was like that, not only in its end, but throughout its whole course. There must have been an element of suffering in his human experience from the very beginning, and this element became more and more dominant as his life moved to its terrible climax.

The Servant Songs, which we considered briefly in chapter 5, show this note entering more and more into his experience. Isaiah 42, which is the first of these 'songs' simply suggests that there would be factors in his ministry which would have made many

another falter or be discouraged (v. 4). The second, Isaiah 49, sees
the Servant looking back and assessing his ministry. In verse 4 he
says, 'I have laboured to no purpose; I have spent my strength in
vain and for nothing and vanity. Yet what is due to me is in the
LORD's hand, and my reward is with my God.' He is then described
as 'despised and abhorred by the nation' (verse 7). Isaiah 50:6
shows the spite of his enemies beginning to take the form of physical
violence: 'I offered my back to those who beat me, my cheeks to
those who pulled out the beard; I did not hide my face from mocking
and spitting.' It is however in the great fourth song (Isa. 52:13-
53:12) that the note of suffering comes to dominate the picture,
and these sufferings culminate in death.

Our concern in this volume is not so much with the work of
Christ as with his person. Because of this, we shall not be giving
theological consideration to the cross as a sacrifice for sin, or,
indeed, giving any thought to the work of Christ as effecting
salvation for us.[4] It is, however, relevant for us to think about his
sufferings in so far as they affect our understanding of his person.

What did Calvary and all the sufferings and sorrows that
preceded it mean to him? We cannot understand this in any full
way, not only because no human being can have a completely
accurate awareness of the sufferings of another, but also because
there were factors of a very special kind in his own sufferings. We
can however reverently follow up any light the Bible throws on
the subject. It should serve to deepen our sense of wonder and
gratitude.

His human feelings
The Gospels make use of language showing us that our Lord
possessed truly human emotions. Mark, in particular, uses a number
of words and phrases signifying strong feeling. He says that Jesus
was 'filled with compassion' when a leper came for cleansing
(Mark 1:41). Almost immediately, in verse 43, he uses another
word, *embrimesmenos*, which is difficult to translate in this context,
because it normally suggests anger. The NIV translation of verses
43 and 44 reads, 'Jesus sent him away at once with a strong warning:
"See that you don't tell this to anyone." ' The fierceness of his

manner which is suggested in the Greek may have been due to his knowledge that the man had every intention of disobedience, as the account itself shows. The main point for us, though, is that both the compassion and the fierceness point to the existence of real human feelings in Jesus. On a later occasion, encountering Pharisaic legalism when he met a man with a shrivelled hand on the Sabbath day, Mark tells us, 'He looked round at them in anger, and, deeply distressed at their stubborn hearts, said to the man, "Stretch out your hand" ' (Mark 3:5).

We could go right through Mark's Gospel, illustrating this point, and could add evidence from Matthew, Luke and John. We shall simply note that the Gospel writers sometimes refer to deep sighing. When the Pharisees were seeking a sign from him in order to test him, 'he sighed deeply in his spirit' (Mark 8:12, RSV). We know what it is to express distress or longing or disgust in this inarticulate way. So did Jesus.

Some thinkers in the early church, especially those of the Alexandrian school[5], found it quite difficult to treat this kind of language with the seriousness it deserves, but it demands to be faced fairly and squarely. No suggestion that his sufferings were just play-acting and not real can possibly be accepted. The passages that record these sufferings do not stand in the Gospels on their own, but in the context of a true human experience in which emotion played a real part.

His sinful environment

The Old Testament contains a number of moving passages which seem to be virtual cries from the heart of God. In Deuteronomy 5:29, God says, 'Oh, that their hearts would be inclined to fear me and keep all my commands always, so that it might go well with them and their children for ever.' In Psalm 81:13f., he cries, 'If my people would but listen to me, if Israel would follow my ways, how quickly would I subdue their enemies and turn my hand against their foes.'

The book of Hosea has much of this kind of language, and Hosea 11:8, 9 is particularly striking and moving. Making an historical reference to two cities destroyed in a divine judgement, God says,

'How can I give you up, Ephraim? How can I hand you over, Israel? How can I treat you like Admah? How can I make you like Zeboiim? My heart is changed within me; all my compassion is aroused. I will not carry out my fierce anger, nor will I turn and devastate Ephraim. For I am God and not man, the Holy One among you, and I will not come in wrath.'

The marvellous affirmation, 'for I am God and not man' suggests that if the rebellious people of Israel had been in the hands of a man and not God, they would have been severely punished by him. This intensifies our sense of wonder when we find this kind of language used also in the Gospels, now of course on the lips of one who was not only divine but human.

Jesus was deeply stirred by the unbelief of the people around him. Mark tells us that he was amazed at their lack of faith (Mark 6:6). When he found failure of faith not just in the people generally but in his own disciples, he cried out, 'O unbelieving generation, how long shall I stay with you? How long shall I put up with you?' (Mark 9:19).

The most poignant of all these sayings is to be found in his mournful cry over rebellious Jerusalem: 'O Jerusalem, Jerusalem, you who kill the prophets and stone those sent to you, how often I have longed to gather your children together, as a hen gathers her chicks under her wings, but you were not willing' (Matt. 23:37). The repetition of the name of the city, the vivid illustration of parental concern taken from the animal world, and the contrasting references to desire, first his and then theirs, all serve to underline the deep concern that must have been in his heart at that time.

It is not easy for us to imagine what the presence of a sinful environment all around him must have meant to Jesus. He was holy, and he had come to earth from the realm where all was holy. Many a Christian has wept tears of anguish over men and women who would rather have the sin that destroys people than the Saviour who blesses them. What must the sinless Saviour himself have felt when he saw on every hand men and women failing to give glory and thanks to the God who had given them everything they ever possessed, and who were determined to go their own way despite the eternal consequences?

His experience of hostility

Christ's coming and the nature of his life and ministry produced deep divisions between people. The Gospel writers show us two processes working at the same time. He was gathering disciples who would stay with him, observing his works and hearing his words, at least until near the end, but his enemies also began to emerge (Mark 1:16-20; 2:13f.; 3:1-6, 13-19).

Mark tells us that at one point the Pharisees and the Herodians got together to plot his downfall and death (Mark 3:6). In fact these two groups were poles apart in their general outlook. The Pharisees held themselves aloof from the occupying Gentile forces, while the Herodians collaborated with them. They became united however by a powerful emotion which they had in common: they hated Jesus. The priestly Sadducees, too, came into this unholy alliance at a later stage (Matt. 22:23-34).

John in his Gospel, in chapter after chapter, shows Jesus in controversy with groups of Jews. Much that he said produced enmity. The chief priests and Pharisees tried without success to arrest him (John 7:32), they accused him of having a demon (John 8:48) and then tried to stone him (John 8:59; 10:31). Finally the high priest gathered together the Sanhedrin, the great council of the Jews. He was its president and its membership included substantial numbers both of Pharisees and of Sadducees. He advised them to seek the death of Jesus (John 11:47-57), and so from that day onwards, they were looking for a chance to do away with him.

Jesus was well aware of their hatred and their plots. The writer to the Hebrews comments on his patient endurance of such hostility. His readers were beginning to face some persecution in their own stand for Christ. There had been no martyrs in their fellowship yet, though, and so he points them to Christ himself as a Model in terms of his reaction to the opposition of sinners. In Hebrews 12:3, 4, he says, 'Consider him who endured such opposition from sinful men, so that you will not grow weary and lose heart. In your struggle against sin you have not yet resisted to the point of shedding your blood.'

His anticipation of the cross

'Don't worry, it may never happen!' Hardly the gospel, and yet it must be said with shame that posters with hardly more of the good news sometimes appear on notice boards outside churches. Despite its obvious lack of real hope, this pathetic piece of counsel does contain the only ray of future light in the minds of some people. They are haunted by gloomy thoughts of what may be their lot tomorrow, or next week, or next year, and their comfort lies in the thought that things may not turn out to be so bad after all. They do not hope in God, only in a change of circumstances. 'Today is the tomorrow you were so worried about yesterday, and all is well' – except that sometimes it is not!

What about Jesus Christ? What was his outlook on the future? Of course, he was trusting in God, for he is the perfect Example of faith as well as its perfect Object. The Gospels show us, however, that he knew long before the crucifixion that he was going to have to suffer and die (Mark 2:18-20; John 2:19-22). Calvary existed in his mind, in his imagination, in all the anticipation of its dreadful agonies, long before he was nailed to the tree. Our own experience reminds us that the expectation of suffering is itself suffering.

Some writers of the past have used the phrase 'Galilean springtime' about the early part of Jesus' ministry. They visualised it as a time when great crowds thronged him, when everybody listened to his teaching with bated breath and when the thought of suffering and death was never in his mind. He would conquer the whole nation, and perhaps the whole world, by his teaching. Only later, when the crowds began to leave him, did he anticipate a tragic end to his life.

This picture is just not true to the facts. Certainly the Galilean crowds were often large. Certainly the realisation of the cost of discipleship only began to take its toll and to cut down the numbers after a while. But the cross was by no means an afterthought. Early in his ministry Jesus, using as an analogy something familiar to his hearers, spoke of himself as the bridegroom. He said, 'How can the guests of the bridegroom fast while he is with them? They cannot, so long as they have him with them. But the time will come when the bridegroom will be taken away from them, and on that day they will fast' (Mark 2:19, 20). The very word employed here strongly suggests violence. We should notice too the hint in the parable of the sower that there would be persecution and tribulation for the followers of Jesus (Mark 4:17). If his followers were to experience this, would their Master escape it?

These hints of a destiny of suffering are followed later by absolutely clear and plain teaching. At Caesarea Philippi, in the far north of the country, Jesus had asked his disciples who they believed him to be. Peter had replied, 'You are the Christ, the Son of the living God' (Matt. 16:16). Straight away Jesus began to teach them what sort of Christ he was to be. 'From that time on Jesus began to explain to his disciples that he must go to Jerusalem and suffer many things at the hands of the elders, chief priests and teachers of the law, and that he must be killed, and on the third day be raised to life' (Matt. 16:21).

This was not an isolated saying on the part of Jesus, but the beginning of a definite course of teaching, which seems to have become more and more detailed as time went on. For instance, Matthew 20:17-19 records Jesus as saying, 'We are going up to Jerusalem, and the Son of man will be betrayed to the chief priests and the teachers of the law. They will condemn him to death and will turn him over to the Gentiles to be mocked and flogged and crucified.' Mark, introducing this same saying, pictures Jesus walking some distance ahead of the disciples, who were huddled behind him in amazement and fear (Mark 10:32-34). They were walking to Jerusalem – he was anticipating Calvary.

Jesus spoke of his destiny as undergoing a baptism or drinking a cup (Mark 10:38), and these images suggest suffering and sorrow as we can see from Old Testament passages, such as Psalm 69:1-3 and Isaiah 51:17 where they are used. His ministry had opened with baptism in water; it was to close with baptism in blood. How he felt about this becomes clear when we hear him cry out, 'I have a baptism to undergo, and how distressed I am until it is completed' (Luke 12:50). This was his destiny, and, as the word translated 'distressed' suggests, he felt hemmed in and under constant pressure because of this.

Gethsemane

From time to time the church has been plagued by heresies in which either the deity or the humanity of Jesus has been denied or under-valued. Sometimes it has been suggested that he was not a real man, but only a kind of phantom.[6] No such theory can be entertained for a single moment if we take the events in the garden of Gethsemane seriously. They may be studied in any of the Synoptic Gospels, for they all record them (Matt. 26:36-56; Mark 14:32-50; Luke 22:39-53).

Mark gives us a particularly vivid account of what happened on that occasion. He tells us that Jesus 'took Peter, James and John, and began to be greatly distressed and troubled' (Mark 14:33). Commentators on Mark are agreed that this sentence is not easy to translate into English. The language is strong, very strong, and no English verb quite expresses either of the two Greek verbs, *ekthambeisthai* and *ademonein,* involved. Distress, horror, dread, amazement – all are indicated as involved in the complex of emotions he experienced on that occasion.

Out of this horrifying experience came a poignant word to his disciples, 'My soul is overwhelmed with sorrow to the point of death' (Mark 14:34). These words too are so very difficult to translate. The New English Bible rendering is rather free, but it does something like justice to them as an expression of deep feeling: 'My heart is ready to break with grief.'

It was while his heart was thus weighed down with horror and grief that Jesus went to pray. He said, '*Abba,* Father, everything is possible for you. Take this cup from me. Yet not what I will, but what you will' (Mark 14:36). The use of the word 'cup' in such a context as this makes us realise what an agony of anticipation must have formed the emotional background to its use by him on earlier occasions, for example when he said to two ambitious disciples, 'Can you drink the cup I drink?' (Mark 10:38). His human nature shrank from the cross, yet his will embraced the Father's will. He would do what the Father wanted him to do, no matter what the cost of it might be to him.

In Gethsemane, he was denied the human comfort his disciples might have given at this time. On the occasion just noted, some of them had said, so glibly, that they could drink the cup he was to drink and undergo a baptism with him (Mark 10:38, 39). Peter had said to him, earlier on the very evening of his Gethsemane agony, 'Lord, I am ready to go with you to prison and to death' (Luke 22:33). Yet when he was feeling the anticipated horror of the cross most deeply, he had to face it alone. Not only did they fail to understand what it meant for him, they could not even keep their eyes open!

Calvary

> But none of the ransomed ever knew
> How deep were the waters crossed;
> Nor how dark was the night that the Lord passed through,
> Ere he found His sheep that was lost.

In these words, Ira D. Sankey speaks for all Christians. There are depths of suffering in the cross of the Lord Jesus Christ that none of us can hope to plumb. One of the most unexpected and impressive features of the Gospels is the fact that their authors make no attempt to exploit the emotional impact of the events. What might the sensationalist press of today have done? What about the cheap modern novel? Even great writers like Shakespeare, Tolstoy or Goethe may well have been sorely tempted to dwell on particular aspects of the physical or inner sufferings of the figure on the centre cross. The Gospel writers simply record the facts, with economy of language, and allow them to speak for themselves – and how they speak!

We shall simply ponder two great utterances that came from the lips of the Saviour himself as he hung on the Roman cross, because they tell us all we need to know. John records that Jesus said, 'I am thirsty' (John 19:28). In these words all the physical agonies of the cross were focused, for a raging thirst always overtook a victim of crucifixion after he had spent some hours on his cross.

This we can say, but who can hope to penetrate beyond the surface of the most awful cry ever to emerge from the lips of a human being? 'My God, my God, why have you forsaken me?'

Luke and John each record three sayings from the cross, but Matthew (27:46) and Mark (15:34) give us this only. It must have impressed them so greatly that they allowed it to stand completely alone – like the lonely experience out of which it came – in their accounts of the crucifixion.

To explore the meaning of this saying with any fullness would be to move beyond the bounds of our subject. Suffering in the place of sinners, taking the punishment that was due to us, knowing in his experience the agonies of the lost, although he was absolutely pure from sin and was the very Son of God – it is along lines such as these our thoughts must move if we are to take these words seriously in the light of his other teaching.

For any human being, to be forsaken by God represents the unthinkable, even though it is exactly what our sins deserve, and, according to Christ, what they will receive unless we turn to the him. But for the sinner it is in fact the logical outcome of a life of sin, and represents the making permanent of his condition along with all the penalties which must accompany it eternally. For Christ, however, it was the very opposite of what he deserved, and represented an awful break in that fellowship which he had known with his Father, not simply throughout his sinless life, but from all eternity. Here was the profoundest suffering, the expression of the profoundest love.

References

1. J.A.T. Robinson, *Honest to God*, London, SCM Press, 1962.
2. In this he followed the lead of Paul Tillich, as he indicates on pp. 21,22, 41,56. On p. 56, he says, 'This, I believe, is Tillich's great contribution to theology – the reinterpretation of transcendence.'
3. e.g. Matthew 8:17; Luke 22:37; Romans 10:16.
4. For this, see John R.W. Stott, *The Cross of Christ*, Leicester, IVP, 1986.
5. Largely for philosophical reasons, although possibly also out of a desire to highlight his uniqueness, the Alexandrians often tended to express the fact of the humanity of Jesus in a less than satisfactory manner.
6. This view, known as Docetism, has surfaced at various times during the history of the Church. There have been milder tendencies towards it even among some writers otherwise theologically orthodox.

Chapter 8

THE ETHICAL ISSUE

The New Testament and the church that bears Christ's name make great claims for him. Not only so, but the Gospels record great claims made by him, claims to be Son of God and Lord. During his ministry and ever since then these claims have made him a controversial figure and human beings have been divided in their attitude to them.

A survey of opinion about him however reveals one striking fact. There is great respect for his character. This is shared by many who do not accept his claims. It is even common among some who, for religious reasons of their own, must reject the claims made for him by the Christian church. For instance, Moslems do not accept either his deity or the fact of his death for human sins and yet they hold him in high esteem for his character. Many Jews too have a respect for him even though they know that many of their people have been persecuted by those who have borne his name. Many Hindus, who, because of their tolerance of all kinds of religious belief, have a rooted objection to the exclusive claims of the Christian faith, admire the compassionate concern he showed to those in need, and the Mahatma Gandhi's deep respect for him is well-known.

In this chapter, we will examine the evidence of the Gospels and the comments of the New Testament writers about the character of Jesus, and offer some reflections on this. First of all, though, it will be useful to survey the various ways in which human character has been assessed by ethical thinkers.

Various approaches to ethics
What lies behind particular ethical judgements such as 'that is right', 'that is good', 'that is loving', 'in the circumstances that seems morally appropriate'? What is a moral or an immoral action?

A great many ethical thinkers and teachers have stressed the

149

importance of law. Their concern often centres in some particular legal code, with a set of moral commandments providing a standard of morality so that all human actions are judged by them. Of course, the most famous of such sets is itself found in Scripture, the Decalogue or Ten Commandments which are the heart of the Mosaic legal system.

Whatever may be our view of the Pharisees[1] there can be no doubt that they gave the Law of Moses a place of considerable importance. Not only so, but a great body of oral applications of the Law to the changed conditions of their day had grown up and they accorded these virtually the same status.

Does preoccupation with law tend to produce harshness and an unloving spirit? It is often thought so, but this is not necessarily the case at all. The author of Psalm 119 was so taken up with the Law of God that he devoted a very long psalm to it, but what comes over so clearly is not harsh legalism but a great love for the Law as the expression of God's deep concern for the good of his people.

The moral judgements which characterise this approach to ethics are normally expressed in terms of right and wrong. If an objective legal standard exists then whether an action is right or wrong is often determined simply by investigating the facts. So, in a law court, evidence is brought forward and there is a strenuous endeavour to secure objectivity so that a clear verdict of 'Guilty!' or 'Not guilty!' may be attained.

Now this approach to ethics raises an important question: can we decide all moral issues by a simple application of the principle of law? If we say we can, then why is it that two people may break the same law and yet a law-court may prescribe different penalties for them? This is due sometimes to a difference in the consequences of each action, but also to the fact that issues of motive and intention are regarded as relevant when it comes to deciding the penalty or even at times defining the crime. For instance, such considerations may determine the reduction of a charge of murder to one of manslaughter. Even when somebody is charged with stealing, it matters a great deal whether he or she can prove an intention to return what has been taken. Borrowing and stealing both involve taking what does not belong to us, but motive and intention are different in the two cases.[2]

We can see then that in such cases other criteria have been brought in to modify the legal criterion. What criteria? Many ethical philosophers have tried to define 'the good' and to discover some all-encompassing moral principle by which all actions may be judged. Some, for instance, have suggested this should be expressed in terms of 'the greatest good of the greatest number of people' or 'the general improvement of mankind'[3] or simply love.

This kind of approach recognises that ethical actions are predominantly relational. We live in a society and we ought to be working for the general good. Can it be said of me at the end of my life that I have left the society to which I belong better than I found it, or, at the very least, that this was my motive, no matter how far short I may have fallen of attaining this objective?

What is known as 'Situation Ethics' is really a particular form of this approach to ethical decisions. The follower of this form of ethical theory, holding to some altruistic criterion (usually 'love'), may maintain, for instance, that there are some situations in which what society regards as legally wrong may be reckoned ethically appropriate. Society may regard it as wrong because it is illegal, but, so the argument goes, it is good because it is loving.

For instance, some would argue that a man faced with the starvation of his family would be right to steal a loaf to feed them, no matter what the law says, and that those who plotted the assassination of Hitler were planning something good because this would have removed the threat he posed to countless numbers of people. Of course others would reckon one or both of these actions to be wrong. What has been so characteristic and moreover so troubling to many of us in recent Situation Ethics has been the tendency to apply its principles to sexual conduct and, for instance, to say that sometimes adultery may be right.[4]

Now most people would agree that there is value both in recognising the place of law and also of motive and intention. It is not easy to set law aside altogether, for quite a number of reasons, not least of which is the difficulty of defining the general good. Put a fascist and a communist together in a room and ask them to discuss what the general good is, and the fur will soon begin to fly!

Perhaps then, it may be suggested, what is most helpful to the ethical life is the recognition of a great human example. What is good is found in that person's character, what is right comes to be based on what he or she is known to have done in a similar situation, or, if a teacher, what he or she requires of a follower or would-be follower. Discussions as to the nature of the good can be too abstract and we often need to see the good in a human life before we can truly recognise it. It is also true that there can be problems in a legal system if we find two laws coming into conflict in a given situation. It may be easier to see the way through at such a time when we know somebody we admire has tackled just such a problem in actual experience.

Now a little thought will show that it can be dangerous for us simply to follow the example of a person we admire. The person concerned may have a strongly charismatic personality and may simply sweep us off our feet.[5] In such a case, however, we have not used true ethical judgement about him or her at all, and our loyalty may become divorced altogether from real ethical criteria. Modern history has seen some disastrous examples of this. It is noticeable that mere loyalty to the orders of a person has not normally been accepted as proper ethical grounds for action in the proceedings of war crimes tribunals.

Sometimes what has been advocated is loyalty, not so much to a person, as to a regime. So totalitarian regimes, especially, have taught that loyalty is the all-commanding virtue. First of all you commit yourself to the political ideology of a regime and then you simply accept without question the legal system imposed by that regime. Most people can see that there are great dangers in such an outlook if in fact we have misjudged the character of the regime.

The nature of biblical ethics
Without doubt there are in the Scriptures several of the approaches we have outlined.

The divine law for Israel set out in the Mosaic system and in particular in the Decalogue had great importance for the Old

Testament. Despite the fact that the New Testament, especially in the Pauline Epistles, makes it clear that, because of human sin, salvation cannot be by the keeping of the Law[6], its influence is still very much felt in the New Testament. To give one example, the Epistle to the Ephesians contains either quotations or distinct echoes of half the commandments, the half concerned with relations in society.[7] Moreover, the New Testament letters themselves contain many commands which are backed by the divinely-given authority of the apostolic writers. Christ himself said that he did not come to abolish the Law but to fulfil it (Matt. 5:17).

The Bible also places emphasis on love. For instance, in the Old Testament the love of God is most movingly presented in the Book of Hosea (e.g. in Hos. 11:1-4, 8,9), and Israel is charged with failing to respond in love to him. God says, 'What can I do with you, Ephraim? What can I do with you, Judah? Your love is like the morning mist, like the early dew that disappears' (Hos. 6:4).

The New Testament presents the claims of love very strongly. Christ underlined the central importance of love by identifying the two greatest commandments as those requiring love for God and for our neighbour (Mark 12:28-34). This shows incidentally that his teaching did not cut across that of the Old Testament but rather confirmed it.

The New Testament writers followed their Lord in this emphasis. Paul's love 'hymn' in 1 Corinthians 13 is deservedly famous. When Peter says of Christ 'he went around doing good', it is clear that his understanding of good is related to love, for Peter expounds the good he did in terms of healing all those who were under the power of the devil (Acts 10:38). 1 John also stresses love, especially in 4:7-5:3, not surprisingly in view of its author's repeated statement 'God is love' (1 John 4:8,16).

It can be well argued that all this biblical teaching rests ultimately on the character of God. It is because he is what he is in his perfect holiness that the Mosaic Law was what it was, and it is because he is love that human beings are commanded to love others.

Because, as we have seen, Jesus summed up the Law in terms

of the command to love God and to love neighbour, some have suggested that the whole concept of Law can be set on one side and replaced by the principle of love. If however God's character is the ultimate basis of ethics, then the Law must be seen as stemming from his character, because it was he who gave the Law. It therefore remains a standard for godly action.

Loyalty or faithfulness to the true God and rejection of all other gods is treated as of great importance in the Bible[8] and, of course, the 'regime' of God is his Kingdom, proclaimed and concretely expressed in Jesus Christ.

It is not surprising that the character of Christ has come to have an important place in the approach of Christians to ethical matters.[9] Christians have recognised, quite properly, that if Christ is in fact God incarnate, then his character must furnish an ethical touchstone for his followers. Not only so, but the very fact that in Christ God came in human form and with fully human experience means that in him we have an ethical standard which is not only deeply challenging but is of great practical value. We see him facing the kind of concrete situations which we ourselves encounter. Therefore it is of great importance for us to raise and to face ethical questions which the fact of Christ has prompted in many readers of the Bible.

This we will now seek to do.

The Gospel facts

The Gospels provide us with several different types of material in relation to the ethical significance of Jesus. They show us his actions and we see not only how these actions conform to the Mosaic Law but also there is reference to his motivation. In speaking to his disciples shortly before his death, he underlined the importance of love, saying, 'Love each other as I have loved you. Greater love has no-one than this, that he lay down his life for his friends' (John 15:12,13). This means that the understanding of what real love is must be determined by Christ's definition of love. His love now becomes the demanding standard, and particularly the ultimate expression of it at the cross.

As we shall see, the Gospels give us statements that he makes of an ethical kind, both about his own character and conduct and about the character and conduct of others, they give us his teaching on ethical matters, and they also record the sayings of others about him.

The witness of the Father

This comes early in the Synoptic Gospels in the word spoken from heaven at his baptism, 'You are my Son, whom I love; with you I am well pleased' (Mark 1:11 and parallel passages in Matthew and Luke). This occurred at the very beginning of his ministry and God's pleasure in him must therefore have covered the whole period of his life prior to his baptism. Its timing was most appropriate, for it makes clear to us that his baptism was not, like that of others, undertaken as a sign of repentance for sin. This is reinforced by his own statement to John the Baptist, when the latter confessed his unworthiness to baptise Jesus. Jesus said, 'Let it be so now; it is proper for us to do this to fulfil all righteousness' (Matt. 3:15). The exact meaning of this saying is a matter of debate, but what is certainly clear is that Jesus did not connect his baptism with personal sin.

The Synoptic Gospels each give an account of the Transfiguration of Christ and in this connection they record a word from the Father about Christ. In Matthew's Gospel the wording of this is identical with that of the Father's declaration at his baptism (Matt. 17:5; cf. 3:17). Here then is another affirmation of God's pleasure in him, this time after much of his ministry has already been fulfilled.

The Johannine Gospel tradition shows us the voice speaking from heaven a third time, this time towards the end of the ministry of Jesus to the world. It came in the context of a passage where the cross is very much in view and where the language Jesus uses strongly suggests that he was then facing – and resisting – the temptation to call on his Father to save him from it (John 12:23-29). It gives a promise that the Father would glorify his own name, with the clear implication that he would do this through the obedient death of Jesus.

So each recorded word from heaven bears witness to the character of Jesus.

The temptation in the wilderness

This is recorded briefly in Mark and in more detail in Matthew and Luke. We will concentrate on the Matthaean version, found in Matthew 4:1-11. Luke's version is very similar apart from variation in the order of the temptations.

The temptations need to be viewed in the light of the Messianic vocation of Jesus. It is true that each of them is presented as offering some advantage to Jesus. The first is about supplying his body's need for food, the second assures him of God's protection, while the last offered him world-wide sovereignty. This last, however, provides us with a clue to the wider meaning of them all, for, when we read it in the light of the whole story of Jesus, it clearly suggested that there was no need for the cross. Moreover, had Jesus turned stones into bread, the people would doubtless have flocked to him as the universal provider.[10] Had he cast himself down dramatically and yet been totally uninjured, the people would have been impressed by this dramatic evidence that he had a special place in God's favour. So we see that yielding to any one of these temptations could have opened the way to high worldly position for Jesus.

So then this series of temptations bears all the marks not only of historical verity but also of situational appropriateness. It is difficult to think of other possible temptations that would have been more alluring to One who knew that doing God's will would lead to suffering and to Calvary.

What resources were available to Jesus when he was faced with these temptations? There are clear indications. Luke tells us that 'Jesus, full of the Holy Spirit, returned from the Jordan and was led by the Spirit in the desert, where for forty days he was tempted by the devil' (Luke 4:1,2). So it was in the fullness of the Spirit that he faced the temptations. He replied to each temptation by quoting the words of Holy Scripture, all of these quotations being, in fact, from Deuteronomy, chapters 6 to 8. The peculiar appropriateness of these chapters to his situation may be discerned when we note that their context in Deuteronomy is the wilderness experience of Israel en route to the Promised Land and that there is considerable emphasis in that context on the importance of doing

God's will and not giving way to idolatry and the worship of false gods.

There are of course major questions to face in connection not only with these particular temptations but with the whole fact of temptation in the life of our Lord. These we will address soon.

Presented as sinlessly perfect in the Gospels

The Gospel writers' recorded sayings of Jesus in which we get a glimpse into his own moral consciousness. When this happens, we see that his conscience was completely void of offence.

He was able to look his enemies in the face and say to them, 'Can any of you prove me guilty of sin?' (John 8:46). He had a strong awareness of the kingdom of evil. Towards the close of his life he spoke to his disciples about the devil, and said, 'The prince of this world is coming. He has no hold on me, but the world must learn that I love the Father and that I do exactly what my Father has commanded me' (John 14:30,31). Again, speaking of his Father, he said, 'I always do what pleases him' (John 8:29). It is interesting to see how perfectly this agrees with what we have already discovered of the Father's approval of him, spoken from heaven at his baptism and transfiguration and recorded in the Synoptic Gospels. His great concern in life was to do his Father's will. On one occasion he said, 'I have food to eat that you know nothing about ... My food ... is to do the will of him who sent me and to finish his work' (John 4:32,34).

The Gospels also record sayings of other people who show how deeply they were impressed with him. They said, for example, 'He has done everything well .... He even makes the deaf hear and the mute speak' (Mark 7:37).

As far as Roman Law is concerned, we have the verdict of no less a person than the Roman procurator, Pontius Pilate, who said to the enemies of Jesus, 'You brought me this man as one who was inciting the people to rebellion. I have examined him in your presence and have found no basis for your charges against him. Neither has Herod, for he sent him back to us; as you can see, he has done nothing to deserve death' (Luke 23:13-15). Pilate's wife took the unusual course of sending her husband a message while he was about his duties, saying to him, 'Don't have anything to do with that innocent man' (Matt. 27:19).

Elsewhere in the New Testament

In his sermon to Cornelius and his friends, Peter puts the matter so simply and yet eloquently, when he says of Jesus, 'He went around doing good' (Acts 10:38). As we have already noted, this assessment was based on keeping close company with Jesus for three years and more. After some years of reflection on the Christian facts, he saw no need to change his opinion, for in his first Epistle, he says of him, 'he did no sin, neither was guile in his mouth, who, when he was reviled, reviled not again, but committed himself to him who judges justly.' The apostle John, too, assuming that he is the author of the First Epistle of John,[11] there says of him, 'in him is no sin' (1 John 3:5), which perhaps takes us deeper for it suggests an assessment of the inner nature of Jesus, not simply of his outward actions.

The writer to the Hebrews, as we have seen already, maintained that Jesus had a full human experience of suffering and of temptation (Heb. 2:18; 4:15), to fit him for the office of High Priest, which required sympathetic understanding of what faced those he represented.

This enables us to put into perspective the teaching of that Epistle about the perfecting of Jesus. The concept of perfecting here means completion. What the writer sees so clearly is that it was necessary for Jesus to experience temptation and its attendant and resultant sufferings in order to give him that all-round experience of human life which a priest needed to enable him to minister to his people. 'He learned obedience from what he suffered' (Heb. 5:8), for his obedience led to suffering and so he learned in that experience what obedience could involve. So, 'once made perfect, he became the source of eternal salvation for all who obey him' (Heb. 5:9).

Jesus as our moral example

It is important for us to consider the sense in which Christ is to be regarded as our moral example. Of course, there is a real sense in which that perfect Life actually condemns us, for, if the sin that is within us prevents us from offering full heart-obedience to the Law of God, we will certainly be found wanting when it comes to the standard of Christ's character, whose commitment to God's will was absolute.

There are however passages where Christians, already accepted in Christ because of his work of atonement, are pointed to him as the great example of some moral quality. This mostly concerns his humble and loving willingness to suffer in pursuance of the will of God for his life. We find this especially in Philippians 2:1-13 and 1 Peter 2:18-25. Christ did not please himself and we are called to follow his example in this (Rom. 15:1-3), and we ought to walk as he walked (1 John 2:6). This involves, at least metaphorically, taking a towel and washing the feet of others (John 13:12-17). Paul says that consideration for others, the kind of consideration Christ had, must guide our moral decisions (1 Cor. 10:31-11:1; cf. Rom. 15:1-3).

Problems in the Gospels
Not surprisingly, the conduct of Jesus as recorded in the Gospels has been subjected to considerable scrutiny, with some passages being quoted against the idea of his sinlessness.

John records a miracle at Cana where he turned water into wine. When his mother approached him to let him know that the wine had run out, John records him as saying, 'O Woman, what have you to do with me? My hour has not yet come' (John 2:4, RSV). It has been suggested that this showed irritation and that it was a rude retort to the mother who had raised him.

This is however to misunderstand it. 'Woman', in an address of this kind, did not have the connotations that it has for us in English. It has been pointed out that Jesus used the term when speaking to his mother from the cross (John 19:26) and also to Mary Magdalene when he met her after his resurrection (John 20:15). Giving the saying a culturally appropriate rather than a literal translation, we might render it, 'Mother, this is something on which I am going to have to take the initiative rather than you, and the time has not yet come for me to do it.' The NIV, in fact, softens the saying by translating somewhat freely, 'Dear woman'.

Then, in response to an appeal by a Canaanite woman for him to deal with the demon possessing her daughter, he said, 'I was sent only to the lost sheep of Israel ... It is not right to take the children's bread and toss it to their dogs' (Matt. 15; 24,26).

There have been two objections to this. The first suggests that he was possessed by a narrow nationalism. But this can hardly be when we find on so many other occasions that he had a positive attitude to people of other nations and races. He responded positively to a Roman centurion, saying that he had not found such faith in Israel (Matt. 8:10). He rebuked the violent prejudice of James and John against the Samaritans who had refused to welcome him (Luke 9:51-55). He spoke well of the Samaritans, who were so hated by his fellow-Jews, and he took time to bring blessing to a Samaritan woman and her whole community (John 4). Moreover, right at the start of his ministry, in a synagogue sermon in his own town, he pointed out that God had shown his love in special ways in the days of Elijah and Elisha, not to Jews but to Gentiles (Luke 4:24-29).

His reference to Israel when speaking to the Canaanite woman must therefore be seen as related to a saving strategy. It is clear especially from Luke/Acts (written by the Gentile Luke), that God's plan for him was that he should labour first predominantly among the Jews and then that, after his resurrection, his disciples should take the message of the gospel also to the Gentile lands.

The second criticism of him raised by this incident relates to the use of the term 'dog'. It is true that 'dog' was a term of abuse used by Jews in relation to Gentiles, but Jesus softens it greatly, using the diminutive term employed of puppies. Although adult dogs were disliked and even feared because they were not pets but scavengers, living on all kinds of rubbish and sometimes threatening human safety (cf. Ps. 22:16), puppies were kept as pets in the home. The woman, in fact, saw hope in the word he used, because the puppies were fed from scraps from the table. Jesus praised her for her faith, which was in fact elicited by the nature of his response to her request.

Then some have questioned his habit of answering questions indirectly and of responding to a question with a question. This kind of thing happened several times, for instance on the Day of Questions prior to his crucifixion (Mark 11:27-12:37).

It is important here to discern something of his motivation. This method of conducting a discussion makes people think, and it was very important that his interlocutors should be stimulated to consider their words and actions more deeply for many of them were pursuing a thoughtless course of opposition to him.

This is probably the key also to the passage which, more than any other, has been quoted as evidence against his sinlessness, as it has been taken to indicate that not even he believed in it. This was the occasion when an enquirer called him 'Good Teacher', and Jesus gave him a gentle rebuke, saying, 'Why do you call me good? No-one is good – except God alone' (Mark 10:17,18).

This was, however, thoroughly in line with the questioning technique which we have already seen to be characteristic of him. The man's language in fact played into the hands of Jesus, for it gave him the opportunity to encourage the man to deeper reflection. The man had probably used the phrase as a somewhat conventional form of address to a respected person. At the deepest level of reflection of all, reflection induced by the Spirit of God, such a question could open the way to a belief in the Incarnation.

Sometimes the fact of his submission to baptism at the hands of John the Baptist is raised, but, as we have already seen, there is no question of this being an admission of sin. Rather, he was standing with sinners because he had come to do them good, as only he, the perfect One, could.

His sinlessness has sometimes been questioned in relation to the Fourth Commandment, which commanded the hallowing of the Sabbath day.

Now it is quite true that the activities of Jesus on the Sabbath day often scandalised the Pharisees, as we see, for example, in Mark 2:23–3:6 and John 9:16. Two things must, however, be borne in mind.

The first of these is that he did not consider himself bound by the many extra regulations which had accumulated around the written Law. For instance, the Rabbis defined rubbing ears of corn between the hands as reaping and therefore as work banned on the

Sabbath (Mark 2:23,24). Jesus did not regard their interpretations of the Law as in any way binding and in fact on this occasion he said, 'the Son of Man is Lord even of the Sabbath' (Mark 2:28). As Lord it is his prerogative to interpret the Law. Not only so, but the performance of good deeds on the Sabbath, including of course the healing of the sick, was not only allowed but commended by him.

It may be said too that he viewed the Sabbath Law in terms of its original purpose. This day was set apart for the worship of God and for the rest of the body. As he said, it was a means to an end, not an end in itself, for 'the Sabbath was made for man, not man for the Sabbath' (Mark 2:27). It was never intended to be the yoke of bitter bondage which Rabbinic Judaism certainly appears to have made it.

Theological Reflection
If God really did become man in Christ, then this is a most stupendous fact and it would be most surprising if it did not raise some deep questions in our minds. Some of these questions are of an ethical nature, and we must now seek, in a spirit of reverence and of submission to Scripture, to address these questions.

Could Jesus have a truly human ethical experience when he was God as well as man?
This apparently straight-forward question in fact leads us on to several further questions, each following necessarily from the last.

We have to ask first of all how we are to conceive the relationship between his divine and his human natures as much depends on the nature of their connection with each other. The formula agreed at the Council of Chalcedon in 451, which was accepted for many centuries as an orthodox Christological formulation, will be examined in detail in a later chapter. What it did was to spell out the implications of the belief that in Christ two natures co-existed in one person. It asserted that he was both truly God and truly man and that the two natures were joined in one person 'without confusion, without change, without division, without separation'.

It is the phrase 'without confusion' which is the most important in connection with this question. It means that although the divine and human natures both belonged to the one person, each of the natures retained all its properties. Nothing essential to either nature was given up when or after the union took place.

If the Chalcedonian formula is right, then the human nature of our Lord had a real human ethical experience, for this is proper to human nature as such and it must have been true therefore of Christ's human nature.

But this answer in fact now raises a further question:

If Christ had a truly human nature, does this not mean that his human nature must be sinful, as ours is sinful?

No! The Epistle to the Hebrews expressly asserts that Jesus was without sin (Heb. 4:15). Whether the writer had a sinful nature or sinful acts in mind we cannot be sure. It seems more than likely that the distinction was not in his mind.

It was evidently one of the purposes of his virgin birth, or rather of his conception by the Holy Spirit (which is simply the positive way of saying what 'virgin birth' says negatively) that his human nature should be free from inherited sin. The angel said to Mary, 'The Holy Spirit will come upon you, and the power of the Most High will overshadow you. So the holy one to be born will be called the Son of God' (Luke 1:35). The double use of the word 'holy' here is significant, as is John's assertion, 'in him is no sin' (1 John 3:5).

It has sometimes been maintained, e.g. by Edward Irving and Karl Barth, following Irving,[12] that our Lord did in fact inherit a sinful nature but that he never committed actual sin. It is true that Paul wrote of God sending his own Son 'in the likeness of sinful man to be a sin offering' (Rom. 8:3). The final phrase here surely implies though that he was sinless in every way, his moral perfection answering to the physical perfection required of the sin offering. In view of this we need to emphasise the word 'likeness', for the text speaks of likeness but not of identity. He was like sinful man in being human but not in being sinful. Otherwise he could not have been an offering for sin. David Wenham is right when he says, commenting on Romans 8:3 and Philippians 2:7, 'It is widely agreed that Paul wants to assert the true humanity of Jesus, while affirming his distinctiveness, particularly as far as sin is concerned.'[13]

The Son of God took human nature in all the fullness of what is proper to it, but sin is not proper to it, for it is an invader.[14]

Another question now follows:

If we say that he did not possess inherited sin, could he have had a real experience of temptation?

Now it is true that, for us, much temptation arises from our sinful hearts within us, but we should not overlook the fact that this was not true of Adam and Eve. What happened in their case was that Satan appealed to legitimate desires, placed in them by God, and what he did was to propose illegitimate exercise of these desires.

In view of this, it is very instructive to compare the records of Christ's temptations with Genesis 3, where verse 6 is important to the comparison. 'When the woman saw that the fruit of the tree was good for food and pleasant to the eye, and also desirable for gaining wisdom, she took some and ate it.'

There are some striking parallels. The connection with food is obvious but so also the appeal to the eyes, for the call to throw himself down from the temple pinnacle was designed to overawe the observer. The desire for wisdom, apart from God, suggests that it was a perverse kind of wisdom which would have its principles dictated by Satan who offered it.

We should not imagine however that Christ's temptations were under the same conditions as Adam's. It is important to remember that, unlike Adam, he came into a sinful human environment, and that, in addition to the direct activity of Satan, the world is full of allurements to sin.

Most of all, perhaps, we should recall that many of his temptations were related to his distinctive vocation, which meant that he had to embrace in experience all the awfulness of Calvary, and that what was proposed would have meant an escape from this. As we have seen, a universal food provider or a wonder worker of the most spectacular kind could soon assume great authority over others. This means that, far from his temptations having less power than ours, they will certainly have had more.

Had he succumbed, however, the great problem of sin, with which he came to deal, would have remained unsolved. In fact, it would have been infinitely magnified. This is what gives the picture of an evil world ruler in Revelation 13 such point as the manifestation of great sin, for in that chapter Satan, the dragon (Rev. 12:9) gives to an evil character that world dominion which he had promised to Christ.

Even though the Chalcedonian Definition declares his two natures to be without confusion, we are bound to ask a further question:

Could he possibly sin, and if not how could his temptations be real?

For centuries two Latin tags have provided the focus of this question. Are we to say that it was not possible for him to sin (*non posse peccare*) or rather that it was possible for him not to sin (*posse non peccare*)? It is important for us not to answer this question too quickly without giving some deep thought to it.

In fact, we need to answer in the affirmative to both. When we are thinking about his divine nature, then of course we must say that it was not possible for him to sin. In fact, in terms of his divine nature, it is not even possible to give a proper definition of what sin would be, for sin is an offence against God. How can God sin against God? What is not logically possible is not morally possible either, for we are talking of the God of the Bible, whose nature is perfect holiness.

But Christ was human as well as divine, and in terms of his human nature the right answer is that it was possible for him not to sin. His human nature was subjected to a real test or rather to a series of real tests. If he really was tempted in all points as we are then certainly his temptations must have been real for ours certainly are!

A further question arises out of the last one.

If it was possible for him not to sin, does it follow that it was also possible for him to sin?

So far we have been emphasising the fact of his two natures. Now we must consider what it meant for him to be one person, as this too must be relevant. The two natures were in his one person without division and without separation. So, because his human nature was joined to his divine nature in the unity of one person we are compelled to say that it was impossible for that person to sin.

Does this then completely negate what we have already said about the reality of his temptations? By no means! In temptation, the moral issue for the person being tempted is not so much the objective possibility of sin but rather the subjective experience of moral challenge. To be a real test, the temptations had to be real as presented to the consciousness of Christ.

We can perhaps gain some understanding of this when we say of a particular person, accused of some sin or crime, 'I know this was an impossible act for him.' We are not saying that he could not be tempted. Rather we are saying that he was a person of proven character and that it would have been utterly out of character for him to do it. But such a person may in fact have had great pressure put on him by the temptation, even though we could have predicted the result.

If that is true at the level of sinful human beings, how much more could it have been true of the sinless Christ?

A final question must now be asked:

In facing temptation did he use any resources not available to us?

This too is a question which requires careful thought before we give an answer. If it had been formulated differently, perhaps as 'Did he use his divine powers in facing temptation?', then we might easily say 'No!' and we would be wrong!

Of course he used his divine powers, but this does not mean that he employed resources not available to us. What often befogs this issue is the fact that we do not first enquire as to what resources Christians have available in facing temptation, and the clear and definite answer given by the New Testament is 'divine resources'. None of us can face the Evil One in mere human resources. We need the power of God, and we see in Ephesians 6:10-20 that God has provided us with a full armoury of weapons against the wiles of Satan. As Paul says in 1 Corinthians 10:13, 'No temptation has seized you except what is common to man. And God is faithful; he will not let you be tempted beyond what you can bear. But when you are tempted, he will also provide a way out so that you can stand up under it.'

We are then greatly encouraged by the fact that through the Holy Spirit the power of God indwells us as Christians and, as we rely on him, God gives us power to quench all the fiery darts of Satan – but not otherwise.

Our Lord Jesus Christ was filled with the Spirit and, in the Spirit's power he did the work for which he was Spirit-anointed, his Messianic work of salvation. The temptations were in terms of his vocation. We do not face precisely the same temptations as he, because we are not Christ, but we do meet temptations in terms of the particular vocations each of us has. Paul plays on the relationship between the verb 'to anoint' and the title 'Christ', meaning 'the anointed One', in 2 Corinthians 1:21, 22. There he says, 'Now it is God who makes both us and you stand firm in Christ. He anointed us ... and put his Spirit in our hearts.' The Spirit of anointing who indwelt him as the Christ is in us if we are members of God's family by the new birth, and we may be confident that resources will be available that are more than adequate to enable us to overcome the temptations we face in our own vocations for God.

Just one question now remains. Did Jesus receive the resources of the Spirit in the same way as we and how are we to relate the possession of the fullness of moral power in his divine nature to this infilling of the Spirit? This profound question we must reserve for consideration until a later chapter.

Before closing this section, we should note that the Scriptures he had are available also to us. In fact, we now have in our hands the Bible in its complete form. Just as he must have spent much time before God meditating on Holy Scripture and its relevance for his own life, so also may Christian men and women. Unless we do this and our minds and hearts are possessed by the Scriptures, how can we expect to overcome temptation? It is the sword of the Spirit we must use, and this is the Word of God.

References
1. See pp. 119-120.
2. See the articles, 'Law, Civil and Criminal' and 'Law, Uses of' in D.J. Atkinson and D. Field (eds.), *The New Dictionary of Christian Ethics and Pastoral Theology,* Leicester, IVP, 1995, pp. 541-543 and 543-544.
3. See the article, 'Consequentialism' in *The New Dictionary of Christian Ethics and Pastoral Theology*, pp. 253-254.
4. Issues raised by Situation Ethics are discussed in the articles, 'Love' and 'Situation Ethics', in *The New Dictionary of Christian Ethics and Pastoral Theology*, pp. 9-15 and 794-795.
5. See Antony Storr, *Feet of Clay: A Study of Gurus,* London, Harper Collins, 1997, whose book warns us of the danger of unthinking devotion to a guru. Storr's fascinating book is worth reading, even though he includes both the sinister and the saintly within his pages.
6. e.g. Romans 3:9-20; Galatians 2:16.
7. cf. Exodus 20 with Ephesians 4:25, 28; 5:3, 5; 6:2 and also Ephesians 4:31 in the light of Matthew 5:21,22.
8. e.g. Joshua 24:14; 2 Kings 17:7-23; 1 Chronicles 9:1; 1 Corinthians 10:14-22.
9. See the article 'Jesus' in *New Dictionary of Christian Ethics and Pastoral Theology*.
10. It is surely significant that John places the people's intention to force Jesus to become king in the context of the feeding of the Five Thousand (John 6:15).
11. Not accepted by all scholars. See the brief discussion in F.F. Bruce, *The Epistles of John*, London, Pickering and Inglis, 1970, pp. 29-31.
12. Karl Barth, *Church Dogmatics*, Edinburgh, T. and T. Clark, I. 2.
13. David Wenham, 'The Story of Jesus Known to Paul' in Green and Turner, *Jesus of Nazareth*, p. 300.
14. Irving felt that the more usual doctrine minimised or even overlooked completely the place of the Holy Spirit in the Incarnation and in the life of Christ. For a thorough and sympathetic treatment of his Christology, see Graham W.P. McFarlane, *Christ and the Spirit: The Doctrine of the Incarnation according to Edward Irving*, Carlisle, Paternoster, 1996.

Chapter 9

JESUS CHRIST IN HIS EXALTATION

The term 'exaltation' when applied to Christ is commonly misunderstood. It is often treated as a synonym for his ascension, but in fact it has a wider application than this. It is the fourfold movement in which God gives him ultimately all that he deserves, not only as God but as man, in fact as the God-man whose work for us on the cross dealt with sin and dealt the death-blow to Satan. The four elements of it are his resurrection, his ascension, his session at God's right hand and his return.

Paradoxically, there is even a suggestion of it in the way Jesus sometimes spoke about his cross, according to John's Gospel. He said he would be 'lifted up' (John 3:14; 8:28; 12:32-34). How amazing that the same event could be thought of both as humiliation and exaltation! The cross was an experience of awful humiliation and agony and yet it was also the glory of Christ as the place of his victory over sin and Satan.

The resurrection of Christ

Life is for living. How good it is to be alive! God has set us in his own universe, in a world full of interest. Everywhere we go we find colour, sound, order, beauty, majestic sights, delicate detail. There is food to eat, water to drink, work to do, air to breathe, and there are people to meet, to love, to serve. It is all there, out there in the world. And what of myself? I have eyes to see it all, ears to hear it all, hands to handle it, feet to walk about it, and a heart to love.

But! But at the end comes death! Life leaves me and I leave this setting – for what?

It has been well said that any true view of life must begin with a true view of death. Yet the impression we so often get is that people are trying very hard not to think about it. Sex used to be the forbidden topic of conversation, but now it is death. Yet experience has a way of breaking this conspiracy of silence, and we have to face it, if only perhaps for a few days.

To spell the matter out more clearly, it is not simply dying that people are afraid of, but death. Dying may fill us with fear but we know that, however unpleasant the mode of it may be, it will soon be over. It is what comes after it that really puts terror in the heart, what the Epistle to the Hebrews calls 'a fearful expectation of judgement' (Heb. 10:27). This is the real sting of death.

In fact, the word 'death' in the Bible covers not simply the absence of physical life, but all the consequences of human sin, and especially the condition of enmity against God and his purposes which we all find in ourselves if we probe deeply enough. God prescribed a very simple test for the man he had made to see if he really loved him and would do his will. He warned him, 'When you eat of it you will surely die' (Gen. 2:17), and die he did in this spiritual sense. He became dead towards God. This death began to work in his whole being and eventually physical death claimed him.

It is the fact that Christ conquered death after bearing God's judgement on sin for his people that makes the New Testament such a joyful book.

Foretold in Scripture

Because the disciples of Jesus resisted his teaching about his coming death, they could not grasp the complementary fact of his resurrection, which he so often linked with that death (e.g. Matt. 16:21; 17:22f.; 20:17-19). The angels who met the disciples at the empty tomb gently rebuked them for this, saying, 'Why do you look for the living among the dead? He is not here; he has risen! Remember how he told you, while he was still with you in Galilee?' (Luke 24:5,6).

His resurrection had also been foretold in the Old Testament. In recording Paul's visit to Thessalonica, Luke tells us, 'As his custom was, Paul went into the synagogue and on three Sabbath days he reasoned with them from the Scriptures, explaining and proving that the Christ had to suffer and rise from the dead. "This Jesus I am proclaiming to you is the Christ" ' (Acts 17:2,3). It has been suggested that on the first Sabbath he may have explained from the Old Testament that the Messiah must suffer, on the second that he must rise from the dead, and on the third that he moved from prophecy to recent history and proclaimed the fulfilment in Jesus.

What Old Testament passages would the early Christians employ to show this? We do not know very fully, but there can be little doubt that they would have used Isaiah 52:13-53:12, which implies that God's suffering Servant would be raised from the dead. It speaks clearly of death, and yet also states, 'See my servant .... will be raised and lifted up, and highly exalted ... I will give him a portion among the great, and he will divide the spoil with the strong; because he poured out his soul to death' (Isa. 52:13; 53:12). Incidentally, chapters 54 and 55 are full of joy, so appropriate in following a declaration of full atonement and resurrection.

Likewise Peter took Psalm 16, argued for its application to Christ, and then showed that it foretold his resurrection from the dead (Acts 2:24-32).

The resurrection appearances

The closing chapters of the four Gospels tell of the empty tomb and also a number of appearances of Jesus to his disciples, both female and male. Just as they tell the story of the cross with great simplicity, so they do with the resurrection. There is no attempt at sensationalism. They simply let the amazing facts speak for themselves.

In 1 Corinthians 15:5-8, Paul gives an impressive list, not necessarily exhaustive, of the post-resurrection appearances of his Lord. It includes two appearances to the twelve apostles. These were the men who had been so devastated by the death of their Master and who had never taken in the promise of his resurrection. There is an appearance to James, a member of his own family who rejected his claims during his ministry (John 7:5). There was an appearance to a great crowd of five hundred. In such a crowd there would be many hard-headed realists who would need real, tangible evidence. Paul too saw him, and his encounter took place during the course of his bitter campaign against the Christians.

John tells us that he too saw the risen Christ many years later on the Isle of Patmos. He says, 'Then he placed his right hand on me and said, "Do not be afraid, I am the First and the Last. I am the Living One; I was dead, and behold I am alive for ever and ever! And I hold the keys of Death and Hades" ' (Rev. 1:17,18).

The special character of Christ's resurrection

The Lord Jesus performed many miracles, many of them dealing with diseases of various kinds or with demon possession. It is as if his touch of life was banishing part of the shadow death casts before it. In his resurrection, though, Christ was both the subject and the object of the greatest miracle.

There are a few examples in both Testaments of the dead being raised (1 Kings 17:17-24; 2 Kings 4:32-37; Mark 5:35-43; Luke 7:11-17; John 11:1-44; Acts 20:7-12). These too are miracles, but not of the same order as his resurrection, for he never returned to death and he conquered it for others.

Was his resurrection body physical at all? Yes! He showed the disciples his hands and feet and said, 'It is I myself! Touch me and see; a ghost does not have flesh and bones, as you see I have' (Luke 24:39). He then ate some food before them. Thomas was absent and would not accept their story. Eight days later, Jesus appeared again, when Thomas was present, and said to him, 'Put your finger here; see my hands. Reach out your hand, and put it into my side. Stop doubting and believe' (John 20:27).

God does not play tricks on us. He deals with us according to truth. These passages mean nothing unless we are being taught in them that the body of Jesus after the resurrection was a real one.

W.L. Craig and Robert H. Gundry have helpfully gathered together the evidence from the New Testament for the essentially physical nature of our Lord's resurrection body.[1] Gundry says 'My position is threefold; (1) the New Testament presents a unified view of the nature of Jesus' resurrection; (2) according to that view, he rose from the dead in a physical body; and (3) the physicality of that body forms an essential element of his risen being.'[2]

The conditions of his life however were changed. He did not need to open the door of the upper room to gain admittance. He simply appeared. He made himself known in two different ways, presumably for different purposes. Apparently during the forty days between his resurrection and ascension he looked much as he had always done. The two going to Emmaus did not recognise him at first, because God prevented this recognition (Luke 24:16), but treated him as an ordinary person. Paul and John however saw him revealed in glorious light and splendour (Acts 9; Rev. 1). Paul speaks of 'his glorious body' (Phil. 3:21), as if this is now its normal state (cf. 1 Cor. 15:42-44).

Divine in power

The resurrection could only have been an act of God. Death is man's most dreadful and dreaded enemy. It rules like a king over every human being. Only a stupendous release of divine power could overthrow that enemy. It is perhaps surprising at first to find that when the New Testament writers want to illustrate the power of God, they do not usually talk about the creation of the universe. To bring into being all the varied features of this vast universe and to sustain it all in its ordered course – what power is this! These men do not dwell so much on that as on the resurrection of Christ, which they must have seen as the supreme act of power.

Paul prays that his readers may be given divine enlightenment, so that they may know 'his incomparably great power for us who believe. That power is like the working of his mighty strength which he exerted in Christ when he raised him from the dead ...' (Eph. 1:19f.).

Whose power raised Christ? According to many passages it was the power of God the Father, as in Peter's sermon at Pentecost (Acts 2:23,24) and in passages like Galatians 1:1 and 1 Peter 1:3. In John 2:19-21, however, Jesus says, '"Destroy this temple, and I will raise it again in three days." The Jews replied, "It has taken forty-six years to build this temple, and you are going to raise it in three days?" But the temple he had spoken of was his body.' Later, he said of his life, 'I have authority to lay it down, and authority to take it up again' (John 10:18). So Christ emerged from the grave by virtue of his own power! Even this does not completely settle the question. In Romans 8:11, Paul's words imply that the Spirit of God too was involved.

None of this should surprise us. In the Holy Trinity, the Father, the Son and the Holy Spirit are one in being and nature, and therefore completely united in purpose, working together in all They do. So this most important act of God was effected by the power of the Triune God.

Far-reaching in results
We should note not only what the Bible teaches but also what it emphasises, or we may embrace error by making central what is really peripheral. The New Testament writers greatly emphasise the death and resurrection of Christ. Paul says, 'For what I received I passed on to you as of first importance, that Christ died for our sins according to the scriptures, that he was buried, that he was raised on the third day according to the scriptures' (1 Cor. 15:3,4). Matthew, Mark and Luke each give about one third of their space to the events of passion week, and John goes further still, with nearly half devoted to it. This underlines the importance of these events.

Why so much emphasis on the resurrection? The victory of Christ over death showed that God had accepted his sacrifice for our sins. Paul says that Jesus 'was put to death for our trespasses and raised for our justification' (Rom. 4:25), that is, our new right relationship with God. We might have expected him to connect justification with Christ's death, but he links it with his resurrection, as this gives the assurance that God accepted his sacrifice. As he says elsewhere, 'If Christ has not been raised, your faith is futile; you are still in your sins' (1 Cor. 15:17).

The resurrection of Christ puts his whole life and claims into divine perspective. Is he really, as he claimed, the Son of God, the Son of Man, the long expected Messiah, the great Servant of the Lord, the Saviour and Judge of men? Not if he is still in the grave. But by raising him God himself signified that all his claims were genuine. He was 'declared with power to be the Son of God, by his resurrection from the dead' (Rom. 1:4).

During his ministry Jesus made many promises. He told his disciples he would be with them (Matt. 18:20), that he would send the Holy Spirit to them (John 16:7) and that he would come back again (John 14:3). None of these promises could have been fulfilled without his resurrection. The Epistle to the Hebrews contains only one express reference to his resurrection (13:20), but its great doctrine of his heavenly priesthood and constant intercession for his people makes no sense at all unless he rose from the dead and is in heaven now.

Because Christ has overcome death, so shall we. To be 'in Christ' in living union as a Christian believer is to be deeply involved in all he did. In Romans 6 and elsewhere, Paul teaches that when Christ died and rose from the dead, this meant the death and resurrection of each one joined to him. This has two stages to it. Firstly, we 'die' to what displeases God and we 'rise again' to a new life in which we are concerned to do his will. Then, if Christ returns after our physical death, we are raised with a glorious body like his (Phil. 3:21). All this depends on his own death and resurrection and so is the fruit of his work.

The ascension and heavenly session of Christ

Young people today often have a real 'hang-up' on the question of authority. They tend to resent parents, policemen, teachers, employers and royalty. Why is this? Is it because they do not accept the idea of authority at all? Not really. If it were this, then there would never be a gang with a leader. Peer leadership is often accepted because of the feeling we have that our peers may well understand us better than other authority figures.

The real problem is often not the authority itself but the way it is exercised, or the way young people think, sometimes mistakenly, it will be exercised. So in this case, it is not so much authority as authoritarianism that is the real issue.

This certainly over-simplifies things, but is there not something in it? What folk are so often looking for is a leader they can really trust, somebody who is fit to lead, not just because he is strong (although that is certainly needed) but because he has the real interests of the group at heart. They may not know who it is for whom they are seeking, but the New Testament writers do. They tell us his name is Jesus. His fitness for leadership cannot be doubted. He is supreme, he loves us, and he works for our good from the place of absolute power.

Taken up into heaven

Luke is a very important writer. In terms of its wordage, he wrote even more of the New Testament than Paul. He is important too because he gives us the facts about the ascension of the Lord Jesus, and does so in both his books. He tells the story very simply in the last chapter of his Gospel: 'When he had led them out as far as Bethany, he lifted up his hands and blessed them. While he was blessing them, he left them and was taken up into heaven' (Luke 24:50,51). This account is supplemented in Acts. 'He was taken up before their very eyes, and a cloud hid him from their sight' (Acts 1:9). The received ending of the Gospel of Mark makes reference to this also. 'He was taken up into heaven, and sat down at the right hand of God' (Mark 16:19).

It is sometimes alleged that the ascension rests on too little evidence. The authenticity of Mark 16: 9-20 has been disputed, as we have seen, leaving Luke alone, and it is said that we cannot accept it simply on one man's evidence. We should not forget though that this is true of almost everything in Acts and yet men as diverse as Sir William Ramsay[3] and Adolph Harnack[4] have tested Luke's historical reliability and given a positive verdict.

There is much more to be said. Peter writes of 'the resurrection of Jesus Christ, who has gone into heaven and is at God's right hand' (1 Pet. 3:21, 22). Incidentally 'gone into heaven' suggests this was his own act. If the resurrection could be viewed as the work both of the Father and of the Son, so could the ascension. We may distinguish the ascension and the heavenly session, but they belong together, as the second is the result of the first. Paul surely presupposes the ascension when he speaks of the power of God that 'raised him from the dead and seated him at his right hand in the heavenly realms' (Eph. 1:20). Hebrews, too, tells us that 'Christ ... entered heaven itself' (Heb. 9:24). The ascension then is a fully authenticated piece of Bible history.

Seated in the place of power

Even the greatest of human rulers have controlled only a restricted area and then only for a time. The great Son of Man vision in Daniel 7:13,14 shows him being given a kingdom that is both truly universal and eternal.

Jesus never had any doubt that this was to be his destiny. He spoke often of the kingdom of God, and when he was to all appearances a helpless prisoner in the hands of his enemies and his disciples must have thought all hope of the kingdom as Jesus had conceived it had gone. He declared before the high priest, 'I say to all of you: In the future you will see the Son of man sitting at the right hand of the Mighty One and coming on the clouds of heaven' (Matt. 26:64). The reference to Daniel's prophecy is unmistakable.

His kingdom does not belong only to the future but also has a present dimension. The Pharisees asked him when the kingdom of God was coming. He answered, 'the kingdom of God is within you' (Luke 17:21, NIV) or 'in the midst of you' (RSV). Wherever the king is, there is the kingdom. The writer to the Hebrews says that Christ sat down when his work was finished: 'After he had provided purification for sins, he sat down at the right hand of the Majesty in heaven' and soon applies the words of a psalm to him, 'Your throne, O God, will last for ever and ever, and righteousness will be the sceptre of your kingdom' (Heb. 1:3,8). This means that Christ is even now reigning in heaven.

So we can have confidence that this world is in the hands of Christ. So, for instance, the Christian who has to live under a tyrannous regime can commit his cause to him in the sure knowledge that he is almighty and that his purposes are bound to be triumphant in the end.

The head of his church
The New Testament contains many illustrations of the church of Christ. For instance, it is the family he loves (Mark 3:33-35), the field he cultivates (1 Cor. 3:6-9), the temple he is building (Eph. 2:20-22), the bride he marries (Eph. 5:25-33). Each of these pictures presents some aspect of the church's life in relation to Christ. None can give us a full understanding of what the church is. All are needed for a complete picture.

Perhaps the most important of them all, certainly in Paul's teaching, is the illustration of the body. On the Damascus road, Christ said to him, 'Saul, Saul, why do you persecute me?' (Acts

9:4). Here Christ movingly identifies himself with his persecuted church. It is not surprising then that it is Paul who writes so much about the organic union of Christ with his church in terms of a head and a body, for the concept is implicit in the first words he heard from his risen Lord.

As the head, supreme lordship in the church must always be his and cannot belong to anybody else. Luke asserts that it is the sovereign Lord who adds members to the church (Acts 2:47). His headship applies to the whole church and to every aspect of its life.

In a most impressive passage, Paul says that God 'raised him from the dead and seated him at his right hand in the heavenly realms, far above all rule and authority, power and dominion, and every title that can be given, not only in the present age but also in the one to come. And God placed all things under his feet and appointed him to be the head over everything for the church' (Eph. 1:22). It looks as if Paul is saying here that Christ is ruling the universe with a constant eye on his purpose for his church. All that happens is put to the service of that purpose. What an encouragement for Christians facing persecution, for missionaries who are expelled from the country whose people they love and for us all in the more distressing circumstances of life!

If Christ is the head of the whole church, he is head also of each local church. The Book of Revelation, with its vivid picture language, speaks of one like a son of man walking in the midst of the seven golden lampstands (Rev. 1:12f.). It is he therefore that joins them to each other because they are all joined to him. He also holds the seven stars in his right hand (Rev. 1:20), symbolising his complete power over each of the churches. Because he has this power, he addresses a letter to each of the seven churches separately, related to the particular needs of each. He does not hesitate to issue commands they must obey and warnings they must heed as well as promises in which they can rejoice.

If he is indeed the head of the church, then every local congregation needs to acknowledge what Christians of an earlier generation used to call 'the crown rights of the Redeemer', and submit to him in everything. No church can 'go it alone' or 'do its own thing', because each church exists for him and for him alone. It is his purposes that must determine everything that is done in the church. If we really took this seriously, a lot of our church programmes would be given an entirely new look.

Active on earth

Did Christ's ascension mean the end of his earthly activity, at least until his second advent? By no means! Just prior to it, he said, 'Surely I am with you always, to the very end of the age' (Matt. 28:20). The age has not yet ended and so the promise holds good today. But if he is in heaven, how can he be still on earth?

He works on earth now through the Holy Spirit. It is because of the Holy Spirit that Christians now have a more intimate relationship with Christ than the disciples had before Pentecost. Jesus had said to the disciples, 'I will not leave you as orphans; I will come to you' (John 14:18). The verses immediately before this statement are about the Spirit and this suggests to many commentators that the promise was related to the gift of the Holy Spirit. This promise therefore was fulfilled on the day of Pentecost, when Peter declared, 'Exalted to the right hand of God, he has received from the Father the promised Holy Spirit, and has poured out what you now see and hear' (Acts 2:33). So there is a special connection between Christ's exaltation and the gift of the Holy Spirit. He was exalted because his work of atonement had been completed, and the Spirit is sent from heaven to make the experience of salvation from sin real in his people's hearts.

Although the exalted Christ and the Holy Spirit are distinguishable they cannot be separated. The three Holy Persons always work together. Christians are 'in Christ' but it is also true to say that the Holy Spirit dwells in us. Paul calls him 'the Spirit of Christ' (Rom. 8:9), so that Christ lives in us through the Spirit. Because of this, he can be in heaven and on earth at the same time. This union with Christ through the agency of the Holy Spirit is a unique fact with no real parallel in human experience.

So then Christ empowers us for the Christian life through the Spirit and in this way he is still active on earth. Ephesians 5:18 and Colossians 3:16 are set in passages which have a number of common features. This strongly suggests that the two exhortations in them, the first to be filled with the Spirit, and the other to let the word of Christ dwell in us richly, are really two sides of the same fact. The Lordship of Christ and the fullness of the Spirit answer to each other.

Praying for his people

Every Christian person lives two lives. There is the life he or she lives among other people, among family and workmates, moving amongst his friends and acquaintances. There is also his life with God, the relationship of worship and love and prayer which operates deep within his heart. The quality of the former is always determined by the quality of the latter.

In the Lord Jesus each of these two lives was perfect, and the two were perfectly integrated. The Gospel writers, and especially Luke, give us much insight into his prayer-life. We see him praying at the great crisis points in his ministry (e.g. Luke 3:21; 9:28f.; 22:40-46). It was not only in such times of special need, however, that he prayed, but throughout his day-to-day life. It was their observance of his own life of prayer that caused the disciples to ask him to give them instruction in prayer (Luke 11:1).

One of the most selfless expressions of prayer is intercession. In it we take the needs of other people on our hearts and bring them to God. Simon, along with the other disciples, was to face a great crisis in his own life when the Saviour was taken from him to death. Shortly before this, Jesus said to him, 'Simon, Simon, Satan has asked to sift you as wheat. But I have prayed for you, Simon, that your faith may not fail. And when you have turned back, strengthen your brothers' (Luke 22:31,32).

The longest recorded prayer of Jesus is to be found in John 17. There we find him interceding for his disciples in the simplest and yet deepest terms. This prayer was not only for the disciples who companied with him during his ministry, but modern Christians are included too, for he said, 'My prayer is not for them alone. I pray also for those who believe in me through their message' (John 17:20). Their message has come down to us in modern times in the written form of the New Testament, and so modern Christians may be encouraged by the fact that this prayer includes them.

What has all this to do with the exaltation of Christ? A very great deal. The Epistle to the Hebrews has a lot to say about the priestly function of Christ. Now according to the Old Testament, the main work of a priest was to offer sacrifice. The writer of this letter never tires of telling us that Christ has done that for us, and done it with complete effectiveness and finality. He sat down, not only because he is a king, but also because his sacrificial work has been completed (Heb. 10:11-14), for a priest never sat down until his work was finished.

A priest was called to pray as well as to offer sacrifice. Hebrews also makes it clear to us that Christ is still our High Priest and that he is occupied constantly in prayer. As the writer puts it, 'He is able to save completely those who come to God through him, because he always lives to intercede for them' (Heb. 7:25).

This theme is not restricted to the letter to the Hebrews. John, in his first letter, says, 'My dear children, I write this to you so that you will not sin. But if anybody does sin, we have one who speaks to the Father in our defence, Jesus Christ, the Righteous One' (1 John 2:1). Paul, in one of his most deeply emotional passages, asks the question, 'Who is he that condemns? Christ Jesus, who died – more than that, who was raised to life – is at the right hand of God and is also interceding for us' (Rom. 8:34). There seems to be a kind of ascending scale in the four facts Paul mentions in this verse, with the highest point reached with his assertion that Christ is praying for us.

Many Christians give little thought to the intercessory ministry of Christ and it figures little in their Christian lives. When the devil seems to be throwing everything against you, when you are overwhelmed by some sorrow, when you pass through some experience of deep discouragement, it is good to remember that Christ is praying. Many of us deeply appreciate the promises of prayer that other Christians have made, but they may forget at times. Christ never forgets to pray. His intercession is continuous and eternal.

Coming back again

The Christian life is a life of faith. Christians know Christ, love him and serve him, without having ever seen him. Yet to us, he is not simply a figure in history, but somebody who lives now and who has brought us into a wonderful relationship with him, which is vibrant with life and power. Yet we long to see him. Shall we be denied this for ever? No, the Word of God promises that he will come again.

What will he do when he returns? It is well known that there has been much debate about the second coming ever since the early Christian centuries and much difference of opinion on matters of detail. This is not surprising. It is important however to realise that the issues of the greatest moment are not matters on which opinions differ greatly. The main purposes of his return are clear, and questions as to the exact programme of events, interesting as they are, must be of less importance.

It is clear that he will take Christians to be with him. He said, 'If I go and prepare a place for you, I will come back and take you to be with me that you also may be where I am' (John 14:3). Paul's teaching in 1 Thessalonians 4:15-18, although somewhat more detailed, also emphasises that the coming of Christ for his church means that his people will be with him for ever. Many Christians will of course be dead, but many will be alive at the time of his return.

Clearly, because his coming is to be an historical event and yet one that will reunite all Christians in his presence, some will be taken from death and some from life, but both groups will be given bodies like his own glorious body (Phil. 3:21). As Paul puts it in one passage, 'When Christ who is your life appears, then you also will appear with him in glory' (Col. 3:4).

We can hardly conceive what this will mean. Paul wrote a long chapter on the subject of the resurrection of believers (1 Cor. 15) and this repays careful study. Some at Corinth appear to have asked questions about the nature of the resurrection body. Paul does not encourage foolish speculation, but he does use the illustration of the death of a seed (1 Cor. 15:35ff.), an illustration employed also by our Lord although in a slightly different connection (John 12:24).

He contrasts the lowliness of the seed with the glory of the plant that springs from it and says that our bodies as sown are perishable, without honour and weak, while the resurrection body is glorious, imperishable and powerful. 'It is sown a natural body, it is raised a spiritual body' (1 Cor 15:42-44). The implication appears to be that our bodies will be freed from the limitations of earth and will be perfectly adapted to the new dimensions of consummated eternal life. This is a wonderful prospect.

What else will happen? The whole of human history has known injustice, evil men apparently getting away with acts of great cruelty, cursing God and refusing to do his will. Sometimes God has judged them within the process of history, but sometimes it seems as though he has not. They seem to go on their way into blacker and blacker crimes, heedless of him and of his claims on all human life. Can this go on for ever? No! The Bible makes much reference to historical judgements but it also warns of a great future judgement which everyone will have to face.

Christ told his disciples that he would judge the world when he returned. 'The Son of Man is going to come in his Father's glory with his angels, and then he will reward each person according to what he has done' (Matt. 16:27). The New Testament writers take up this teaching and amplify it. Paul speaks of the time 'when the Lord Jesus is revealed from heaven in blazing fire with his powerful angels. He will punish those who do not know God and who do not obey the gospel of our Lord Jesus' (2 Thess. 1:7, 8). This gives great seriousness to the proclamation of the good news of the Lord Jesus Christ, and every Christian ought to regard this as a priority of the highest kind for his or her own life.

The true Christian longs for the Lord Jesus to come back. John, in the Book of Revelation, using one of the illustrations of the church, declares, 'The Spirit and the bride say, "Come!" ' A few verses later he writes, 'He who testifies to these things says, "Yes, I am coming soon." Amen. Come, Lord Jesus!' (Rev. 22:17, 20). When he came to earth the first time the human beings he had made mocked and rejected him, and killed him. He is coming to be vindicated by his Father where he had been rejected. Nothing could be more fitting. 'Come, Lord Jesus!'

References
1. W.L. Craig, 'The Bodily Resurrection of Jesus', in *Gospel Perspectives, Vol. 1* (eds. R.T. France and D. Wenham, Sheffield, JSOT, 1980, pp. 47-74; Robert H. Gundry, 'The Essential Physicality of Jesus' Resurrection according to the New Testament' in Green and Turner (eds.) *Jesus of Nazareth*, pp. 204-219.
2. *Op. cit.* p. 206.
3. e.g. in *The Bearing of Recent Discovery on the Trustworthiness of the New Testament*, London, Hodder and Stoughton, 1915
4. A. Harnack, *The Acts of the Apostles* (trans. J.R.Wilkinson), London, Williams and Norgate, 1909.

Chapter 10

THE SUPERNATURAL ISSUE

Why is it that the claims Christians make for Christ are not accepted more widely than they are?

It is often said by preachers that resistance to these claims is basically moral and spiritual, that those who resist them do so because of the disturbing effect Christ would have in their lives if they really took those claims seriously and accepted his Lordship in terms of personal commitment. There is of course real truth in this, as many of us for whom conversion was associated with considerable moral struggle know only too well in our own experience.

Yet, although this factor is of quite crucial importance in the conversion experience, there are many who face genuine theological problems on the road to conversion, and it is the task of the apologist to seek to help them. The major problem for many people is one that is perhaps better described as philosophical, because it relates to a clash between the biblical world-view and their own world-view. It is the supernatural element in the Christian faith that they find a great stumbling block.

Now this would be troublesome, but not so serious, if it related only to peripheral elements in Christianity. What makes it so crucial is that it is the central elements, and particularly what the Bible teaches about Christ, which are affected. He is the very centre of the Christian faith, and the presentation of him in the Bible is strongly supernatural.

Natural and Supernatural

What do we mean by these terms? It is important for us to give them careful definition and to consider carefully the relationship between them.

The term 'natural', at least when employed in philosophical discussions, normally relates to features of the observable universe as we know it that can be explained purely in terms of other features we find within that universe. The assumption is that all these features are bound up together, and that there are totally consistent principles, scientific laws, which govern all these phenomena and their interactions. So we may say that one event is the cause of another, and that both cause and effect are parts of an interlocking system.

This view of the universe has been quite a basic one for modern science, being taken for granted by scientists, no matter what their area of science might be. If they found something which had not yet been explained from phenomena related to it in some way within the universe, then they regarded this as a challenge and they laboured at it until they found such an explanation. As a result such a scientist might deservedly gain a Ph.D or even a Nobel prize.

It needs to be said though that in the twentieth century scientists working in the areas of quantum theory and chaos theory have raised questions as to the completely inviolable character of the natural universe. The most basic building blocks of nature have turned out not simply to be particles but waves of mathematical information, and nature now seems to many scientists to be more open than pre-quantum scientific thinking would have admitted, although of course the quantum physicists, like other scientists, are concerned to demonstrate the inner consistency of the universe as fully as they can.[1]

It is difficult for us to realise that the modern scientific outlook has not always prevailed. It was once accepted (and still is accepted in some societies) that a whole range of phenomena in our experience have a source that is independent of an inter-related system of cause and effect. There are still societies in which almost all of their members feel that they have always to take account of the influence of spirits, good and evil. Because these beings are personal, their influence is largely unpredictable. This is not only the case in what are known as animistic societies, where the animation of material things by such beings dominates people's outlook, but also in some with a religion which is much more sophisticated but where people often feel that the influence of such spirits is very important in the affairs of everyday life.

Predictability is of course a major feature in the modern scientific outlook. A scientific hypothesis is regarded as unproved until it can predict the way the phenomena with which it is concerned will act under certain controlled conditions. To quote a famous example, one billiard ball striking another will always cause the second to move unless some other object is so placed as to prevent that movement.

It is not surprising then that there has been so much debate as to whether or not psychology and the social sciences are truly scientific. The desire to establish them as scientific is probably one of the main reasons why theories have arisen which explain the actions of human beings in a somewhat mechanistic way, as if people are highly sophisticated machines. It is to secure for these subjects the credibility and respect that we accord to the physical sciences.

We need too to face the fact that the concept of the purely natural is now under attack even in Western society. The New Age movement is a somewhat amorphous outlook with many different varieties, but common to it is the recognition of a spiritual dimension to life and the possibility of the intervention of supernatural forces in the life of the individual.[2] This is in fact all part of the still wider movement known as Post-Modernism, to which reference has already been made.

Despite all that has been said, of course, there are whole areas of life where the most thorough-going animist or New Age devotee normally anticipates that life will be predictable. Even such people do not expect the intervention of the 'supernatural' to take over completely from the natural.

What then do we mean by 'supernatural'? There is no doubt that this term has somewhat diverse connotations or nuances,[3] but, for our purposes, it is best understood in terms of phenomena within the observable universe, that is the universe that can be observed by the methods of science, which are not capable of explanation in terms of other phenomena within that same universe.

Notice the phrase 'not capable', for it is very important. This means that we are not identifying the supernatural with the puzzling, for what puzzles us today may not puzzle us, or our children, tomorrow. Nor are we identifying it with the wonderful. We may wonder at a great waterfall or a glorious sunset but that does not make it supernatural. The supernatural is anything which by its very nature is incapable of explanation in terms of other phenomena within the observable universe. It therefore belongs to a different order from the natural.

To try to make this abundantly clear, we are not saying that it is something for which we can find no natural cause, but rather something which can, in the very nature of things, never be found to have a natural cause. So we define the supernatural more in objective than in subjective terms.

Why are we insisting on this? Because Christians have often been accused of believing in a 'God of the gaps'. What is meant by this is that we attribute to God features of the world as we know it which are mysterious and for which no explanation has yet been found. 'God' fills the gaps left by science, but the more science advances the more these gaps are filled and so, it is argued, the less place is there for God.

Now it would be foolish to deny that Christians have sometimes assumed such an attitude as this or that there are Christians today who sometimes do this. Such an attitude is not however really defensible. It is, in fact, extremely unstable and provides little or no defence against determined unbelief. It is only truth that can withstand the assaults of error and this view simply is not true.

It is of great importance for us to recognise that the one God is God both of the natural and of the supernatural. The natural testifies to the amazing order of his mind, while the supernatural reveals a very special purpose which is in a different dimension from the normal order of the universe. The supernatural does not introduce disorder, but rather shows that the divine order has a dimension beyond what we can observe.

For the believer in God, what we call scientific laws are really simply evidence of his amazing consistency, his wonderfully ordered mind.[4] If that believer is a Christian, the coming of the supernatural Christ and his victory over sin and death reveal that God has other purposes than simply keeping an ordered universe of time and space in being, and these too show the great values which, although internal to his eternal mind, govern his every action.

Christians have sometimes been troubled when what they thought to be supernatural has turned out to have a perfectly natural explanation. In principle, this should not trouble us at all. In fact, it should lead us to praise the God whose amazing order it has revealed. We should praise him for the supernatural and we should praise him for the natural, for he is the God of both.

Is there then any room for the concept of the supernatural at all? In terms of the Christian faith the answer must be 'Yes!' Christians believe that in Christ the God who created the natural order has intervened supernaturally to bring salvation to men and women. An 'unsupernatural Christianity' is certainly not the Christian faith that is found in the Bible.

We have to face the fact, however, that there are theologians and commentators who do not accept the supernatural. From Strauss (and even earlier) to members of the Jesus Seminar they have ruled out the supernatural in seeking to understand the witness of the New Testament. It has to be said that this outlook is a serious departure from historic Christianity, and shows that in this respect some naturalistic philosophical position has come to exercise the function of a filter through which the biblical facts have been put.

If the natural and the supernatural are different and yet both are manifestations of the activity of the one God, are there any definite links between them? Without doubt there are. We have already suggested that both are related to God's purpose, although clearly to different aspects of it. It can even be argued that the supernatural testifies to a higher purpose, for its unusual and exceptional character would appear to bear witness to this. Even human beings who act habitually in certain ways do not normally act in quite different ways unless they feel it important to do so.

Then, as C.S. Lewis argued so persuasively,[5] the supernatural and the natural have an important link in that the former impinges on the latter. Take, for example, the miracle of the feeding of the five thousand by Jesus. If loaves and fishes are supernaturally multiplied because of some special purpose of God, when they come to be eaten they are absorbed into the body through the digestive system just as well as loaves and fishes that have not been supernaturally multiplied. This means that although the supernatural is different from the natural it does not introduce a discordant note into God's universe.

The Supernatural in the Christ-Event

Why all this philosophical discussion? To clear the ground so that we may give thought to the supernatural in the life and experience of Jesus Christ, for its presence is a most marked feature of the New Testament revelation.

The New Testament records his virgin birth, his miracles, his resurrection and ascension and promises his second coming. All of these are important and are parts of the Christ-event, and as we have already seen the resurrection is of very great importance indeed. We should note though that they all rest on something which was both an event and a continuing fact and which was the cause of them all, namely the event and continuing fact of the incarnation, that permanent union of God and man in Christ which began in the womb of the Virgin Mary but which will never end.

In our present discussion, we propose to take the incarnation for granted as it is to be discussed quite fully in Chapters 11 and 12. We will however include the virgin birth, which was the method of the incarnation. The ascension and second coming of Christ both rest on his resurrection. Unless he really did rise from the dead, the ascension could not have taken place, for it is presented in the New Testament in physical and not purely spiritual terms. In other words, at the ascension the resurrection body of Jesus actually moved from the earthly to the heavenly sphere. The second advent too is presented as a physical event, for, as the angels said to the disciples who watched him ascend, it will be the same Jesus who will return and he will come back in a similar fashion to his going, and this surely includes the fact of his resurrection body.

His miracles too need to be discussed. If we take seriously the presentation of them in the Gospels, we see that they are presented as real events of a supernatural character. They are not trickery nor are they the result of hallucinations. Some of the healing miracles are often regarded as the least 'shocking' to those who reject the supernatural because of the wide recognition of psychosomatic illnesses today and so of the relationship between the inner life and the health of the physical body. Also various 'natural' explanations of some of the other miracles have been given. For instance, the feeding of the five thousand has been 'explained' by suggesting that the generosity of the boy who donated his loaves and fishes put to shame many in the crowd who actually had food with them but did not wish to share it with others. Even if this is a plausible explanation (which is highly doubtful), it would explain only one alleged miracle and would leave a multitude of others unexplained.

The greatest of the miracles are those that involved the raising of people from the dead. These and all his other miracles are validated by his own resurrection, for in emerging from the grave he conquered death once and for all. This must surely mean that all his claims were true. He actually was the Son of God and the Lord of all[6], and so nothing would be impossible for him. This does not mean, of course, that there can be no discussion of particular miracles performed by him, but it does mean that his actual ability to perform them is beyond all doubt. If he can conquer death totally and permanently he can do anything.

The Central Apologetic Importance of the Resurrection of Christ

Apologists for the Christian faith have sometimes been divided into minimisers and maximisers. These terms should not be misunderstood. It is not that the maximisers have a fuller faith than the minimisers. The two groups do not in fact disagree at all as to the nature and contents of the Christian faith. Their only disagreement concerns the task of the defence of that faith.

Let us picture the Christian faith as a walled city which is under siege from outside. The Christian apologist rallies forces of truth to defend the city from attack. If he is a maximiser he will endeavour to station a defender at every point on the wall. If a minimiser he will not do this, but instead, recognising the various places on the wall where the enemy is most likely to attack, he will concentrate the defence of the city at such points, producing one argument after another to vindicate Christian belief in the areas of essential and central belief.

The maximiser is concerned to defend everything. Every feature of the biblical revelation needs to be defended, every problem passage in the Bible investigated and explained. There is a sense in which many Bible commentators are maximisers in apologetics, for they seek to tackle every problem as it occurs in the text before them, whether that problem be historical or theological. Such commentaries are, of course, of great value and we can be thankful for the work of such meticulous scholars. The commentaries of Albert Barnes, the nineteenth century commentator,[7] are an example of the maximising apologist's approach. You may not always be satisfied with his handling of a difficult passage, but you will never find him ignoring it!

We may applaud the diligent work of the maximiser and be thankful for it, while having some reservations if it reflects a particular mentality. You see, it may induce or even be the product of a certain nervousness, a certain over-defensiveness. Maximising has sometimes surfaced in a somewhat unhealthy way when the Christian faith has been under severe attack by rationalists. To believe in the infallibility and inerrancy of Scripture is one thing, but to feel that the whole Christian faith is insecure unless every problem in it can be solved is quite another, and is the product of a faith which feels itself insecure. Of course, it is important also to say that many who pursue this method are robust Christians and anything but insecure in their faith.

An analogy with the scientific enterprise may be helpful. The scientist believes in the consistency of the phenomena within the universe, but this is not because he can give a complete account of this consistency. There are still puzzles,[8] but they do not undermine his faith that full consistency exists. The minimiser, on the other hand, selects certain features of the Christian faith and concentrates on defending these. He may be a minimiser for purely practical reasons. After all, life is not long enough to enable him to defend everything! He may, on the other hand, be a minimiser by conviction. Once defend the great central truths and the whole Christian faith is secure.

All minimisers regard the defence of the resurrection as important, and the extreme minimiser concentrates completely on it in the conviction that this is absolutely central to the apologetic task, and that, once this has been successfully defended, the whole Christian faith is secure.

The present writer must confess to being a minimiser. He greatly values the work of maximisers for their work has shed a great deal of light on passage after passage in the Bible, but he believes that the resurrection is so central that this should be the chief focus of the apologetic task.

The historical evidence for the resurrection of Christ

This has often been explored. The treatment of the subject by Frank Morison[9] is justly famous. Morison started out as somebody who was much attracted to the character of Christ and yet could not believe in the miraculous. He decided to investigate the records of the passion and death and resurrection of Jesus. He expected that as a result of his investigations he would be confirmed in his rejection of the miraculous. Instead, the exact opposite happened, for it was by examining the facts themselves that he became totally convinced of the truth of Christ's conquest of death.

The necessary limits of our present volume make it impossible for us to look at the facts in the detail which they deserve, but we will concentrate on certain central features of the argument for the reality of the resurrection. Those who wish to pursue the matter further are recommended to read Morison's book.

There can be no doubt that Jesus actually died on the cross

It has been suggested that Jesus never really died at all as a result of his crucifixion, or at least that there was a postponement of that death. Perhaps, it is suggested, he only swooned on the cross. The tomb would have been cold and this was just what would be necessary to revive him. Some time later he could have emerged from that tomb, spending time again with his disciples before being finally taken by death.

This view at first sounds plausible, but a little thought reveals that it leaves far too many questions unanswered.

Remember that there were Roman soldiers at the cross, that one of them examined Jesus to see if he was dead or not, that to make absolutely certain he drove his spear into his side and that blood and water, the evidence of a ruptured heart, emerged from that pierced side.

Remember the stone that was placed over the entrance to the tomb. The stones used were huge and heavy. Such a stone could never have been removed by one fit man, let alone by one so cruelly wounded that the observers thought him dead.

Remember too the guard of soldiers placed outside the grave. The stone could not have been removed by human hands without their being aware of what was happening. In the unlikely event that they had fallen asleep (most unlikely because of the dire consequences to them), his escape from the tomb could hardly have been effected sufficiently quietly. If he had managed it, this would soon have been discovered, and the authorities would have spared no pains in tracking him down.

Remember too the note of victory and joy which throbs in the accounts of the first Easter Sunday and that never dies to the last page of the New Testament. Can we really assert that a man's narrow escape from death was the cause of this? Not only so, but on this theory, whatever happened to the man Jesus eventually?

There can be no doubt that the grave itself was empty on the first Easter Sunday

The Gospels make it clear that the disciples were not expecting the resurrection of Jesus. He had of course told them that this would happen, but they had been so troubled by what he had told them about his sufferings and death that they did not really take this in. The women went to anoint a body but found an empty tomb. The disciples, Peter and John, went also, and they too found the grave empty.

It has been suggested that they may have gone to the wrong grave. This too sounds plausible, but this theory also does not bear investigation. After all, we are talking about a man who was greatly loved by his followers. How very unlikely that all of them should have wrongly identified the grave of somebody they had loved so dearly! Is it not much more likely that the spot would be for ever imprinted on their minds?

Moreover on the day of Pentecost they proclaimed these facts in Jerusalem itself, the very city where the trials and death of Jesus had taken place. This proclamation must have had an electrifying effect on the authorities. Both the Jewish leaders and the Romans had a vested interest in disproving the resurrection and there can be no doubt at all that they would have done so if it had been possible. All these men had to do was simply to produce the disintegrating body of Jesus, but they did nothing of the sort.

There can be no doubt that he appeared to people alive from the dead

The Gospels record the resurrection appearances of Jesus on the day of his conquest of death, while Paul gives a list of appearances in his first Letter to the Corinthians (1 Cor. 15:5-7). Now all these appearances had their purpose and each must have been very precious to the people concerned, but from an apologetic point of view some of them are particularly significant.

There was the appearance to Thomas a week after the resurrection, recorded in John's Gospel. He comes over in the Gospels as the most hard-headed of the disciples. He had been absent when Jesus had appeared to his disciples in the Upper Room on the day of the resurrection itself and he had manifested considerable scepticism when told by the others. A week later however Jesus appeared to him and he was utterly convinced (John 20:19-29).

Then there was the appearance to James, the eldest of the brothers of Jesus. The Gospels make it clear that his whole family had refused his claims during his ministry. We learn however from the Acts of the Apostles that he became a leader of the infant church at Jerusalem (Acts 15:13-21; cf. Gal. 1:19). It must have been that resurrection appearance that led to his change of outlook.

Then there was the appearance to Saul of Tarsus.[10] Saul was a man of great promise who had been trained in the Pharisaic Judaism which was the theology of many members of the Sanhedrin which had condemned Jesus. He shared their rejection of the claims of Jesus, and he was so anti-Christian that he was bent on the destruction of the followers of Jesus. It was while he was on his way to put many of them in prison that the risen Jesus met him. As a result of this, he became utterly convinced that Jesus had risen from the dead.

Paul tells us too of his appearance to more than five hundred Christians at once. A mass hallucination experienced by such a large number takes some believing.

There can be no doubt that he has continued to work since his death

In the preface to his second volume, Luke implies that the Acts of the Apostles is the story of what Jesus, whose deeds and words he had recorded in his Gospel, continued to do and teach (Acts 1:1,2). He records the coming of the Holy Spirit at Pentecost very early in this book, and records that Peter, in his Pentecost sermon, declared that the Spirit's advent was itself evidence of the exaltation of Jesus. Referring to the visible and audible manifestations of the Spirit at that time, he says, 'Exalted to the right hand of God, he has received from the Father the promised Holy Spirit and has poured out what you now see and hear' (Acts 2:33).

This means then that we may see the activity of the Spirit in the origin and growth of the church and in the multitude of blessings that have come to people through the gospel as evidence that Jesus conquered death and is now in heaven, still active on behalf of his people through the Holy Spirit.

The living church of Christ today, when it is true to its calling and is utterly dependent on the Holy Spirit, will always provide contemporary evidence in the lives of people that Jesus is alive. So many people have had their lives revolutionised and have become God-orientated, deeply caring disciples of Christ, that each one adds to the accumulation of evidence of his risen life and of his continued activity.

There can be no doubt as to the honesty of the witnesses

Is it possible that everything that has been recorded is simply a fabrication, one gigantic confidence trick? It is anything but easy to believe that it is.

For one thing, the accounts are so straight-forward, almost matter of fact. They are certainly not the normal stuff of fantasy or of artificial contrivance. There is a sobriety about the Gospels that is immensely convincing and, if anything, this is most marked in the accounts of the last week in the life of Jesus. They certainly do not read like romancing.

Then there is another and, on the face of it, very odd piece of evidence. This is the fact that the accounts of the first Easter day given in the four Gospels are not easy to harmonise. Many have worked at this and proposed different solutions to the problems, some more helpful than others. Harmonisation is possible but it has to be worked at.

Now these very difficulties testify to the fact that we are dealing with independent witnesses. The resurrection was vital and central to the claims Christians made for their Lord. If those claims were based on a lie, we can be certain that the witnesses would have taken as much trouble as possible to make certain that their accounts could be harmonised with ease. This is in fact what often gives conspirators away in a court room. Their accounts are too much alike, and they are so because they have agreed on the story beforehand. No two people describe the same event in identical terms.

There is nothing of this unconvincing and contrived harmony in the accounts of the resurrection in the Gospels. Why? Because they are true!

A number of sceptics have set out to study the New Testament references to Christ's resurrection, with the clear expectation that it would not stand up to scrutiny, only to find themselves utterly convinced by the evidence itself that Jesus Christ really did emerge from the grave, alive from the dead. Frank Morison's account of his search, entitled *Who moved the Stone?* [11] makes compelling reading.

The resurrection and other supernatural features of the fact of Christ

Later we will consider the question as to whether we may neatly divide the fact of Christ into natural and supernatural features.

Meantime, however, we will look at certain events which, as recorded, bear very evident marks of the supernatural, and ask how they appear in the light of the resurrection of Jesus.

The birth of Jesus

In many ways the birth of Jesus was perfectly normal, perfectly natural. It was not so much his birth as his conception which was so unusual, indeed unique. As the Creed says, and as the Gospels of Matthew and Luke testify, he was 'conceived by the Holy Spirit'.

Now this raises all kinds of questions for us. What does this conception by the Spirit really mean? How are we to relate it to the findings of modern genetics about genes and chromosomes and especially about the combination of genetic inheritance brought about by the productive union of a man and a woman?

The biblical text does not answer these questions. In fact it does not even raise them. If it had, it might well have been unintelligible to people of the New Testament period for whom genes and chromosomes would have been meaningless terms.

We have frankly to recognise that the birth of Jesus was supernatural. The most significant feature was not so much the absence of a human father, although that was not without its importance, but the special work of the Holy Spirit which took place. Here in the womb of Mary the amazing fact of the incarnation became a reality, for it was at his conception, not at his birth, that the union of God and man took place.

If we accept the resurrection of Jesus there is no reason whatever why we should not accept the virgin birth. It should however be noted in passing that there are some theologians who have fully accepted the resurrection but not the virgin birth. It is obvious that their reason for this must be quite apart from the question of the supernatural, for, in accepting the resurrection, they have already in principle accepted the supernatural.

Foremost among such theologians was Emil Brunner. His objections to the doctrine were not on the grounds of its miraculous nature but rather about its appropriateness.[12] It can be well argued, however, that nothing could be more appropriate than a miraculous beginning to the life of Jesus. If his exit from this world was so markedly supernatural, how apt that his entrance to it should be also!

If however the issue is not appropriateness but possibility, then the resurrection ought to settle the issue completely. If Jesus could so overcome sin by dying for sinners on the cross and could so triumph over all the consequences of sin that he actually vanquished death, its greatest consequence in human life, then nothing in the physical realm can be reckoned impossible, and this includes the virgin conception.

The miracles of Jesus

None of these can be regarded as impossible. Not one of them is of a higher order (or even of a comparable order) to his resurrection. C.S. Lewis made a useful distinction between miracles of the old creation and miracles of the new.[13] The former often simply speeded up processes that normally operate within the natural world as we know it. There is a multiplication of bread and fish in the natural world by the ordinary processes of generation affecting cereals and fishes and water becomes wine as the vine absorbs water for purposes of its healthy growth.

Miracles of the new creation, however, mean the introduction of a new order or the impinging of a new order on the old. Human beings do not walk on water or come back to life under the old order, but Christ effected both. Even however in terms of the new creation, Christ's resurrection with its total defeat of death was unique. His raising of others from death was not of course of the same order as his own conquest of it, for this was permanent, and, moreover, as the New Testament witnesses, it became the cause of the future resurrection of believers. Accept his resurrection and all the miracles he performed, both those of the old creation and those of the new, are easily acceptable.

The ascension of Jesus

The ascension must be thought of as taking place in two stages, the first visible to human eyes and the second invisible but just as physical.

In the first stage he was taken up from the earth and a cloud hid him from their sight (Acts 1:9). The visibility of this stage gives the event apologetic value. They saw him with their physical eyes.

What happened at the second stage we do not know. Obviously if Christ has a resurrection body, as the New Testament testifies, then that body exists now. Just what the properties of a resurrection body are we do not fully know. We do know that Christ could appear and disappear, that he could pass through closed doors and yet also that he could eat fish and that he had real flesh and bones, real hands and feet (Luke 24:39-43; John 20:19,20). All this gives us clues but does not supply full answers. We may perhaps assume that the possession of a body implies location. We do know also, of course, that this is not the whole story and that Jesus is present with his people spiritually through the Holy Spirit.

His ascension was the entry to his heavenly session. He is seated at the right hand of God the Father, which is clearly language expressive of a place of supreme power in the government of the universe.

It is of course fitting that he should have this place, not only because he is God incarnate, but also because of his conquest of sin and death. If the resurrection had really taken place, then his entry into heaven was assured and his government of the universe most fitting.

His second advent

Acts 1:11 ('in the same way') certainly seems to imply that Jesus will return physically and visibly for that it is the way he went This physicality and visibility are of course made possible by his resurrection, and the purposes of his coming are completely appropriate, when we consider who he was and what he has done. He is coming to establish his kingdom, the kingdom which he constantly proclaimed, which he inaugurated and which he promised would be brought to its consummation on his return (Matt. 26:29, 64; Rev. 11:15). If he is in fact Lord of the universe, it is utterly fitting that, through his Kingdom, his rule over all kinds and conditions of human beings should be fully established.

He is also coming to complete the salvation of his redeemed people (Luke 21:29), so that, already quickened spiritually through vital contact with him through the Holy Spirit, they may now come to have resurrection bodies also (Phil. 3:20,21). He is coming too to judge the world, for as the God who made them and as the man whose life was one long fulfilment of his Father's holy will, he is eminently and uniquely fitted for this great task (John 5:22,23; Acts 10:42).

References
1. For a Christian approach to this type of thinking, see John Polkinghorne, *Reason and Reality: The Relationship between Science and Theology*, London: SPCK, 1991. I am grateful to a friend and colleague, the Revd. Howard Taylor, lecturer in Apologetics at Glasgow Bible College, for very helpful comments on the relationship between the natural and the supernatural.
2. For a useful exposition and Christian critique of the New Age movement, see Peter Jones, *The Gnostic Empire Strikes Back: An Old Heresy for the New Age,* Phillipsburg, Presbyterian and Reformed, 1992.
3. In the thought of the philosophical theologian, Paul Tillich, an attempt was made to transcend the dualism of the natural and the supernatural, but his fellow philosophers did not find it convincing. See S. Hook (ed.), *Religious Experience and Truth* (London, Oliver and Boyd, 1966), much of which shows philosophers and theologians engaging with his thought.
4. For exposition of this view of the relation between God and nature, see Donald Mackay, *Christianity in a Mechanistic Universe and Other Essays*, London, IVP, 1965.
5. See his book, *Miracles,* London, Geoffrey Bles, 1947, especially Chapter 8.
6. Peter saw clearly that the resurrection of Jesus follows logically from the nature of his person, when he said, 'it was impossible for death to keep its hold on him' (Acts 2:24).
7. Albert Barnes, *Notes, Explanatory and Practical on the New Testament* (in 11 volumes), Glasgow, Blackie and Son, 1832. He also wrote some Old Testament commentaries.
8. Heisenberg has promoted the idea of an 'uncertainty principle' in Physics.
9. Frank Morison, *Who Moved the Stone?* London, Faber and Faber, 1944.
10. He mentioned this in the 1 Corinthians passage and Luke records it three times, in Acts 9, 22 and 26.
11. Morison, *Who Moved the Stone?*
12. Emil Brunner, *The Mediator*, London, Lutterworth Press, 1934, pp. 322-327.
13. C.S. Lewis, *Miracles,* Chapters 15 and 16.

Chapter 11

GOD INCARNATE

The person who has had all his or her questions answered and for whom the universe has no mysteries does not exist. Everybody is perplexed about something. In fact, we seem to need some mysteries to satisfy one side of our make-up. In my teenage years, I met an old man out in the country. We were talking about the beauties of nature, and I said, in response to some comment of his, 'That's wonderful!' 'Wonderful, young man?' said he; 'Everything's wonderful!'

That old man had not lost the wonderment and enquiring mind of a child. In a child everything raises questions. Why this? Why that? How does this work? What does this mean? As we get older, our questions may become less clamorous but we are still just as puzzled. We may be able to understand gravity or electricity, at least at a basic level, but what about DNA? What about the relationship between the mind and the body? What about the presence of evil in the world?

Many of the deepest questions we ask are about the meaning of life itself. There is a story told about a nineteenth century German philosopher. He was seated one day on a park bench. Seeing this elderly, shabbily dressed man and thinking him a tramp, a policeman accosted him, saying, 'What are you doing here?' The philosopher replied that he wished he knew, and that he had given the best years of his life to that problem and yet still did not know the answer.

Those who met Jesus and got to know him found themselves in the presence of a mystery of the profoundest kind, for they found that they ran out of human categories when it came to describing who he was, and yet, in a strange paradox, these human categories still had a certain appropriateness.

A real man

Martin Luther used to maintain that the proper way to come to a proper understanding of Jesus Christ was to begin with him as a man. For instance, he said, 'Scripture begins very gently by leading us first to Christ as to a man, and afterwards to one who is Lord of all creation and finally to one who is a God. Philosophy and the wise men of the world want to begin at the top and have become fools. We must begin from below, and after that come upwards.'[1]

This was in fact the way the earliest apostles came. If we take the New Testament at its face value, we can see that, although their eventual view of his person was the same in substance as that of Paul, the way they came to it was different, for it was through their experience of Jesus as human Master and Companion of the way.

What then do we learn about Jesus the man? We learn that his manhood was real. He bore all the marks of real and genuine humanity and such marks are clear in each of the four Gospels. Luke tells the story of his birth and gives a glimpse into his boyhood in the story of his encounter with the teachers in the temple when Mary and Joseph took him to Jerusalem at the age of twelve. After this he tells us, 'And Jesus increased in wisdom and in stature, and in favour with God and men' (Luke 2:52). He ate and drank, was weary and showed emotions like joy and sadness, anger and compassion. We saw in an earlier chapter just how deeply he experienced sorrow and suffering. If this was not a real man, then the Gospels are totally unreliable as historical documents.

The concerns of the modern Liberationist theologians may be thought to belong more to questions about the nature of the work of Jesus rather than those that centre in his person, Nevertheless, they do influence our conception as to the kind of person he was. They have emphasised the deep social concern of Jesus and particularly his compassion for the poor and the disadvantaged. This is a prominent element in the Gospel of Luke and is present also in the other Gospels. They have stressed that those who profess to be his disciples should be deeply committed to the dispossessed just as he was and should strive for justice for them. They have no time for theologians who seek to do their work without any evidence of such personal commitment on their part.[2]

This challenge can be recognised, faced and accepted by us without our endorsing the kind of Liberationism that would treat 'salvation' exclusively or almost exclusively in social and political terms. If we are concerned to have a Christology, an understanding of Christ, based on the whole Bible, then we must not be one-sided. Some forms of Liberation theology can be criticised on the grounds that they think of salvation exclusively in terms of the Book of Exodus rather than of the Epistle to the Romans, and in terms of the Gospels rather than the Acts sermons and the New Testament Epistles. On the other hand, some Evangelical Christians have majored in the great doctrines to be found in the Pauline Epistles largely to the neglect of the Gospels. To embrace the whole Christ we must embrace the whole Bible. This may mean that both the Liberationist and the more traditional Evangelical Christian will have some adjustment to make in their thinking.[3]

There are other elements of humanity in his life which are not always given the recognition they deserve. This particularly applies to his prayer-life. It is only human beings who pray. It is quite true that there were profound dimensions to his praying, and that he gave every appearance of knowing God in a particularly deep way. But these are special qualities in an experience which was genuinely human. It is only a dependent being who prays, for it is only a dependent being who needs help from God. The prayer-life of the Saviour shows every evidence of being as real as other elements in his life. In fact, in Gethsemane prayer and suffering were merged into one. 'And being in anguish, he prayed more earnestly; and his sweat was like drops of blood falling to the ground' (Luke 22:44).

The Gospel of John records a great deal of his teaching. One phrase occurs over and over again in its pages, and is highly relevant to our subject. He described God as 'him who sent me' (John 4:34; 5:23f., et al.). In fact, after 'Father' and 'God', this is the most frequent designation of the Almighty to be found in this Gospel. Jesus lived his life therefore as the Agent of God, committed to doing his will and walking in his ways. This too shows real manhood.

We also find him asking questions. It is quite true that many of them were rhetorical and did not expect an answer. Many were intended to make his hearers think deeply about him and his teaching, so that they were asked for their benefit rather than his own.

He seems however to have asked other questions because of a genuine desire to know. When confronted with a demoniac boy, he asked the father, 'How long has he been like this?' (Mark 9:21). When Lazarus was in his grave, he asked, 'Where have you laid him?' (John 11:34). These would seem to be perfectly straightforward questions asked simply out of a desire for information, for it is difficult to find a teaching motive behind them.

One striking saying takes us further still. Mark 13 contains much of his teaching about the future and about his second coming. Towards the close of it, he says to his disciples, 'No-one knows about that day or hour, not even the angels in heaven, nor the Son, but only the Father' (Mark 13:32). For the moment we shall simply note this saying, but will consider it much more fully in the next chapter.

Here then is a man. A most wonderful person, yes, but despite that a real man, with flesh and blood, hands and feet, thoughts and feelings, coming to maturity of growth by increase in size and accumulation of knowledge and skill in using it, and then taking the Jerusalem road that led to arrest, mockery, scourging, brutal execution and death. It is important too to emphasise that it was a real man they took down from the tree and put in the grave – and a real man that came out of it!

When we consider humanity as Jesus expressed it, we begin to realise what poor shadows of what a human being should be we often are as a result of our sinfulness. As one theologian has put it, the real question is not whether Jesus was truly human but whether we are!

A first century Jew

It is strangely easy for us to forget this, despite the fact that it is so patently obvious.

Schweitzer criticised the nineteenth century quest for the

historical Jesus because of the fact that the questers seemed to be looking for somebody like themselves, a nineteenth century German or American or British liberal Christian dressed in first century Jewish clothes. There was much truth in this criticism, and it was the recognition of it that brought the quest, in its old form, to an abrupt halt.

Schweitzer substituted for this conception of Jesus the picture of a radical apocalyptic preacher, that is, somebody who proclaimed the imminent inbreaking of the Kingdom of God and challenged people to get ready by radical repentance. There was more truth in this than in the Liberal Jesus, but it is now widely recognised that Schweitzer's own view does not do justice to the whole presentation of the person of Jesus in the New Testament, and that there are other features to him as we see him there.

Schweitzer's work however had its positive side, for it compelled attention to the first century Jewishness of Jesus. This has been greatly explored since his day.[4]

More recently the westernised concept of Jesus has undergone further attacks from a somewhat different angle. Many of the Christian churches of Asia, Africa and Latin America have been influenced by Liberation theology and have come to think of salvation, not simply in spiritual but also in political, social and economic terms. The 'blond Christ' of the West has been set aside and the identification of Jesus with the so-called 'Third World' has been stressed. Asian theologians in particular have underlined the fact that he was an Asian, and African and Latin Americans that he was a member of a race oppressed by an alien ruling power. All have pointed out his compassion for the outcasts and the dispossessed of society.

All this is and needs to be fully recognised, and yet this view of Jesus should not be accepted in a completely uncritical way. To many of us the true humanity of Jesus is a very wonderful thing, but there is the danger that, in our deep realisation of his oneness with us as a human being, we may be guilty of 'domesticating' him. Rembrandt and many other great artists have depicted Jesus in surroundings that have more in common with their own lands and times than with the land and time of Jesus. At one level there is nothing wrong with this, for he is 'the universal Man'. We must never forget, though, that he is also Jesus of Nazareth and that historically he belongs to the first century. Undoubtedly there are similarities between the world of his day and ours but there are also profound differences, and we should recognise both.

This is in fact a lesson we all need to learn from the original 'quest'. Jesus was not a nineteenth century liberal but neither was he a twentieth century social revolutionary. He was himself. Paradoxically, in our thinking about him, he needs to be both localised and universalised.

So we should welcome every attempt to understand him in terms of his Jewish background and all research into the history, culture and religion of first century Galilee. This may from time to time produce some somewhat eccentric or one-sided pictures but we should accept any valid insights while working towards a balanced, all-round picture of Jesus of Nazareth in terms of his background.

Among much that is positive, the development of Third World Christologies has had two features which are somewhat disturbing. One is the tendency on the part of some to play down the uniqueness of the Christian faith and of Jesus himself. For instance, Sebastian Kappen says, 'The message of the reign of God would be welcomed by all men and women. Not so the lordship of Christ, as it implies the superiority of Christians over the rest of mankind.'[5] But we should not forget that Jesus exercised his Lordship from a cross before ascending to the heavenly throne and this implies that the Christian should think of himself as the servant of others, not their superior. The issue of the uniqueness of Jesus will be taken up in Chapter 13.

As thoughtful consideration of these words of Kappen may suggest, one aspect of this general movement is an increasing tendency to focus on the Jesus of the Gospels and to play down or even reject the Pauline doctrine of Christ. This is very marked in some writers. Byung Mu Ahn, in fact, rejects the emphasis on the kerygma[6] which, he admits, dominates the New Testament. He says, 'Even up to the present time the New Testament scholars of the West are giving preference to the Christ of the Kerygma in comparison with the historical Jesus ... It is true that the Christ of the Kerygma is dominant in the New Testament. And this fact serves as the basis for the Christology and the doctrine of salvation ... But besides the Kerygma, the stories about Jesus were transmitted as well. Jesus in these stories is entirely different from the Christ in the Kerygma.'[7]

This savours of the old quest for the historical Jesus in which so-called Paulinism in the New Testament was discarded in an attempt to find Jesus as he really was. What, we wonder, would Schweitzer have said about this?

Even if we find this point of view to be open to criticism, we should not discard the positive point being made about the fundamental nature of the Gospels and their true accounts of the compassionate life of Jesus the man. To read the Gospels is surely to be reminded that the Object of our faith is not a mere abstraction, nor is he simply the heavenly Christ. He is the Christ who has been here and has shared our life and has shown deep compassion not only for our lostness but also for our hurts, and who is now gloriously alive, with the same character still.

A male human being

In our day, a new issue has been raised in connection with the humanity of Jesus, and this is the question of his maleness. Feminist theologians vary in their approach to theological issues, from those who simply wish to see all the offices of the church to be open equally to women and to men to those who wish to substitute a Mother God for a Father God. What about Christology?[8] Was God unconcerned about female humanness when he became a man?

Nothing can alter the fact that Jesus was a male human being, but then not all modern feminists are in fact women. There are many men who have enlisted in the feminist cause, in either its moderate or more extreme forms. What about Jesus?

The feminist writer, Elizabeth S. Fiorenza has sought to promote a picture of Jesus as a radical feminist. She discounts the strong Gospel tradition that Jesus thought of God especially as his Father and considers that this was not an original part of the teaching of Jesus, but was a later accretion due to the general patriarchal atmosphere that prevailed in first century Judaism.

Ben Witherington III well summarises her standpoint when he says, 'It is Fiorenza's view that Jesus saw God as Sophia, not as Abba, and that he was part of a wisdom resistance movement that opposed the domination systems in place in his land. Jesus himself should be seen as a radical prophet, liberating women and the marginalized from oppressive patriarchal structures.'[9] The Greek Sophia is of course feminine, Wisdom is personified as a woman in the Book of Proverbs, and Fiorenza lays great stress on passages like Matthew 11:28-30, Luke 7:35 and 13:34 where Jesus relates Wisdom very closely to himself. Rosemary Ruether has a similar approach.[10]

Certainly such passages must be treated seriously, as everything in the Gospels must be, but it has to be said that they are few in number and do not furnish strong grounds for challenging 'Father' as our Lord's main designation of God.

Unfortunately, many women have experienced deep hurts through male chauvinism and sexual and other forms of physical abuse from them. To some women 'father' is a dirty word. The present writer had a long correspondence with a Christian woman for whom the use of the word 'Father' of God was a great stumbling-block. Light began to come when she realised that we are not to see God's relationship to us as modelled on our human fathers, but that God is himself the judge of all human fatherhood, and that the challenge to human fathers is to be like him. It is important that Christian men realise this, and that the elements of great tenderness in the biblical character of God should be fully recognised, not only in preaching but also in worship and in the shaping of Christian character.

B.O. McDermott makes a very important point when he says, 'While Jesus necessarily had individualizing characteristics, these were not principles of salvation. Jesus' human point of contact, his human ground of relatability to other human beings, was and is his humanity as such, not his being a Jew of the first century, a carpenter, of a certain height and weight – or a specific sex and gender. This does not mean that sexuality is not an extremely important dimension of our humanity, but it does mean that, *soteriologically*, Jesus' sex was not important.'[11] Rosemary

Ruether, after discussing various possible images of Jesus, comes to a position not far from this, when she says, 'His ability to be liberator does not reside in his maleness, but, on the contrary, in the fact that he has renounced this system of domination and seeks to embody in his person the new humanity of service and mutual empowerment.'[12]

As these quotations remind us, the 'scandal of particularity' in the Christian faith relates to more than to the maleness of Jesus. It relates to every aspect of his life, for no two human beings are exactly alike. The uniqueness of Jesus therefore relates not only to his deity but even to his humanity. As God he was unique in a sense which is completely untrue of us, but as man he was unique in a sense at least partially true of us, for every human being is unique.

The more sensitive a human being is the more he or she is able to empathise with the concerns of others. We may ask whether all who opposed apartheid were black? Were all who fought against the slave trade themselves slaves or former slaves? A deeply sensitive woman may have a profound understanding of what concerns and motivates men, and, most importantly for this issue, the most deeply sensitive man who ever lived must have had an understanding of women without equal.

It is interesting to find that the maleness of Jesus is not such an issue in some parts of the world. Virginia Fabella, who is from the Philippines, says, 'Feminist theologians in the US have raised the question of the maleness of Jesus. Among Asian women, the maleness of Jesus has not been a problem, for we have seen it as "accidental" to the salvific process. His maleness was not essential but functional. By being male, Jesus could repudiate more effectively the male definition of humanity and show the way to right and just male-female relationship, challenging both men and women to change their life-patterns.'[13]

As we read the Gospels, we discover the deep concern of Jesus for women. He commended, not the ostentatious giving of rich men, but the sacrificial offering of a poor widow (Luke 21:1-4), and he criticised the discourtesy of the Pharisee while pardoning the sins of a woman who had shown her faith in her love (Luke

7:36-50). One of his most significant resurrection appearances was to Mary Magdalene (John 20:10-18).

Far more than man

We cannot stop at this point. The evidence compels us to go further, much further. It is difficult to read any chapter of the Gospels without wondering whether Jesus of Nazareth was more than a mere man, more even than the most wonderful man in human history.

Think, for example, about his miracles. Now it is quite true he is not the only worker of miracles in the Bible. There were miracles performed by God through Moses and Joshua, through Elijah and Elisha and other characters of Old Testament Scripture. Some of them even restored people to life (1 Kgs. 17:17-24; 2 Kgs. 4:31-37). It is not any single miracle he performed, but the sum-total of them that points beyond mere humanity. The frequency and the fullness of range of this man's miracles are simply staggering.

The impression given as we read of all these miraculous deeds is that he was able to exercise control over any and every situation he found. Even when Mark tells us, writing about his home town, 'he could not do any miracles there, except lay his hands on a few sick people and heal them', it is clear from the context and from Mark's further comment, 'he was amazed at their lack of faith' (Mark 6:1-6), that the impossibility was moral. It was morally not physically impossible for him to bless them by the use of his miraculous powers in such a situation.

Healings, exorcisms, multiplying loaves and fishes, walking on water, raising the dead – this combination of miracles is utterly without parallel in the Old Testament. But the supreme miracle, as we have already seen, was one he performed not on nature nor on other human beings but on himself. He rose from the dead. It is true that his resurrection is most often attributed to the Father or to God *simpliciter,* but there are passages in the Gospel of John where it is seen to be his own act (John 2:19-22; 10:17,18). For believers in the Triune nature of God there is no contradiction in this.

By our own power most of us cannot lift ourselves off the ground for more than a few seconds, let alone out of the grave and from the grip of death. Moreover that victory over death was permanent. As the risen Christ puts it in Revelation 1:18, 'I am the Living One; I was dead, and behold I am alive for ever and ever!'

Then there was his teaching. Officers sent by the religious leaders of Israel were instructed to arrest him. On their empty-handed return, the chief priests and Pharisees said to them, 'Why didn't you bring him in?' They answered, 'No-one ever spoke the way this man does' (John 7:45f.). It may be that they were referring specifically to his great dramatic utterance on the last day of the Feast of Tabernacles, 'If anyone is thirsty, let him come to me and drink' (John 7:37), but it was of course true of his teaching as a whole.

Now it is true that the Holy Spirit had been inspiring human beings and giving them truth to teach and words in which to teach it for many centuries. The Old Testament is the product of this work of inspiration. Nevertheless, the teaching of Jesus possessed some unique features. Once again, as with his miracles, it is the fullness and comprehensiveness of it that strikes us so forcibly.

More than this, however, is the manner in which he conveyed this teaching to his hearers. Rabbis were for ever quoting other rabbis, and even the inspired writers of the Old Testament often gave the source, the divine Source, of their inspiration, by the use of phrases like 'the word of the Lord came to me'. It is very noticeable that Jesus did not use this kind of language. He said, 'I tell you' or 'I tell you the truth'.[14] Very often, the 'I' in such a phrase is emphatic in the Greek in which it is recorded. This therefore places great emphasis on the One who uttered the words. No earlier human teacher had dared to speak in this way, even under the inspiration of the Holy Spirit.

Most significant of all was his perfect character. We thought about this in an earlier chapter. He was absolutely flawless in his manner of life before men, and enjoyed the most perfect, unbroken fellowship with his Father until that awful experience on the cross when, because he was taking the place of sinners, he endured the wrath of God for us (Matt. 27:46).

It has been well said that no miracle he ever did can equal the miracle that he was. H.R. Mackintosh says, 'No miracle of Christ equals the miracle of His sinless life. To be holy in all thought and feeling; never to fail in duty to others, never to transgress the law of perfect love to God or man, never to exceed or come short – this is a condition outstripping the power of imagination and almost of belief. Here is a casement opening on a divine world.'[15] As we have seen already, the New Testament writers do not hesitate to use the strongest language about his character. They regarded his holiness of life as absolute.

In Old Testament days, men and women were called to do many different kinds of work in the service of God. There were prophets, priests and kings, there were judges and great national leaders, like Moses and Joshua. What differentiates Jesus from all who came before him is the fact that in him all the most significant offices are found in one person. He is the supreme Servant of God because not only do all these forms of service find their point of union in him but he brings each to its final realisation, performing each with utter perfection. This puts him entirely in a class of his own.

This is really what being the Christ or Messiah means. He is the one who brings the purposes of God for his people to their fulfilment, not only as a great king but as God's great 'man of many parts'. It is sometimes said of an exceptional man that it would take two or three others to replace him. The total resources of the human race could not replace Christ. This makes him unique.

The question has been asked as to whether Jesus really thought of himself as the Messiah. It is true that the use of the term by him is infrequent and that he tended more to respond to the use others made of it than to use it himself. Can we be sure he had a Messianic self-consciousness? I. Howard Marshall makes the point that the answer to this question does not rest only on whether or not he used the title. He says, 'It is impossible to see how the unique functions and person of the Messiah could have been separated in his thinking. The indirect approach to Christology demonstrates that Jesus spoke and acted as Messiah. The presence or absence of Messianic titles cannot alter this proof.'[16]

Lord of all

To say that Jesus Christ is man and more than man is true but it is not enough. We must go further and name him as Lord of all. We saw earlier that the New Testament preachers and writers employed the title 'Lord' of him, and in chapter 1 that it also occurs in some of the Gospels.

Without doubt, this great word is used more frequently than any other in the New Testament to indicate the belief of the first Christians that Jesus Christ is divine. The fact that it was used by the Greek translators of the Old Testament to render the great name of the Almighty made it quite special when employed by a Jew. In fact, the divine name it translated was regarded as so awesome that the Jews gave up using it altogether. Peter and others were therefore really claiming deity for Jesus Christ in calling him 'Lord'.

This means then that we must not only say he was far more than man. If we would be New Testament Christians, we cannot refrain from saying also that he was not less than God.

This use of the term 'Lord' by the early Christians was probably based largely on the way our Lord himself employed it on one particular occasion. The Day of Questions (Mark 11:27-12:44) took place during the week which came to its climax in the crucifixion. On this day, Jesus was teaching in the temple of Jerusalem. People came to him with questions. They belonged to different religious and political groups within Judaism, and many of these questions were clearly intended as traps. He countered every one and answered them with great wisdom. The most important question of the day, however, came at its close. Its importance is underlined by the fact that it was asked not by them but by him, and moreover on his own initiative, not in reply to one put by them

Mark records it thus: 'While Jesus was teaching in the temple courts, he asked, "How is it that the teachers of the law say that the Christ is the son of David? David himself, speaking by the Holy Spirit, said, 'The Lord said to my Lord, "Sit at my right hand, until I put your enemies under your feet." ' David himself calls him "Lord". How then can he be his son?"'

Here, in a psalm apparently acknowledged by his hearers to be messianic[17], the inspired writer calls the Messiah Lord.

Because he is Lord, this means everything in the universe is under his sway. It may be that sinful men do not acknowledge him now, but one day they will have to bow the knee to him and confess him Lord (Phil. 2:9-11). The Christian needs to take Jesus' Lordship very seriously in practical terms. In what has been described as the most illogical sentence in the Bible, Peter once said to him, 'Surely not, Lord' (Acts 10:14). You just cannot use this combination of words without talking nonsense. The Saviour himself put this very pointedly when he said, 'Why do you call me, "Lord, Lord," and do not do what I say?' (Luke 6:46).

The lordship of Christ extends far beyond the scope of human life. In his letters, the apostle Paul uses a number of terms denoting authority which appear to have been applied to various angelic beings in his day. In Colossians, he employs them when he says of Christ, 'By him all things were created, things in heaven and on earth, visible and invisible, whether thrones or powers or rulers or authorities – all things were created by him and for him' (Col. 1:16). Later in the same letter he says that 'he is the Head over every power and authority' (Col. 2:10) and then, speaking of his cross, he declares that 'having disarmed the powers and authorities, he made a public spectacle of them' (2:15).

So, as Creator, as Redeemer, as Victor, his supremacy is absolute. There may be many powers in the universe but there can be only one Lord, and all other powers exist only beneath his sovereign sway.

Son of God

The terms 'Lord' and 'Son of God' have something in common. Both of them are used in the New Testament in connection with the deity of Jesus Christ. In fact, they are the two chief terms employed. They are also both terms of relationship. We should notice however that the relationship indicated by each is a different one. When we use the term 'Lord' we are thinking of the relationship of the Lord Jesus to the universe and to us. It is one of sovereignty and supremacy. He is in control of everything. The term 'Son of God', on the other hand, points to his relationship with God the Father. Both underline his deity, but they do it in different ways.

We noted some aspects of the New Testament use of the term 'Son of God' in earlier chapters. There is no doubt, however, that the chief exposition of its meaning comes in the teaching of our Lord given in the Gospel of John. We shall now concentrate on this.

The Lord Jesus used the terms 'Father' and 'Son' in such a way as to suggest that the relationship between him and God was without any parallel. God is the Father and he is the Son (John 3:35; 5:19-27, etc.). He spoke of him as 'my Father', in an intimate way which, to say the least, was not characteristic of Jewish practice.[18] After the resurrection he said to Mary Magdalene, 'I am ascending to my Father and your Father' (John 20:17). Why not 'our Father'? This would have been more natural if he had not been aware of a special relationship with God. In fact, although he taught his disciples to address God this way in the Lord's Prayer, there is no evidence he ever prayed that prayer with them.

He clearly believed and taught that he had an existence in heaven before he ever came to earth. He said, for instance, 'I have come down from heaven, not to do my own will, but the will of him who sent me' (John 6:38; cf. 3:13, 17; 6:33, 50f., etc.). John 16:27, 28 is particularly impressive. Here, in consecutive verses, he says he came from the Father. The first statement uses the Greek preposition *para,* which really means 'from the side of', but the second, *ek,* goes far beyond this in its meaning, for it means 'out of', and so suggests that the Son is from the very being of the Father. C.H. Dodd says that the words of verses 28 'can hardly mean less than "I issued out of the Father and came into the world" .... He had His origin in the being of the Father .... In this sense, applicable to no prophet or messenger, Jesus is Son of God.'[19] This then tells us something about his real nature and is not simply a statement to the effect that he had a previous existence. We note too that his exalted status is suggested when he speaks of his glory with the Father before the very foundation of the world (John 17:5, 24).

There are some things that God and God alone is able to do. Only God can raise the dead to new life, only he can give eternal life, only he sits on the great throne of the universe to judge all men. All these Christ claimed to do, although not independently of the Father but as perfectly expressing his will (John 5:21-29). As we have seen earlier, he also claimed that he would take back his own life from the grave and so break the power of death (John 2:19-21; 10:17f.).

He said also that he was able to meet the very deepest needs of men. All those who came before him in Old Testament times pointed men to God as the answer to their needs, but he pointed men to himself. He promised to give them living water (John 4:10-14), the bread of life (John 6:27), in fact to be himself that bread (John 6:35), to set them completely free from slavery to sin (John 8:34-36) and to bestow both peace and joy on them (John 14:27; 15:11). Those who have put their trust in him know these claims are by no means idle and that every one of them is true.

One of his most staggering claims is linked with the words 'I am', which occur so frequently in the Gospel of John. In this expression special emphasis in the Greek is placed on the pronoun.

On one occasion, Jesus and the Jews were talking together about Abraham. The Saviour said to them, 'I tell you the truth, before Abraham was born, I am' (John 8:58). The implications of this are quite staggering. If he had wanted simply to indicate that he was pre-existent and therefore lived before Abraham (in itself a considerable claim) all he needed to say was, 'Before Abraham, I was.' But the words he actually used clearly reminded his hearers of the great revelation God made to Moses when he called himself 'I am' (Exod. 3:14). Jesus was claiming to be God!

In this passage in Exodus, God also said 'I AM WHO I AM', which may also be translated instead 'I will be what I will be'. It is as if he is saying to his people that he is going to show many different sides of his nature and his character to them throughout the years ahead. Perhaps this is what the Lord Jesus is himself saying when he says, 'I am the bread of life,' 'I am the way, the truth and the life,' 'I am the resurrection and the life,' and so on. All that his people need, that will he be to them as life proceeds.

John 18:1-8 records a most striking event. Soldiers had come into the garden of Gethsemane to take Jesus. The account goes on,

'Jesus, knowing all that was going to happen to him, went out and asked them, "Who is it that you want?" "Jesus of Nazareth," they replied. "I am he," Jesus said ... When Jesus said, "I am he," they drew back and fell to the ground.'

This incident is at first difficult to understand. It is the reaction of the soldiers that is so puzzling. Then we notice that Jesus used the majestic phrase 'I am', and that the word 'he' which follows it in most of our English versions is not in the original. Like several other passages in the Gospel of John, the answer of Jesus can be understood at two levels. On the face of it, he is simply identifying himself as the man they are seeking. It may be, however, that he said the words with such majesty that they linked them with the great revelation of God in Exodus, and so fell to the ground.[20]

Several times in this Gospel we find the Jews taking up stones to stone him, and it was normally when they realised he was claiming to be divine (5:17f.; 8:58f; 10:30f.). In the last of these passages, Jesus was using the pastoral language of the Holy Land and applying it to his relationship with his disciples. He was the Shepherd and they were the sheep. He would look after them and keep them safe. Then he says, 'My Father, who has given them to me, is greater than all; no one can snatch them out of my Father's hand. I and the Father are one' (John 10:29f.). It was at this point the Jews took up stones to stone him.

What does the last statement of that quotation mean? The word 'one' is in the neuter gender in Greek. Jesus is not saying that he and the Father are one person. Is it enough simply to say – as some have said – that they are one in will or in purpose? This could perhaps imply that Jesus is different from Christians only in degree, that is in the extent of his submission to God's will. The passage must mean more than this. It is power which is being discussed. If he and the Father are one in power, then this means that he is almighty, and if he is almighty he is God!

Space does not permit us to pursue this immensely rich topic much further, but if you want to do so yourself, you should study the following passages from the Gospel of John: 11:4; 12:44f.; 14:6-11, 23; 15:23f.; 16:3, 15.

It is possible that some reader will raise an objection at this point. We have been looking at many passages from John's Gospel, but what about the other Gospels? Is it possible that John has not been true to the actual facts and that he has given us material he has constructed himself and which does not really show us the mind of Jesus himself? No, for the term 'Son of God' occurs in all four Gospels, not just in one.

There is one passage of special importance. In Matthew 11:27, the Saviour says, 'All things have been committed to me by my Father. No-one knows the Son except the Father, and no-one knows the Father except the Son and those to whom the Son chooses to reveal him.' This passage, with its parallel in Luke 10:22, has been called 'a bolt from the Johannine blue'. Yet, although it sounds so Johannine, it is here in two of the Synoptic Gospels, and all attempts to dislodge it from the text have failed. The claims made by Jesus here are deeply impressive and are right along the same lines as the teaching we have found in the Gospel of John.

Peter Stuhlmacher, a major contemporary German New Testament scholar, commenting on the widely-held view that Jesus did not use the titles 'Christ', 'Son of Man' or 'Son of God' but that the church after Easter gradually attributed them to him, then goes on to affirm: 'Although scholars continue to repeat this viewpoint, it remains an abstraction of research that the texts and historical probability contradict. One makes considerably more progress in the attempt to retrace the rise of faith in Christ by following the text tradition carefully and by realizing that, given the conspicuous deeds of Jesus and his remarkable message among his contemporaries, the question was inescapable: Who then is this man? ... That Jesus would not have answered that question at all ... is altogether unlikely and renders the human Jesus a walking enigma. In any case, the texts describe him (historically quite credibly) otherwise.'[21]

So then, we will ourselves go on to ask that same question.

Who was Jesus – really?
What are we to make of all the Bible tells us about the Lord Jesus Christ? The teaching of the various New Testament books is wonderful, but it raises all sorts of questions in our minds. This is

just as it should be. Every major phenomenon in the universe has
made human beings think deeply. The nature of life, the existence
of evil, the meaning of suffering, all these and many more have
kept philosophers busy since serious thought began, and a great
many ordinary folk who would never claim to be philosophers
have in fact thought about them quite deeply. It would be a great
surprise if, assuming he really is all he claimed to be, his presence
in the world raised no questions or problems in our minds.

What sort of questions occur to us? Was he really both God and
man at the same time or was he some being occupying a kind of
intermediate position between the two? If he was in fact both God
and man, did he stop being God when he became man? When he
went back to heaven did he stop being man? Was he both God and
man right from the beginning of his life, or was he raised to a
higher level of existence at some point in time? If he was divine,
how could he suffer, how could he be tempted? If he was human,
how could he save helpless humans from their sins? God knows
everything and is everywhere. A man grows in knowledge but is
always more notable for his ignorance than for what he knows,
and he can only be in one place at a time. How then could the Lord
Jesus Christ possibly be both God and man at once?

These are just a few of the questions people have been asking
about him ever since his earthly life, and every one of them is
being asked today. We will devote much of the next chapter to a
consideration of them.

True God, perfect Man, one Person

It is clear that the New Testament writers believed him to be both
true God and also perfect man. We do not need to expound this
very fully as we have already noticed it over and over again. Just
to emphasise the point, however, we will take the teaching of the
Letter to the Hebrews. We looked at this in chapter 2, but now we
should think about its significance. Paul, in Romans 9-11, deals
with the vexed question of the apparent rejection of the Jews by
God. The way he deals with it, at least in the first two of these
chapters, is simply to set side by side the two great facts which
bear on this, namely the sovereignty of God (Rom. 9:1-29) and the

responsibility of men (9:30-10:21). Where the two meet and how they relate to each other is a mystery, but Paul does not deny either factor, but sets them alongside each other. Now the anonymous writer to the Hebrews does just the same in relation to the person of the Saviour in the first two chapters of his book. In Hebrews 1:1-2:4 it is his deity which is in view, while in 2:5-18 it is his humanity.

Great terms like 'Son', 'Lord' and 'God' are used in the first chapter, while in chapter 2 (verse 9) he uses for the first time the name 'Jesus', the name of his humanity, the name his family gave him at his birth. He is very interested in the high priesthood of Jesus, and such an office could of course only be performed by a real man. He has a lot to say also about his sufferings and his temptations as qualifying him for his work (Heb. 2:17f.; 4:14-16). So Jesus really understands what human life is like. At the same time, it is to a throne of grace that we come, and the one who sits there is a King and the very Son of God. His humanity enables him to feel with us; his deity gives him power to help.

There is, in fact, one phrase used by the writer of this letter which perfectly sums up the two basic facts about his person. He is 'Jesus, the Son of God' (Heb. 4:14). All the experience of his human life is in this phrase, and all the power and authority of the eternal Son of God.

One Person

The New Testament provides us with three basic facts about him, not just two. Not only was he both God and man; he was both of them at once. His unity therefore provides the third fact.

Psychologists often lay stress upon integration of personality. There is, of course, a pathological condition in which somebody has a split or multiple personality. This is a sad condition which raises great problems both for the sufferer and for those who are brought into contact with him or her. There are also, of course, many people who have more than one 'personality' although not in this pathological sense. They are 'two-faced'. They present different faces to different people. They may do it quite deliberately; sometimes though they may hardly be aware of it.

Another defect in human beings is a lack of balance. This does not have to be extreme for us to recognise it. One man or woman may be excessively stern and strict in dealing with others, while another may be much too soft and pliable. There is a middle way between these extremes. A human being who is mature in character and in his or her relationships inspires great confidence in others.

What about the Lord Jesus Christ? Here we have a person with the most beautifully balanced character. In him holiness and love found their perfect point of integration. Moreover, he was always the same, and did not 'put on an act' before any group of people or any individual. Whether he was talking to his disciples, or to interested enquirers or was confronted by his bitterest foes, he was always the same. He was, in fact, before all kinds of people, exactly what he was before God.

In his great 'high priestly prayer', recorded in John 17, he prays for his disciples, and so his true attitude to them stands revealed. There is absolutely no discord between what he said then in the place of prayer and what he said and did when he was with them. The same motives of love for God and love for men controlled all he ever did and said and prayed and was.

Now this perfect balance, this total integration, applied supremely to his deity and his humanity. We cannot go through the Gospels distributing his deeds and words between the divine and human elements in him. We may be inclined to say that he performed his miracles as God and suffered and was tempted as man, but it is not as easy as that. Did he not stretch out a human hand to touch the leper when the divine power flowed from him in cleansing? Was it not divine as well as human love that kept him on the cross when his enemies were taunting him and yelling to him to come down?

No doubt this raises problems for us, but the problems raised by driving this kind of wedge between the activities of his two natures are in fact even greater. Jesus was one person, although a person with both divine and human characteristics. This is how he confronts us in the pages of the New Testament and, although not fully understanding, we move through wonder to worship.

References

1. See P. Althaus, *The Theology of Martin Luther*, (trans. R.C. Schulz), Philadelphia, Fortress, p. 186, n. 18.

2. See e.g. G. Guttierrez, *A Theology of Liberation*, Maryknoll, Orbis, rev. edn. 1988.

3. See A. Kirk, *A New World Coming*, London, M. M. & S., 1983; Ronald J. Sider, 'An Evangelical Theology of Liberation,' *Christian Century 97* (1980), pp. 314-318; Craig L. Blomberg, '"Your Faith has made you Whole": The Evangelical Liberation Theology of Jesus', J.B. Green and M. Turner, *op. cit.*, pp. 75-93.

4. For a useful survey of recent work in this field, see B. Witherington III, *op.cit.*

5. Sebastian Kappen, 'Jesus and Transculturation' in R.S. Sugirtharajah (ed.), *Asian Faces of Jesus,* London, SCM, 1993, p.174.

6. For the Kerygma, see Chapter 4.

7. Byung Mu Ahn, 'Jesus and People (Minjung)', in R.S. Sugirtharajah, *op. cit.*, pp. 165-166.

8. Mary Daly has taken the extreme position that a male Saviour as Liberator and Model cannot be acceptable to women at all and of course this breaks completely with historic Christology. See her book, *Beyond God the Father,* Boston, Beacon, 1973.

9. Ben Witherington III, *op. cit.*, p. 242. Witherington gives extensive and sympathetic consideration to her view (pp. 163-185 and 242-244) although he arrives finally at a somewhat negative verdict.

10. R.R. Ruether, *Sexism and God-Talk: Toward a Feminist Theology*, Boston, Beacon, 1983, especially pp. 44-71.

11. B.O. McDermott, *Word Become Flesh: Dimensions of Christology*, Collegeville, Minnesota, Liturgical Press, 1993, p. 243

12. R. R. Ruether, *To Change the World: Christology and Cultural Criticism*, New York, Crossroad, 1981, p. 56.

13. V. Fabella, 'Christology from an Asian Woman's Perspective', in R.S. Sugirtharajah (ed.), *Asian Faces of Jesus,* London, SCM, 1993, p. 212.

14. This is the way the NIV renders the Greek which lies behind the AV's 'Verily I say unto you'.

15. H.R. Mackintosh, *The Doctrine of the Person of Jesus Christ,* Edinburgh, T. and T. Clark, 1912, p. 403.

16. I.H. Marshall, *Origins of NT Christology,* Leicester, IVP, 1977, p.55. A.C. Thiselton in 'Christology in Luke, Speech-Act Theory, and the Problem of Dualism in Christology after Kant' in Green and Turner, *op. cit.*, p. 453, supports Marshall's point from the modern Speech-Act theory of language of J.L. Austin and J.R. Searle, in which they maintain that the force of many utterances and their power to bring results depends on the 'institutional status' of the person making the utterance. The application of this to Jesus is evident.

17. We have no clear documentation for this in contemporary Judaism, but the very argument of Jesus implies that he and his hearers were agreed as to its Messianic significance.

18. See J. Jeremias, *New Testament Theology* I (trans. J.Bowden), New York, Scribners, 1971, pp. 61-68.

19. C.H. Dodd, *Interpretation of the Fourth Gospel,* Cambridge, CUP, 1953, pp. 259-260.

20. See the brief but helpful comment on this in R.E. Brown, *The Gospel according to John,* London, Geoffrey Chapman, 1971, Vol. 2, *ad loc.*

21. P. Stuhlmacher, *op. cit.*, pp. 24,25.

Chapter 12

THE CREDAL ISSUE

The present unpopularity of creeds

Creeds are not very popular today. There are several reasons for this.

For one thing they are expressed in the language of certainty. There never was a creed with the word 'maybe' in it. Everything is certain; they brim over with assurance. Now, as we have seen, ever since Kant modern thinkers have largely rejected the very idea of certainty. This is not because such claims seem arrogant, but rather that, for philosophical reasons, it is held that they cannot really be made at all.

Now we have seen already that the orthodox Christian faith avoids Kant's criticism by means of its doctrine of biblical inspiration, not as a piece of tactical evasion, but because of its deep convictions about Scripture. If in fact the Bible is inspired by God, this means that it is authoritative, and authority means certainty when the authority we are talking about is that of God himself. If God cannot give us certainty, where can we find it? Indeed, if we suggest he cannot, are we sure that we know the meaning of the word 'God'?

That very question can introduce an objection that is sometimes made to the Christological Creeds, and especially to the Definition of Chalcedon. It is said that they assume too easily that we know what a divine and what a human nature are and how we are to understand a person, for only if we do can we make sense of a Christological statement that speaks of two natures in one person.

It is quite true, of course, that the Definition does not define the divine nature at all, and simply says of the human nature of Christ that he is 'of a reasonable soul and body'. This latter phrase, however, simple as it is, indicates a desire to say that in Jesus there was all that is proper to a man. By the same token, his divine nature was all that is proper to God. This is easy enough to say but the implications of it are simply staggering.

In some ways, however, the very absence of full definition is an advantage. There *may* have been some elements in what the Chalcedonian fathers believed about God which were more Greek than biblical, although this is controversial, but if there are, they do not appear in the Definition because of its brevity. Its language too enables us to conceive manhood along fully biblical lines and leaves plenty of room for research as to what the Bible teaches about what a human being is. Because of this, therefore, the Definition can still have its place today among those who wish to be biblical.

If, on the other hand, we wish to take our concepts of God and humanity from the general religious field or from modern psychological and sociological views we will find ourselves in difficulty, for both sets of views are extremely diverse. To do this, though, would be to depart from historic Christology altogether and not simply from its Chalcedonian statement.

The concept of person can, of course, be analysed from several different points of view, and all manner of psychological considerations can be brought to bear on it. We must ask though if this is really necessary? We must treat the ancient Creeds in their historical settings and not in the setting of sophisticated modern psychological or philosophical discussions. They had their own technical terminology available and both Greek terms used in the phrase 'one person (*prosopon*) and one hypostasis (this is itself a Greek word)' had a long history of philosophical and theological discussion behind them. There can however be little doubt though that they were thinking in terms of separate individuality with the normal capacities that go with that individuality, capacities such as reason, feeling and will and, of course, of relating to other persons. The biblical doctrine of the image of God in man helps us here, for it means that there are qualities a human being has, as a person, in common with God. This points the way to a real possibility of Incarnation.

Then it is objected that creeds misunderstand the real nature of the Christian faith. What matters in that faith, it is said, is not its intellectual content but rather the religious experience it creates for the individual. This idea goes back at least as far as Friedrich Schleiermacher, sometimes dubbed 'the Father of Modern Theology'. He wrote his book, *The Christian Faith*, [1] nearly 200 years ago. A glance at the contents page of this volume would give the impression that it is an exposition of historic Christianity, but the reading of the book itself makes clear that this is anything but the case. To him the essence of religion is the feeling (note the word) of dependence on God, and the special importance of Jesus for the Christian faith lies in the fact that he had a perfect God-consciousness.

There are a number of reasons why Schleiermacher came to this conclusion. One was the fact that in his day the Enlightenment was calling the received doctrines of the Christian faith into question and so he was concerned to find another basis for that faith, in which certainty would be based not so much on authoritative documents but on religious experience. Another was probably the influence of the Jewish philosopher, Spinoza, some of whose mystical ideas he appears to have imbibed.

Schleiermacher was reared as a Moravian, and the Moravians, who were certainly orthodox Christians, tended to stress the role of feeling in Christian experience. The Wesleys were influenced by the Moravians, and there is a touch of Moravianism in such hymns as Charles Wesley's 'My God I know, I feel Thee mine'.[2] Now we ought of course to feel deeply about Christ, and there can be few things more deadening than a totally emotionless religion, but feeling must always be the by-product of our faith, never its basis. If it is, we are in great danger of creating our own religion rather than accepting God's disclosure of himself, and everybody's version of the Christian faith, on this basis, would be different.

Then others maintain that the creeds place the emphasis wrongly. What matters, it is said, are not the doctrines of the Christian faith but its ethical content. We can certainly agree that Christian ethics are important, but an examination of the New Testament makes it very clear that its ethical teaching rests on its theology. Perhaps the most obvious example of this is to be found in the Epistle to the Romans, where the practical exhortations of the later chapters rest on the great doctrinal exposition contained in chapters 1 to 11, with the exhortations which begin chapter 12 as the link between them.

Finally, it is said by critics of the ancient creeds that they use categories that are no longer really meaningful for us. The creeds with which we are chiefly concerned belong to the period of the early church. It is pointed out that the Greek words employed in them are taken from the philosophical jargon of the day, and that they do not really relate to the categories which modern thinkers use.

Now there may of course be some truth in this, but it does not settle the matter. Modern philosophy is dominated by epistemological questions, that is by questions about knowledge and certainty. It is less interested in metaphysics, which is concerned about the nature of things and especially with realities that lie beyond the world of time and sense. But are not such questions important? To be concerned only with questions of knowledge and not with the nature of things is like exploring the driveway to a great mansion without ever going inside the building.

The Christian faith is concerned about the nature of things, with its great doctrines of God, creation, redemption and the end of things. If a philosopher gives his mind to issues of this kind, he is facing metaphysical and not simply epistemological questions. Now Scripture is not human philosophy but divine revelation. If we are there dealing with material which is divinely authoritative, this means not only that we can have certainty but also that we are given a true understanding of the nature of things. In other words certain matters which the philosopher considers his province are settled by the revelation of God.

This does not mean of course that philosophical epistemology and metaphysics are irrelevant or even illegitimate pursuits, but it does mean that, for the Christian, religious certainty and knowledge of God and divine things do not come primarily this way but from the Word of God. The great certainties of the biblical faith find classic expression in the creeds.

The function of creeds

What are creeds for? A study of their historical context makes it clear that they arose as a result of the challenge of heresy.[3]

Adolf Harnack, who has been called 'the greatest Liberal of them all', had a lively dislike of creeds. At one stage in his life he went round Germany trying to get support for his campaign to abolish them altogether in the German churches. He was surprised at how little support he got. Even though many to whom he spoke shared his Liberal approach, they felt it important to retain the creeds, conserving as they did what Christians have believed historically.

Harnack's objection to the early church creeds was due to the fact that he believed they were products of the malign influence of Greek philosophy on the simple message of Jesus, which, he held, was not about the Son at all but about the Father, about the universal Fatherhood of God and the universal brotherhood of man and the infinite value of every human soul.

It is clear enough, of course, that his view would discount a very great deal of the material in the New Testament. He did in fact believe that the process of philosophising the Christian faith started within the New Testament itself.

Harnack's interpretation of the creed-making process in the New Testament and early patristic church is open to criticism. It has been pointed out that the creed-making movement was in fact going against the main currents of philosophy that were contemporary with it. The creed-makers were concerned not to philosophise the Christian faith but to preserve the purity of the biblical doctrines. Neoplatonism, for instance, provided a philosophical structure into which any religion could fit. If Christians had uncritically accepted the Neoplatonic outlook, the Christian faith would have lost its distinctiveness altogether. Of course, they used terms current in the language of their day, but they could hardly avoid doing so.

The creeds were not intended to present a complete statement of the Christian faith. Most are comparatively short, and they lack the greater detail to be found in the Reformation Confessions, most of which do aim at greater comprehensiveness. Their categories provide a hedge round the doctrines of the faith that were coming under attack. They are protective; they erect barriers against error.

For our subject there are two creeds of special importance, the so-called Nicene Creed (more accurately described as the Niceno-Constantinopolitan Creed) and the Definition of Chalcedon. They are far more important for Christology than any others, and, although there was much difference of opinion over doctrine at the period of the Reformation, both the Roman Catholic Church and the main Protestant bodies were agreed on the main issues concerning the person of Christ, issues which had already been settled at the early councils that agreed the language of the creeds. We will also look briefly at the so-called Apostles' Creed.

The Apostles' Creed

The churches of the second century began employing brief summaries of the great doctrines of the Christian faith. These gradually assumed a standardised form, known to us as the Apostles' Creed.

After expressing belief in the Father, the creed reads, 'And in Jesus Christ, his only Son, our Lord, Who was conceived by the Holy Ghost, Born of the Virgin Mary, Suffered under Pontius Pilate, Was crucified, dead and buried, He descended into hell; the third day he rose again from the dead, He ascended into heaven, and sitteth on the right hand of God the Father Almighty; From thence he shall come to judge the quick and the dead.'

All this can be very simply documented from the New Testament, with the possible exception of the words, 'He descended into hell', which seem to have been based particularly on 1 Peter 3:18-4:6, especially the last verse of this passage. This verse was widely understood to mean that Christ, between his death and resurrection, visited the Old Testament saints and assured them of his victory over Satan The whole passage in 1 Peter is difficult and the exact significance of the credal clause itself is not beyond debate. Those particularly interested in the matter should consult the commentaries on 1 Peter, some of which, especially the commentary by E.G. Selwyn[4], go into great detail, and also J.N.D. Kelly's work, *Early Christian Creeds*.[5]

The Nicene Creed

This was the creed accepted by the Council of Nicaea in 325, but which then became the subject of considerable debate for several decades before it was reaffirmed, in a slightly longer form, by the Council of Constantinople in 381.

As in the Apostles' Creed, a clause affirming belief in the Father was followed by the words, 'And in one Lord Jesus Christ, the Son of God, Begotten from the Father, Light from Light, very God from very God, Begotten, not made, Sharing one being with the Father, By means of whom all things came into being, both the things that are in heaven and the things that are on earth; who on account of us men and on account of our salvation came down and was incarnate, became man, suffered, and rose again on the third day, went up into heaven, and is coming to judge living and dead.'

The debate that followed Nicaea focused on the words, 'sharing one being with the Father', read in the light of the preceding words, 'begotten, not made'. The Council had been called by the Emperor Constantine because of the trouble that had arisen in Alexandria and had spread more widely and that was associated with the name of Arius. Arius denied the true deity of Jesus, believing him to have been the first of all the creatures of God to be created. To quote a sentence that was to become famous, 'there was a time when he was not'.

After Nicaea, it became evident that the creed was not going to win general acceptance easily.

The Greek word *homoousios*, translated 'sharing one being' was disliked by the Arians, because they did not believe it. Another group, led by the church historian, Eusebius of Caesarea, was prejudiced against it because it had been used, in a somewhat different way, by an earlier heretical group. The great advocate of it after Nicaea was Athanasius who was to become Bishop of Alexandria. He saw that the matter was of immense importance, that the whole basis of the Christian faith would be destroyed were the debate to be lost. He was criticised, reviled, persecuted, exiled, but he stood as firm as a rock.

Eventually he and his friends won the day. He was a man of outstanding Christian spirit as well as a clear-sighted theologian.

It cannot be said that the two have always been united! Some genuine believers in Christ preferred the term *homoiousios* ('of similar being') to *homoousios*. Athanasius was convinced that their term was not a sufficient hedge against heresy, but he recognised that they were true Christians and, especially in the period from 360 to 362, he laboured to convince them that they should accept the Nicene formula. In this he was largely successful.

The Definition of Chalcedon
In the late fourth century and particularly in the fifth there was much discussion of the person of Christ. It was not so much his relationship to God the Father, the Nicene issue, that was now to the fore. All the leading participants in the debate fully accepted the deity of Jesus. Now the question was how we are to think of him as God incarnate. He is God in the fullest sense, he is man in the fullest sense, he is one person, not two. These facts can be simply stated, but Christians did not find it easy to think through what the relationship between deity and humanity in one person meant.

One highly respected Christian teacher, Apollinaris, suggested that we should think of the Logos (that is, the pre-existent Christ) as replacing the rational soul in Jesus. This suggestion was made in order to preserve the integrity of his person. Gregory of Nazianzus, however, pointed out that this was an inadequate idea, for it meant that Christ was not really fully man.

Another teacher, Nestorius, is alleged to have taught that Christ was really two persons in fellowship, God and man. Whether he did actually teach this has been much discussed, particularly in the twentieth century, and the matter is by no means clear. Certainly if he did he was wrong. What does seem clear is that Nestorius was not a good theological communicator and took insufficient pains to make himself understood. His pronouncement caused confusion. As one modern writer has put it, no good purpose is served by replacing inscrutable mysteries with incomprehensible explanations! The whole debate between Nestorius and his great adversary, Cyril of Alexandria, was bedevilled by other considerations, political and personal as well as theological.

Another theologian, Eutyches, went to the opposite extreme and thought of Christ as having one nature only, a kind of compound of divine and human qualities. Inevitably the divine qualities came to be thought of as swamping the human and so this raised question marks particularly about the true humanity of Jesus.

The Council of Chalcedon was called in 451 and it issued its famous definition of the person of Christ. It is carefully worded. It asserts the presence of a rational human soul in Christ (so ruling out Apollinarianism). At its heart it asserts belief in Jesus as 'one and the same Christ... proclaimed in two natures, without confusion, without change, without division, without separation'. In this language both Nestorianism and Eutychianism are ruled out.

The four 'without' phrases are, of course, negative, and the definition has been criticised for this. Again however we must insist that these creeds were intended to exclude heresy not to give full positive expositions of the truth, and the Chalcedonian Definition certainly does exclude all the Christological heresies that were current at the time of its composition and acceptance.

Credal reinterpretation

It is important for us to insist that the articles of a creed, on the assumption that they are biblical, should not be re-interpreted. It is of course, perfectly alright for them to be translated. After all, the very words we have quoted from them are themselves translations of them into English. Just as the unchanging gospel needs to be preached in ways that relate to the various cultures in which it is proclaimed, without any loss of its essential content, so it is with the creeds. The really important thing however is that they should not be interpreted in a way that does violence to their original sense.

This is not because the creeds themselves should be regarded as untouchable simply because they are creeds and are hallowed by tradition. Like all human documents, apart from those produced by the special inspiration of the Spirit, they are subject to fallibility, however much we may value them. What makes reinterpretation a matter for concern, however, is the very fact that they are summaries of biblical truth. To reject them either quite frankly or by radical reinterpretation often means a rejection of the biblical doctrine they contain and express.

The history of theological liberalism contains many examples of this.

It was very evident for instance during the period, in the second half of the nineteenth century, when the theology of Albrecht Ritschl was influential. We have already seen how Adolph Harnack, himself a Ritschlian, tried to get German ministers and theologians to join him in a move to abolish the use of creeds in Germany. In fact, this was all of a piece with the way many of the Ritschlians treated the New Testament.

Many German New Testament scholars were Ritschlians, and on one issue they tended to be divided into two camps. Some took Harnack's point of view and frankly said that Paul and others had altered the gospel and imported ideas of Greek origin into it. They declared too that the Gospels contain a certain amount of Paulinism. Others, however, produced new exegesis of passages in the Gospels, in which they tried to show that they did not really mean what Christians, including Christian scholars, had traditionally held them to mean. A great many of these Ritschlian interpretations are now things of the past, as they have been seen to be contrived and not true to the text.

The most serious examples of reinterpretation are connected with the cardinal doctrines of the person and work of Christ. Our concern in this volume is with his person. We need to remember, for instance, that the word 'divine', often quite properly used in theology to describe the deity of Jesus, has a weaker sense, meaning 'originating from God'. Some, in asserting the divinity, have evidently meant nothing more than to say that he was a great (perhaps even unique) messenger of God, but not himself God.

John McQuarrie refers to the nineteenth century philosopher, Henry Jones, and says, 'There is a well-known story of Jones relating to the days when, as a young man, he used to preach in Welsh chapels. It was explained to him that he had not been invited back to one of these chapels because he was said to deny the divinity of Christ. He replied: "I deny the divinity of Christ! I do not deny the divinity of any man."'[6]

We have already seen how important the doctrine of Christ's resurrection is. There has been a very considerable tendency, even among some professing to write and teach Christian theology, to treat Christ's resurrection as the release of his spirit from his body, or, more frequently, simply the continuance of his influence. This is most emphatically not what the doctrine means in the creeds and in the New Testament.

It is important that those who believe in the historic Christianity of the creeds and of the New Testament should stand firm on such truths as the incarnation and the resurrection, resisting all reinterpretation, for to surrender them is to surrender the Christian faith itself.

The example of Athanasius is a helpful one here, in the way he combined theological firmness with brotherly love for those who differed from him in terminology but agreed with him in essential belief, for he was able to distinguish between inadequate statements and outright heresy.

Christological Reflection
We will now seek, in a spirit of reverence, to understand as far as we can what the creeds are saying when they proclaim that in Jesus Christ two natures, one perfectly human and the other perfectly divine, are joined in the one person.

Before the incarnation
John, in the great prologue to his Gospel, tells us that the eternal Word was both with God and was himself God (John 1:1). He then goes on to say, 'And the Word became flesh and dwelt among us, full of grace and truth' (John 1:14). The term 'became' needs to be taken seriously. The eternal Word had to become flesh, because he was not flesh when he was in heaven. He was in no sense man before the incarnation took place.

The Creator/creature distinction is never broken down. When, in 2 Peter 1:4, Christians are said to 'participate in the divine nature' it is clear from the context that moral qualities are in view. God does, through grace, impart qualities of his character to us, so that, as he is holy so we may pursue holiness, and something of his love and wisdom may be reproduced in us by the Holy Spirit. In this way the image of God, seriously marred through the Fall, is being restored in us. There are, however, many qualities of God which are never communicated to other beings, qualities like self-existence and omnipresence.

Why are we saying all this? In order to emphasise the distinction between the two natures of our Lord, so that we must not imagine the one contained the other before he came to earth. God brought the world into being by an act of creation; it was not simply an extension of his own being. What a man creates is not himself although it may bear the marks of what he is. The very same is true of God.

Some early Alexandrian teachers maintained that the Son of God possessed 'heavenly flesh' (whatever that is!) before his birth, while others said he gained nothing from Mary, but that she was merely the vehicle through whom he passed into the world. Both these ideas must be rejected. He became what he was not before he came; he became flesh, that is, human nature in its entirety, apart from sin. As we have seen, the pre-incarnate manifestations of Jesus anticipate the incarnation, but are by no means identical with it.

The very most we can say is that God, because he is God, always possessed the power to do what he actually did do at a particular time and place in the incarnation. At any time he could have assumed human nature and been born on earth. The timing of it was a sovereign act, in line with his great purpose. As Paul puts it, 'When the time had fully come, God sent forth his Son, born of a woman, born under the law' (Gal. 4:4).

The virgin birth

It is true that the incarnation and the virgin birth are not identical, but they are very closely related. The incarnation is the fact that God became man, while the virgin birth is the method by which this took place.

Some have objected that only Matthew and Luke record this fact, but this simply reflects the fact that the Gospels are not stereotyped. Mark starts with the ministry of John the Baptist. It is not simply that he does not tell of the virgin birth, but rather that he does not record the birth at all, yet we cannot doubt that he believed Jesus was born! John takes us right into eternity in his prologue. The other New Testament writers say nothing that militates against this doctrine. In fact, some passages might just suggest a knowledge of it (e.g. Gal. 4:4). It is well worth noting that the only Gospel writer who uses the term 'his parents' in relation to Jesus is Luke, and he had already provided against misinterpretation of this conventional expression by recording the virgin birth.

The doctrine known as adoptionism is the idea, which keeps on recurring at different periods in church history, that Jesus was not the eternal Son of God but that he was adopted by God at some time. He started life as a man, but at some point or other he 'became' the Son of God, because he had been so obedient to God. Adoptionists have not agreed as to the particular point in time when this happened. Some identified his baptism as the moment, others his resurrection, while others thought of this 'deification' as going on gradually throughout his life, to be completed at his resurrection.

Such a view cannot stand scrutiny in the full light of the New Testament teaching. All that we have seen of its teaching on his divine pre-existence militates against it. Jesus Christ was both God and man from the very beginning of his earthly existence, even before he became visible as a distinct individual and was still in the womb of his mother. This is why it is important to emphasize that this was a virgin conception.

Some views of his person are in danger of viewing him as if he were different only in degree from the Christian. It is the glory of the gospel that forgiveness brings the life of God right into the soul of man, so that the Christian is 'in Christ' and Christ is in him. He is indwelt by the living God himself. This is not, however, what the New Testament teaches us about Christ. God was not simply in Christ (even though that statement is not objectionable simply as it stands) but he was incarnate in Christ. God actually became a man in Christ, he did not just indwell a man. God and man were not just united in fellowship, or in purpose, they were united absolutely. They constituted one person. This is what theologians mean by the Hypostatic Union.

This means that a nature which can neither diminish nor develop was joined to a nature in the raw, a nature destined, like every human nature, to grow physically and to mature intellectually, emotionally and in other ways. At every stage of this development he was the God-man. In the development of a human being, the man or woman is not more human than the child nor the child than the baby, nor even (so often overlooked or denied today) the baby than the foetus. The human nature is complete as a nature at every stage, although it is developing constantly, just as the oak tree does from the acorn. We can consider our Lord's life at any point from the womb to the tomb (and even, as we shall see, beyond the tomb) and say, 'This is God; this is also man.'

He emptied himself

A term that is often used in connection with Christology is *kenosis*, a Greek word meaning 'emptying'. The reason for its use is that Paul employs the corresponding verb in Philippians 2:7. It comes within the body of a glorious passage, which the NIV translates as follows: 'Your attitude should be the same as that of Christ Jesus: Who, being in very nature God, did not consider equality with God something to be grasped, but made himself nothing, taking the very nature of a servant, being made in human likeness. And being found in appearance as a man, he humbled himself and became obedient to death, even death on a cross!' (Phil. 2:5-8). It is the words 'made himself nothing' that translate this Greek word.

What was this kenosis? Some have suggested that Jesus emptied himself of his divine qualities, or at least certain of them, when he became a man, and that this is what Paul means here. This surely cannot be its meaning! Even on general grounds we see its impossibility. How can God divest himself of some of his qualities and remain God? A being who is not all-powerful, all-knowing and present everywhere is just not God. God as he is made known to us in his Word has all these qualities and we can no more conceive him without them than we can conceive matter without form and substance.

But we are not left to general considerations. The idea does not properly fit the passage. Verse 6 speaks of equality, verse 7 of service and between the two ideas comes the self-emptying. Moreover, verse 8 is also controlled by the ideas of humility and obedience, which are intimately related to the role of a servant. In the focal verse itself, Paul says that Christ emptied himself, taking the form of a servant. What he surrendered for the time being was his equality with God, to replace this with the role of a humble and obedient Servant.

This means that the passage is not about giving up qualities that belonged to his essential nature as God but about the willingness to obey. In fact the word translated 'servant' really means 'bond slave'.[7] He placed himself under the Law (Gal. 4:4). He said, 'I seek not to please myself but him who sent me' (John 5:30). Later, he declared, 'I have come down from heaven, not to do my will but to do the will of him who sent me' (John 6:38). When the terms of that will pressed so hard upon him in the garden of Gethsemane, his utter surrender to it was expressed in the words, 'Not my will but yours be done' (Luke 22:42).

In fact, the whole record of the Gospels could provide us with a commentary on this passage in Philippians. What is quite notable is the fact that the Gospel of John, which is the one that most emphasises his greatness and his deity, is also the one that most clearly and extensively reveals the completeness of his obedience to his Father.

If then it was the Father's will that governed every action of his life, it must have been that will which controlled his use of his divine powers. During his ministry he multiplied loaves and fishes, but during the temptation in the wilderness he would not turn stones into bread. The first was his Father's plan; the second was contrary to it.

When we give further thought to this, we realise that although, in one sense, everything changed when he became incarnate, in another nothing changed. If we believe in the Trinity, we believe that, because the three holy Persons are one in their being, there can never be any question of independent action. Father, Son and Holy Spirit always work together in the most perfect harmony. This is eternally true. Here then, while on earth, the total harmony between the will of the Father and the will of the Son continued, but now within the sphere of action of a human life, a sphere necessarily bounded by the purposes of that life. The distinctive thing therefore about his human experience is that this oneness of purpose was expressed under human conditions of life, requiring him to render a human obedience to the Father. As a true human being he was a dependent being and his reliance was on the Father. So faith and obedience were joined in his experience, as of course they must be also in the experience of the Christian.

Perhaps the key to the problem of Jesus' knowledge lies here. He said that he did not know the date of his second advent (Mark 13:32). Yet, if he was God, he must have known everything. How can absolute knowledge and limited knowledge coexist?

An idea that has helped the present writer arises from the fact that none of us ever uses as much knowledge as he possesses. Most of the knowledge we have is not present to our conscious minds. Consciousness is like a very small tip of a very large iceberg. It is our conscious knowledge that we are aware of using. If I have learned something in the past and yet it is hidden in my subconscious mind at the moment awaiting the appropriate stimulus before it can come into my consciousness, can I be said to know it? In a sense I do and in a sense I do not. Perhaps such items as these were below the level of Jesus' consciousness so that, at that moment, for purposes of conscious action, he could not be said to know them, and yet they were present in the great unlimited reservoir of divine knowledge which was in union with his human nature. I cannot give you biblical chapter and verse for this, but it has helped me.

Mysteriously, it seems necessary for us to say that, in some sense, Christ was still present everywhere even while he was present on earth. This is very difficult to understand. Perhaps the key to it lies in an analysis of what we mean by the term 'present'. God is present in his universe in different ways. He is present everywhere, upholding the whole universe from within. It is also true that he was present in a special sense on Mount Sinai and in the temple at Jerusalem. It is also true that he is present in an even more special way in the heart of the Christian. He was present in the most special way of all in Christ, in fact, in a way that was completely without parallel. If some of these modes could be true simultaneously, as they clearly were, why not the first and the last?

Indwelt by the Holy Spirit

At this point it is helpful to remember the function of the Holy Spirit in the life of Jesus. The Spirit was related to Jesus in his deity, because of their unity in the Triune life of God. This relationship was eternal. He was also related to him in his humanity, because the Lord Jesus was filled with the Spirit (Luke 4:1).

Some early church writers appear to have confused Christ and the Spirit, and there have been a number of notable attempts this century to treat the Holy Spirit simply as the divine nature of Jesus, virtually producing a Binitarian instead of a Trinitarian theology, but this has rested on a mistaken exegesis of a number of Pauline texts, as Gordon Fee, among others, has shown.[8]

Christians have sometimes debated whether Jesus did his miracles in virtue of his own divine power or in the power of the Holy Spirit. You can make out a case for each. Jesus said, 'If it is by the Spirit of God that I cast out demons, then the kingdom of God has come upon you' (Matt. 12:28). Does that settle it? Remember that after his first miracle, John tells us, 'This, the first of his signs, Jesus did at Cana in Galilee, and manifested his glory; and his disciples believed in him' (John 2:11; cf. John 20:30f.). Surely both sides are right!

He used his divine powers, but only as he exercised them under the constant control of the Holy Spirit. In a Christian, submission to God's will and the fullness of the Spirit belong together. This was surely true also of Jesus.

In practical terms, this presumably meant that it was the Spirit who restrained the exercise of Jesus' divine powers in the 'silent years' before his ministry began. Except in character and in his sense of special relationship to God (Luke 2:41-52) he would be an ordinary intelligent child. Then from his baptism onwards, those powers would be exercised in his special ministry, but only as God's purpose determined this and so only under the control of the Holy Spirit.

Does this mean that Jesus' human experience was just like that of the Christian? Yes and no! He was one with us because divine power was channelled into his human life through the mediation of the Holy Spirit (cf. Luke 4:14 and Eph. 3:20). He was unlike us because the true Source of this power was in his own divine being, while for us the power of God is a gift of his grace, his favour which we do not deserve (2 Cor.12:9). Incarnation (God becoming man) is the key to the first, indwelling (God living in man) the key to the second.

This makes him truly human and yet truly divine.

He is exalted

The exaltation of the Lord Jesus can be viewed from two different and yet complementary angles. From the standpoint of his divine nature it was simply the restoration of that glory which was his before the world was (John 17:5, 24). This does not mean, of course, that he now acts independently whereas in the days of his flesh he only acted under instructions from his Father. It is again important to remember that there is never, in heaven or on earth, any division of purpose between the Father and the Son.

From the standpoint of his humanity, it is the exaltation of his human nature. In the great passage in Philippians Paul, having spoken of Christ's obedience to death, goes on to say, 'Therefore God exalted him to the highest place and gave him the name that is above every name, that at the name of Jesus every knee should bow, in heaven and on earth and under the earth, and every tongue confess that Jesus Christ is Lord, to the glory of God the Father' (Phil. 2:9-11). This means that we need to think of Jesus as man still. Glorified humanity is still humanity. (Christians are going to be glorified, but we shall not cease to be human because of it.)

This is a wonderful fact. It means that we can come to him, confident that he understands exactly what human life with all its pressures and temptations and sufferings is like. He has gone deeper in terms of each of these than any of us will ever go. So his sympathy and human understanding are full-ranging. At the very same time he is God and so has all the resources to come to our aid.

In a family, one parent is often the child's refuge for sympathy and the other for strength. In Christ the two are combined and carried to the highest power, in fact multiplied by infinity.

References
1. F. Schleiermacher, *The Christian Faith*, (ed. H.R. Mackintosh and J.S. Stewart), T. and T. Clark, Edinburgh, 1928.
2. *Methodist Hymn Book,* London, Methodist Conference, 1933, No. 387.
3. For the history of the development of the ancient creeds, see Gerald Bray, *Creeds, Councils and Christ*, Christian Focus, 1997, and J.N.D. Kelly, *Early Christian Creeds*, London, Longmans, Green and Co, 2nd Edn. 1960.
4. E.G. Selwyn, *Commentary on the First Epistle of Peter*, London, MacMillan, 1949.
5. Kelly, *Early Christian Creeds,* pp. 378-383.
6. John McQuarrie, *op. cit.*, p. 27, n.4, where he refers to his source as Sir H.J.W. Hetherington, *The Life and Letters of Sir Henry Jones*, p. 43.
7. For a study of the Philippians 2 passage, see B.B. Warfield, *Biblical Foundations*, London, Tyndale Press, 1958, pp. 130-136.
8. Gordon D. Fee, 'Christology and Pneumatology in Romans 8:9-11' in Green and Turner (eds.), *op. cit.,* pp. 312-331.

Chapter 13

THE UNIQUENESS OF JESUS

The Christian faith and its uniqueness

Historically, Christians have always held their faith to be unique. This is chiefly because of one great fact, the uniqueness of Jesus Christ himself. For other religions, other issues may be crucial, but for the Christian faith the status of its Founder is all-important. Other faiths may, like Christianity, have sacred books, systems of salvation and communities brought together for purposes of worship, but only Christianity has Jesus – and that, or rather he, is its glory.

During the second century and the early part of the third Gnosticism posed a great threat to the church of Christ. There was considerable variety among the Gnostics, but in the main Gnostic systems Christ was not viewed as unique, nor as the incarnation of the only God there is, but as a being much lower in the scale of existence. The struggle with Gnosticism had to be won.

The Christian claim for the uniqueness of Christ is rejected by some people today on purely pragmatic grounds. It is said, for example, that it is not appropriate to contend for such a potentially divisive issue in human society when the world's most desperate need is to find unity in the face of the grave threats posed by economic collapse, ecological disaster and possible nuclear oblivion.

In response to this, it needs to be said that that is a doubtful wisdom which seeks unity at the expense of truth. It is said that whereas doctrine divides, love unites, and with the implication that a concern for doctrine and the urge to love are mutually exclusive. This is highly questionable. Christ was himself the incarnation of both truth and love and a major expression of his love was to show people the truth – truth about God, truth about himself and truth about themselves.

The Christian gospel has demonstrated its power to bring unity at a deep level to people of all nations and races. Gatherings like the two great Lausanne Congresses on World Evangelization brought together men and women from virtually every country in the world whose one point of unity was mutual devotion to Christ as the unique Son of God.

This is not to deny that there have been and still are times when Christian groups have shown a deep-rooted and bitter antagonism to each other. Christians are sinners still, and it has to be said clearly and plainly, as Christ himself said (Matt. 7:21-23) that many who profess his name have never known him. Christ in his self-sacrificing love and in his prayer at the moment of his enemies' greatest hatred and cruelty (Luke 23:34) has shown us the way. At the height of the bitter conflict that brought untold misery to former Yugoslavia, one observer noted that the one place where he found Serbs and Croats united in a spirit of love was in a particular Christ-and-gospel-centred local church. Here, in the midst of so much that was a grievous denial of Christian love, the love of Christ asserted its power to unite.

The classic expression of historic Christology, as we have seen, is the Chalcedonian Definition of 451, which emphasised the true and perfect deity and humanity of Jesus and the perfect union of these two natures in his one person.

We have surveyed the biblical evidence that lies behind this Christological definition fairly fully in earlier chapters. Despite variety of terminology, the New Testament writers are at one in teaching a high Christology, consonant in general with that of the great creeds and of the Definition of Chalcedon.

What then do we mean when we talk about the uniqueness of Jesus? We mean that he and he alone is the incarnation of God. The New Testament teaches his pre-existence, and before his coming to earth he was always fully divine, while as man he was and is the incarnation of the only God there is. These claims are simply staggering.

When did this union of God in Christ take place? We have seen that it was not at his baptism, at some time during his ministry nor at his resurrection. It did not even take place at his birth. It was effected at, and was therefore effective from, the moment of his conception in the Virgin's womb. In other words, there was never a single moment of which we can say, 'then he was man but not God.' His human nature developed always in perfect union with his divine nature.

The implications for other important issues
It must surely be clear that all the great issues of religion are deeply influenced by the great doctrine of our Lord's incarnation. If God really became man in Jesus Christ this is bound to alter everything that matters in the relations between God and the human beings he has created.

The implications of this for our view of revelation
If Christ and Christ alone is God incarnate, the revelation given through him must be the standard against which all that claims to be divine truth needs to be tested.

This does not, of course, rule out, of necessity, the possibility that there may be some disclosure of truth in other religions. After all, the New Testament itself contains quotations from pagan writers which are clearly accepted as true. There are notable examples of this in Acts 17:28 where Menander and Epimenides are quoted. This, of course, validates only the particular extracts quoted and not the writings of these men as a whole. It is also worth pointing out that these approved extracts do not convey any new truth, but simply indicate points at which the writer's thought coincides with something in the biblical revelation.

The finality of the revelation in Christ does however mean that a great deal that claims to be truth must be rejected. If it is incompatible with what he revealed, then faithfulness to him requires its decisive rejection.

The implications for our view of salvation
The New Testament teaches that salvation from sin cannot be secured by human effort but only by the grace of God. Not only so but it must come through the channel of Jesus Christ and by faith, the condition God has laid down.

In this connection, it is helpful to consider briefly what the situation was in the Old Testament. At that preliminary stage of

God's revelation of himself, his salvation was experienced at two levels. On the one hand, there was deliverance from trouble such as physical danger or, more often, the evil designs of enemies, and, on the other, deliverance from sin. The latter was connected chiefly with the sacrificial system.

Of all the New Testament writings, the Epistle to the Hebrews is the one that deals most fully with the relations between the Old Testament and the New. In this book the writer argues that the Old Testament sacrifices did not have any real atoning efficacy, for it is not possible for the blood of bulls and goats to take away sin (Heb. 10:1-4).

What then were these bulls and goats? They were provisional means of restored fellowship with God, and their value depended entirely on the great coming sacrifice of Christ (Heb. 9:15). Just as the person of Christ was unique (and the writer declares this in the first two chapters of his book), so also was his work of atonement. Ultimately and in terms of real as distinct from provisional atonement, Christ's sacrifice is the only one there is.

Hebrews makes it clear too that even these God-given sacrifices had no validity once Christ had died for sin (Heb. 10:8, 9, 18, 26). How could they possibly have any validity? The ultimate necessarily invalidates the provisional. Who tries to get light from the moon to read by after the sun has risen?

It is not surprising then to find the writer asserting twice, within a few verses, that 'there is no longer any sacrifice for sin' (Heb. 10:18) and 'no sacrifice for sins is left' (Heb. 10:26). The first time it is because of the joyous fact that Christ has dealt so fully for sin in dying for it, while the second time it is the solemn fact that no other sacrifice is any longer acceptable, but that rejection of him means exposure to the condemnation of God.

If then there was nothing in the Old Testament sacrificial system, the only such system given by the one true God, to which the recipients of the Letter to the Hebrews could return if they retreated from the cross, how impossible that sacrifices or other devices to secure salvation from sin found within some other system should have a scrap of validity!

The implications for our view of judgement
In the New Testament, final judgement is Christ's prerogative. We need to distinguish between the purposes of his first and his second comings. It is true that he himself declared that he did not come to judge but to save, but this must be understood in reference to his first advent, as he also declared, as recorded in the same Gospel of John, that he was to be the Judge of all human beings.

God alone is fit to be the ultimate Judge of those he has made and over whom he rules. For this reason, the judicial function of Jesus must rest on the uniqueness of his person. Deny his deity and you remove the appropriateness of his claim to judge.

Is his true humanity also relevant to this function? Yes. In the nature of the case, the God who knows all things is fully aware of the moral situations human beings face and in respect to which they are to be judged, for his knowledge and understanding are infinite. Nevertheless, the humanity of Jesus is a kind of bonus factor assuring us of his understanding of such situations 'from the inside'. It means that we can never say that the One who is on the throne has not been where we have, for he has.

Revelation, Salvation, Judgement
There can be little doubt but that these are the three great issues in religion, at least as far as individual human beings are concerned. It is the historic Christian position that Christ's relationship to each is unique, decisive, final.

To sum up what he had said so far, the uniqueness of Jesus lies in the fact that he alone is the incarnation of the one true God, and that in virtue both of his Godhood, and of the great historical acts associated with him, he is the final revelation of God and the one Saviour and Judge of the whole human race.

Arguments against the uniqueness of Christ
Writers of many different kinds have argued against the uniqueness of Christ, from atheists through agnostics and students of world religion to devotees of other religions and professing Christians. It is important for us to face these arguments and to weigh and evaluate them.

First of all, though, we will look at one issue that could arise, not from the arguments of those who reject the biblical revelation, but from serious study of that revelation itself.

From his true humanity
Richard Sturch raises, although without identifying himself with it, the possible objection, 'if every event in Jesus' life was capable of being part of a human life, how can any such event be evidence of his being divine?'[1] In other words, it could be argued that the more we press the fact of his true humanity, the more questions this raises about the possibility of his being divine.

It is of course true that others in Scripture uttered divine teaching, including prophecies which were fulfilled, that others performed miracles, even raising people from the dead, that others displayed true godliness of life and even died in faithfulness to God. They were able to do all this because of God's active presence with them. In what way then did Jesus differ in anything but degree from them?

We have already noted that God is present in his universe in a variety of modes, but that his unique presence in Christ must be placed in an altogether special category. Here, and here alone, Christians believe, there is total union between God and man in one person.

It is not always realised that biblical typology, which enables us to understood much of the language used by the New Testament writers about Jesus, could also constitute a problem for us. The whole principle of typology is 'the like in the unlike'. If we emphasise the first of these nouns rather than the second, and if we stress that the Old Testament types are like Jesus, the Antitype, then we have to ask whether we can really hold to his uniqueness.

We need to note that if we insist that Jesus was in every way unique we are really undermining the gospel! His oneness with us and his likeness to us are vitally important. To be our Saviour he needs to be genuinely human as well as eternally divine.

When we examine the great events which make up the fact of Christ, events which, although taking place in the experience of One who was truly human, nevertheless point to a transcendent origin and to a divine life, we discover that there is something about each of them that differentiates them from anything in the Old Testament background to Jesus. There are unique qualities about every one of them.

Before him there had been special births. Both Isaac and John the Baptist, for instance, were born when their parents had given up all hope of having a child, and, at least in the case of Isaac, when the age of both parents would normally have made such a birth quite impossible. The birth of Jesus, however, was not only special but quite without parallel, for his was a virgin conception.

Before him there had been godly lives. There is real beauty of character to be seen in some of the people of the Old Testament. We find ourselves inspired and challenged by the sexual purity of Joseph, Ruth's deep commitment to the true God and his people, and Hosea's amazingly persistent love for Gomer despite her infidelity. Fine godly people as they were, however, not one of them had a perfect character. The moral perfection of Christ shines out, beyond equal in a sinful world.

Some men and women who lived under the Old Covenant paid for their faithfulness to God with their lives. This was true even of our Lord's immediate predecessor, John the Baptist. It is one thing to be a martyr for God but quite another to be a sacrifice for the world's sin. Like all the martyrs who came before him, Jesus suffered because he stood firm in his commitment to the will of God, but unlike them his death was a sacrificial offering in which he bore the wrath of God against our sins, as our great Substitute.

As we have seen already, there were some in Old Testament days who, in the purpose of God, were restored to life as God's power was demonstrated through people like Elijah and Elisha, who were his servants and his instruments. The resurrection of Jesus, however, was unique, not just a return to life but a total triumph over death. Moreover, this triumph was not for himself alone, but for all those who benefit from his redeeming work.

There were also notable cases of exaltation after humiliation. Joseph's consignments to a pit and then to prison were followed ultimately by his exaltation to the highest office under Pharaoh and with great international influence. David, hunted in the hills, deserts and forests of Judah by Saul was eventually exalted to be king of Israel and to rule over a much wider area than was subject to Saul. In the case of Jesus, however, the humiliation was deeper, for he was subjected not only to shame, mockery and terrible pain but to death itself, and the exaltation was much higher, for he is King of the whole universe.

Some of God's servants were used by him to bring great blessing to his people and to others. We have only to think of such men as Abraham, Moses, Joshua and Isaiah, and there are many other names that could be added. In the case of our Lord, however, the blessing was so great that none greater could even be conceived. Through his work on the cross and his resurrection and exaltation, God's Spirit has come to indwell believers. Could even God the Son give us a greater blessing than the gift of God the Spirit to indwell us as a permanent presence, bringing with him untold blessing?

Some Old Testament characters manifested great authority and power. It would in fact be quite appropriate to describe David and Solomon as emperors, for they ruled over a number of states beside Israel itself. Not only, however, does Jesus rule the whole universe, but he does so, as the Book of the Revelation clearly shows us, in such a way as to bring the whole of human history to its great consummation.

So then we cannot view Jesus simply as one of a series, even as the greatest in the series. This is true whether we are thinking of him as a prophet, a priest or a king, a servant of God or a son of man. In none of these realms nor in any other can we say that he is like others without at the same time saying that he is also One on his own.

In every case there was something special pointing to his uniqueness, because of some unusual supernatural feature (as in his birth), or because of his absolute perfection (as in his character), or because of the divine efficacy of his act (as in his death), or because what he did was the cause of all others in the series (as in his resurrection).

Such an unparalleled sequence of events led the hymn writer, Benjamin Russell Hanby, to ask, 'Who is He in yonder stall at whose feet the shepherds fall? .... Who is He in deep distress fasting in the wilderness? .... Lo, at midnight, who is He prays in dark Gethsemane? .... Who is He, in Calvary's throes, asks for blessings on His foes? .... Who is He that from the grave comes to heal and help and save? .... Who is He that from His throne rules through all the worlds alone?' The answer has more than a touch of inevitability about it:

> 'Tis the Lord, O Wondrous story!
> 'Tis the Lord, the King of Glory!
> At His feet we humbly fall;
> Crown Him, crown Him Lord of all.

The special character of any one of these events would point us in the direction, not simply of an agent of God (although he was this), but beyond this to an incarnation of God himself. Each of them is enormously impressive in itself and the cumulative effect of them is simply overwhelming in its impact on our minds. With great awe, we ask, 'Who then is This?'

From the nature of reality
Some might object to the Christian assertion that Jesus is unique because uniqueness is foreign to the nature of reality. What is the Christian answer to this objection?

The Christian might be tempted to take refuge in factors within the natural universe which have the appearance of uniqueness. He might point to the snowflake, the fingerprint or the marvels of DNA. But to base an apologetic for the uniqueness of Jesus on such as these would be most unwise. The most that could be demonstrated, if the expression may be permitted, would be that he was not unique in being unique!

As we have seen, there are supernatural features that are quite inseparable from what the New Testament teaches about Jesus. It might be asked if there is really room for the supernatural in a universe governed by natural law. Do we need then to follow Strauss in rejecting or Bultmann in demythologising the New Testament presentation of him, and see this as the writers indulging in the deification of a mere man?

It is important to appreciate that to do this would be to exchange a religious faith for a philosophical one. There is no doubt that the doctrine of strict natural causation with the exclusion of everything allegedly supernatural, although widely accepted, is as much an article of faith as the Christian doctrine of the incarnation. It can never be proved.

This does not mean, of course, that Christians reject the notion of natural law. This concept owes a great deal to the influence of the Christian doctrine of God and creation. There have been many scientists who have been, at the same time, reverent Christian believers. Such scientists view themselves as simply thinking God's thoughts after him. For such people the rational principle in the universe to which their own rational minds respond is evidence of the mind of the Creator.

This is not however all they believe. The Scriptures they accept for their view of God and creation also indicate God's intervention supernaturally in his universe, in Israel's history and particularly in Christ. Believing scientists therefore accept both the natural and the supernatural.

What links the natural and the supernatural is the concept of a higher purpose. God will sum up everything in Christ for whom the very universe itself exists. In other words, his uniqueness is a deeper principle even than that of natural law in the universe, for the latter exists for the former.

Such a view of Christ's relationship to the universe is to be found, for example, in the Christian philosophy of Herman Dooyeweerd.[2] According to Dooyeweerd, God has created the universe in such a fashion that every feature of it is subject to a particular set of laws. There are, for instance, mathematical laws, physical, chemical and biological laws, laws governing the psychological, sociological, ethical spheres and so on. All these spheres are found in human life. So Christ as man sums up in himself all the law-spheres which God has set in his universe, and, not only so, but he is both God and man, so that he represents both the uncreated Creator and the fullness of created being.

Such a view, although its author modestly describes it as a tentative Christian philosophy,[3] is quite as coherent and rational as any naturalistic philosophy, and the uniqueness of Christ is basic to it.

Some modern writers who reject the uniqueness of Christ have approached the matter somewhat differently, from the standpoint of what is known as Process philosophy. The Process philosophers maintain that it is a mistake to conceive of reality as static. Rather it should be conceived dynamically and along evolutionary lines. Classical philosophy and historic Christian theology have always tended to think of reality as *being*, that is, of course, in terms of what actually exists. Process philosophy and the Process theology to which it gave birth want us to think more in terms of *becoming* than of being. Everything is constantly moving and changing.

Norman Pittenger has applied Process theology to Christology.[4] He says that Christ himself must be understood in evolutionary terms and that if he is, it is quite impossible to treat him as unique. David Wells, in a critique of Pittenger's views, says that for Pittenger 'Jesus was a remarkable effulgence of the divine, but one which differed from other such expressions in degree but not in kind. Every actuality in the world – both in human and nonhuman forms – is an incarnation of God. It is, of course, for this reason that process thinkers have a deep affinity for much eastern thought.'[5]

To seek to refute this would require a detailed critique of the Process theology and of the Process philosophy which lies behind it and this would take us far from our subject. Whatever we may think of his outlook generally, however, it is worth noting that Teilhard de Chardin, a theologian who was also a thorough-going evolutionist, was able to conceive of the uniqueness of Christ even on the basis of an evolutionary philosophy because he thought of him as the Omega point (the final divine Reality) entering history in Christ and so anticipating the final goal of all things.

From the nature of knowledge

Various arguments for the existence of God have been used at one time and another. Kant criticised the arguments which took the visible universe as their starting-point. These are the arguments usually described by the term 'metaphysical'. His basis for rejecting them was that he held, as we have seen, that there can be no certainty about things as they really are on the basis of an examination of the world that is accessible to our senses. We have to take the evidence of our senses on trust and so, in the nature of the case, absolute proof is impossible.

Theological statements in Scripture, as in the history of Christian doctrine, profess to be statements about things as they really are. In Kant's terminology, they profess to be about noumena, not simply phenomena. So, it has been said by writers who show the influence of Kant, theological statements are as open to question as philosophical ones. All they can give us is godly opinion and not authoritative divine truth.

The effect of this outlook on Christology has been very serious. The Ritschlian theologians of the late nineteenth century said that, although we may consider that Christ performs divine functions, we cannot either assert or deny that he is himself God. We have to rest content with saying that he has the value of God for us. This means that we can say that Christ does for us the kind of things we would anticipate that God would do, but that this does not necessarily mean he is God!

Without doubt there are twentieth century theologians who agree with Ritschl and his friends.

So there has been a tendency towards a functional rather than an ontological Christology, that is a Christology which is able to say what Jesus did and does but not, in any deep sense, who he is.

An approach to Christ's person through his work is, of course, by no means illegitimate. It may be found, for example in the works of writers as historically far apart as second century Irenaeus and sixteenth century Luther. It is not absent even from Athanasius, even though he made very strong statements about who Christ is. Functionalism has its place provided it does not lead to a denial of the possibility and importance of ontological affirmations, that is to statements as to who Jesus actually was and is.

Suppose we were to agree with Kant in denying that transcendent realities can be demonstrated with absolute certainty from the phenomena of the universe, it would not follow from this that we would agree to set aside Christian theology. It is not, for instance, on the basis of philosophical inference that we accept Christ's uniqueness but rather on that of divine revelation.

Is this a coward's retreat? By no means! It is, in fact, absolutely basic to the historic Christian position. The Christian accepts by faith what Scripture says about Christ and his uniqueness as divine revelation, and this faith then becomes the basis both for his or her life and thought. Anything more remote from philosophical speculation is hard to imagine. This is why it is so important for a theologian to have a strong and unvarying objective basis for his theology, and Holy Scripture fulfils this important function.

From the nature of truth

Much modern philosophy, Existentialism, for instance. combines Kant's rejection of metaphysics with Hegel's approach to truth. G.W.F. Hegel, a generation or so after Kant, held that human thought always progresses dialectically, that is by a series of antitheses. This means that absolute or ultimate truth is always being sought but not found, although of course there is gradual progress towards it. It is only at the end of the historical process that absolute truth is understood. Until then there is always 'another side to the matter'.

This means then that Hegel as well as Kant maintained that strong assertions of particular truths are always subject to qualification. There is a fundamental incompatibility of this idea with the claims for absolute truth that are made in the Bible. Particularly, biblical Christians are committed to Christ's uniqueness as an ultimate truth.

A further feature of modern thought is the tendency in much modern theology to assert that God does not reveal himself in words but in deeds.

Now there is no doubt that we can accept, and accept gladly, the positive side of this, but not the negative. Certainly God does reveal himself in deeds. He made himself known, for instance, at the Exodus and at the Cross, as a gracious Redeemer-God, delivering his people from Egyptian bondage under the Old Covenant and from sin under the New.

It is one thing, though, to say this and quite another to set aside the statements of Scripture in which these deeds are interpreted. God has not in fact left us to our own understanding as we contemplate these great acts of his. He has opened up their meaning to us by appointing prophets and apostles and by constituting them as channels through whom the Holy Spirit would make known his truth. The revelatory deeds are interpreted by revelatory words.

A further idea, closely linked to the 'deeds, not words' view is that we know God through encounter with him and not through statements about him. This then is not simply a view of the way the historical revelation was given, but of the way in which today people may have a living experience of the living God.

We may readily agree, of course, that revelation does not reach its proper goal when statements are simply accepted by the intellect. It is possible to read the Bible as if it were simply a religious text-book and to try to get some understanding of it as we might a book of geography or chemistry or mathematics. We insult God if we do this, for all the time, in our reading of it, we find it confronting us with challenge after challenge, and these challenges are not just intellectual but moral and spiritual.

Once again, however, it is the negative side of this idea that we must query. How can we be sure that our encounter with 'God' is an authentic one? It is vitally important for us to insist that what purports to be an encounter with the living God must be tested by the words of Scripture which reveal what, in Christ, God is like. The consequences of self-deception or of succumbing to Satan's deceptive counterfeits are too great.

Yet another modern idea has to be considered. Some have maintained that truth is not something objective that ought to be recognised by everybody, but that what is true for one person may not be true for another. This idea is very widespread today. Many Christians find themselves quite surprised when their witness to the gospel and their personal testimony for Christ is listened to with respect. Sometimes, of course, this is because of a deep interest created by the Holy Spirit, but we should also be aware of the fact that it is often due to this idea of the subjective nature of truth. 'So', the hearers is really saying, 'I am glad you have found something that is true for you. Mind you, it is not true for me!'

Now those who take this point of view have not always realised how serious the consequences of it would be if it were to be taken to its logical conclusion. If all truth is subjective, then the basis of all rational communication between human beings is completely destroyed. If I tell you that truth is only subjective, then I am actually telling you (without perhaps realising it) that this very statement I am making is subjective. I am destroying any reason for your taking my statement about truth seriously, because it means that even this statement might only be true for me and not for you!

What then of Christology? Historic Christology assumes that there are objective truths which are universally applicable. It asserts by faith that the Bible's claims for Christ as unique are true and that therefore they should be preached to all for acceptance.

This means then that, for the Christian, faith is ultimate. Are Christians unusual in this? No, for in fact this is true for everybody. We all need some faith by which to live.

For instance, as we have seen, it was Rudolf Bultmann who called for the demythologising of the New Testament. He sought to eliminate the truths on which classic Christology is based, but this does not mean he was without faith. He accepted as true Heidegger's existentialist philosophy as a proper means of approaching the New Testament and of facing life. Surely this was really a virtual abandonment of one faith for another!

From the nature of history
In Chapter 2 we explored some of the implications of the fact that Christianity is a strongly historical faith, based on events and especially on the great event of Jesus. We also looked at ways in which modern theology has often been affected by developments in the understanding historians have of the nature of their discipline, and the fact that they see that a fully objective approach to history is impossible.

It is obvious that many of the biblical writers were writing history, and that, if this view of history applies also to them, we cannot be completely sure that they have given us an accurate picture of Jesus as he actually was. For instance, can we be quite sure that he made claims to uniqueness?

Ultimately a strong doctrine of biblical inspiration is the one complete guarantee we have of the truth of the picture of Jesus we have in the Gospels. In other words, this picture, although coming through eye-witnesses, has its ultimate guarantee in God, for the eye-witnesses were writing through his inspiration.

Apologetics and the work of the Holy Spirit

It is sometimes objected that to take this point of view is to present people who are interested in Jesus but are as yet uncommitted to him with the need to come to important convictions about the nature of the Bible before they come to the kind of certainty about Jesus that will be a basis for true faith in him. It would mean that we would have to say to people, 'Do you accept the inspiration and authority of the Bible?' If they answered 'No!' we would have to tell them that we could do nothing for them!

Happily, this is not the case at all, and for a very sound theological reason. We may tell interested enquirers that they do not need to begin with a doctrine of inspiration but only with willingness to treat the New Testament documents as having general historical reliability.

Why? Because it is the work of the Holy Spirit to convince men and women of the inspiration of the Bible. It means that Christians need, not only to encourage people to read the Bible, but also then to pray for the faith-creating activity of the Holy Spirit and his testimony within people's hearts to the truth.

Does this mean that there is no place for apologetics, no point in seeking to help people with their problems? If this were the case, a number of the chapters in this book would have to be scrapped! It is not in fact the case, for we recall that the New Testament itself contains apologetic material, especially in connection with the resurrection of Jesus, to support the claim that he is unique.

The apostolic preachers of the good news of Jesus did not simply assert that he had risen from the dead. They declared that they had actually seen him. This apologetic material was addressed to the minds of the original hearers or readers. So, the preaching of the gospel took account of the fact that people might well have problems with what was being declared. This apologetic material then was an aspect of the preaching which the Holy Spirit used to bring people to faith in the first years of the church.

If this was so then, why not now?

Apologetics is not, however, simply of value to help interested enquirers as they move towards definite faith-commitment. It also helps Christian believers and strengthens the faith they already have. Faith may be real, even if it still has questions, and it is helpful for those questions to be faced in the light of the wealth of evidence the New Testament contains that Jesus was and is the unique incarnation of the only God there is.

References
1. R. Sturch, 'Can one say, "Jesus is God"?' in H.H. Rowdon (ed.), *Christ the Lord: Studies in Christology presented to Donald Guthrie*, Leicester, IVP, 1982, pp. 326-340.
2. In his *magnum opus*, *A New Critique of Theoretical Thought*, 4 vols. combined in 2 vols., n.p., Presbyterian and Reformed Publishing, 1969.
3. Note, e.g. the very modest tone of the original Foreword to his work, *op. cit.*, pp. v-ix.
4. Norman Pittenger, *Christology Reconsidered*, London, SCM, 1970.
5. Teilhard de Chardin, *The Phenomenon of Man* (trans. B. Wall), New York, Harper and Row, 1959.

Chapter 14

THE INTER-FAITH ISSUE

This issue is of paramount importance today. More people in Britain belong to non-Christian faiths now than at any time since the Viking invaders were converted to the Christian faith. Clearly Christians have to think about their relations with them.

Theological pluralism and the uniqueness of Christ
Theological pluralism is the point of view that reckons all religions to be equally valid, so that devotees of particular religions should abandon all attempts at proselytism. A pluralist may, at least in theory, be himself a Buddhist, a Moslem or a Christian, and there are plenty of other possibilities. His chief concern, if he has any standing as a theologian in his community, will be to convince its members that pluralism is compatible with the faith he and they profess. In Christian terms, this means that a pluralist theologian needs to convince the Christian that he or she is free to worship God in Christ but that all missionary work of an evangelistic type should cease.

Religion is notoriously difficult to define. As the world community is so varied in its faiths and life-stances it is probably best for us to think of religion quite broadly in terms of belief in some transcendent reality, however vaguely defined, and in the fact that certain attitudes and actions are consonant with and required by that belief. Usually, of course, the transcendent reality will be a personal being or beings. Most religions think of men and women as being in some threatening situation and so they prescribe a way of salvation.

In the pluralism debate there are two main issues, the nature of the being or beings worshipped and the way in which salvation may be obtained.

Obviously theological pluralists may emerge from many different religious traditions. We are concerned of course only with the so-called Christian pluralists. What should biblical Christians say in the context of this debate, and what should our stance be if we would be faithful to Christ and to the Word of God? Several points need to be made:

Theological pluralism necessarily calls the uniqueness of Christ into question

David Wright has said, 'Only too predictably *The Myth of Christian Uniqueness* followed in the footsteps of *The Myth of God Incarnate*. Thus the surrenders of liberalism have come home to roost.'[1] Clearly the surrender of the distinctiveness of Christianity and in consequence withdrawal from the Christian evangelistic mission in a pluralistic world must follow inevitably from the abolition of the incarnation.

John Hick and Paul Knitter, the editors of *The Myth of Christian Uniqueness,* describe theological pluralism as 'a viable, though still inchoate and controversial option for Christian believers.'[2] We will argue that this is not the case at all.

According to historic Christianity, the only religious system which ever supplied a valid way to God was the God-given religion of the Old Testament. This was given by him on his initiative and it showed him to be a God of grace. As we saw in the previous chapter, the Old Testament sacrifices were provisional means of salvation until the coming of Christ. This means then that the salvation experienced by the Old Testament believers had something in common with that of New Testament believers, for it rested totally on what God himself would do in Christ.

The Gospel of John contains many sayings of Jesus in which he uses the phrase *ego eimi* (I am). Not only do these passages identify him with Yahweh, the God of the Old Testament, as we have already seen, but David Ball has argued that they deliberately refer to similar sayings in Isaiah, sayings in which Yahweh is emphasising his uniqueness over against pagan deities.[3]

If Christ is the incarnation of the only God there is, it follows that he alone is worthy of worship. Can we claim though that the Christian doctrine of the incarnation is unique? Some have suggested that it is not, and it has been pointed out that the idea of a god entering human history at some point in human guise occurs in a number of religions. It was said, for instance, of Zeus, in Greek religion.

It is widely agreed that the closest parallel to the Christian incarnation doctrine is the doctrine of avatars in Vaishnavite Hinduism. This type of Hinduism is devoted to the god Vishnu, and is based on the idea that this god made a number of 'descents' into the world. He came, for instance, as Rama, while at another time he appeared as Krishna.

There is however a difference of a really major kind. The very multiplicity of Vishnu's avatars highlights this difference. The avatars did not involve any assumption of human nature, as distinct from mere human appearance, by him. This is a vital difference. The Lord Jesus Christ entered into a full human experience. Not only so, but the union of God and man in Christ is not only unrepeatable but permanent. The ascension of Christ is sometimes misunderstood. It was in no way a reversal of the incarnation, but rather the taking of his glorified manhood into heaven.

We saw in our last chapter that the incarnation of God in Christ means that he is the supreme channel of revelation and the only Saviour and Judge of the human race. It therefore follows that to say there are many valid ways to God, or even only two, means that the special claims of Christ must be set aside.

Historic Christianity has always denied the name 'Christian' to those who reject the deity of Jesus and/or the doctrine of the Trinity. They may profess many of the articles of Christian belief, but they have missed the very heart of things. Even such a broad grouping as the World Council of Churches has a doctrinal basis which speaks of Christ as 'God and Saviour'.

This means therefore that the uniqueness of Christ is the central issue in the pluralistic debate within the Christian tradition. It is in fact so central that everything else rests on it.

Theological pluralism involves a mythological or symbolical interpretation of the doctrine of the incarnation

The doctrine of the incarnation is necessarily linked to belief in the supernatural. If God really became man in Christ, then this certainly means that eternity has entered time, that the infinite has embraced the finite, that a stupendous supernatural event has taken place.

In an earlier chapter, we saw that David Strauss and Rudolf Bultmann both rejected all the supernatural elements in the story of Jesus as belonging to unhistorical mythology. We noted too that Bultmann's view differed from that of Strauss in that he did not treat this 'mythology' as valueless but as providing a vehicle for the essential message, the personal challenge of Jesus.

In terms of the concerns of this chapter, however, Bultmann's view is no better than Strauss's. The doctrines of the incarnation and the Trinity, according to Bultmann, do not belong to the kerygmatic kernel, that is the kernel of Christianity as a message to be preached, but to its mythological husk. In other words they are not essential to the message of the gospel but are simply the clothing that message wore in New Testament times. He said that we should recognise the challenge to be found within the mythology and then discard it as quite unacceptable to the modern scientific view of the universe. Jesus was not therefore *really* unique in his person although he does confront us with a unique challenge.

Bultmann has now been dead for some years and it is sometimes said that his thought is no longer anything like as influential as it was. Demythologising of the New Testament, however, was one of his main ideas and it is presupposed in much modern theological pluralism.

Paul Tillich's thought has also been influential. His theology is anything but easy to understand, largely because of his strange use of terms. As we have seen, he used some words in an unusual technical sense, for instance the term 'transcendent'. He used other terms ambiguously, so that, for instance, it is often quite unclear whether 'finding God in the depths' means finding him deep within the universe or finding him in the depths of our own souls.

The idea of symbolism is a key one for the thought of this theologian. Symbols point to realities which lie beyond them. Tillich held that the concept of incarnation, among other Christian doctrines, is not ultimate truth, but only a symbol of it. Many theologians may give it a high status, but the philosopher-theologian sees that there is a truth lying beyond it. What then is this truth?

For him it was simply the somewhat colourless idea that God is being and the ground of being.

This is certainly not what the church of Christ has claimed in asserting uniqueness for the Christ who according to the New Testament, declared, 'I am the Truth'. There is no hint in the New Testament that this claim is anything but ultimate. Tillich's concept of symbolism would certainly have been foreign to its writers and first readers, emerging as it does from a sophisticated modern philosophy.

In some respects Bultmann and Tillich may be thought of as opposites. Bultmann's view was rather like that of the deists of the Enlightenment. For him the universe was a closed system with which God did not interfere. Tillich, on the other hand, had strong pantheistic tendencies. As is so often the case with apparent opposites, though, there were some important similarities also. Both were in danger of losing God, Bultmann by removing him far from his universe and Tillich by identifying him with it.

So we may see that both the mythological interpretation favoured by Bultmann and the symbolical interpretation championed by Tillich represent a radical break with historic Christianity. The implications of this fact need to be faced.

The status of theological pluralism as a monotheistic faith is highly questionable

From a pluralistic perspective it has been suggested that religious differences may be thought of simply as personal preferences. They may be based on upbringing in a community of faith or they may be due to a religious conversion. It makes little difference to the point at issue.

If this is really true, a proper 'Christian tolerance' would accept it. In this case, for me, as a Christian, religious faith would be focused on Christ and on Christ alone, but I could accept as equally valid for him or her another person's sole attachment to another religious object of devotion and trust.

Those familiar with the way scholars influenced by evolutionary philosophy used to approach the Old Testament may perhaps be forgiven for thinking they have heard this idea before. When this philosophy had a major influence on biblical studies it was maintained that full monotheism was only attained at the end of a long evolutionary process, and that the full monotheism of parts of the Old Testament was preceded historically by a monolatrous or henotheistic stage.

Monolatry or henotheism is the view that many gods exist but that the believer has chosen (or been chosen by) one god to whose service alone he will be devoted. Joshua's challenge to his fellow-Israelites was treated as an expression of this outlook, when he said, 'Choose for yourselves this day whom you will serve, whether the gods your forefathers served beyond the River, or the gods of the Amorites, in whose land you are living. But as for me and my household, we will serve the LORD' (Josh. 24:15).

This whole theory is, of course, open to many objections and the passages from the Old Testament which were employed to support it, such as the one just quoted, may be interpreted quite differently.

The point we wish to make just now is that whatever monolatry is or is not, it is not monotheism. Monotheistic belief banishes every being from the heavens except the only God there is. In the final analysis, monolatry is simply a sophisticated form of polytheism.

Not only so, but the scholars who embraced this interpretation of the Old Testament certainly took it for granted that monolatry was inferior to monotheism, a stage in the evolution of religion which had to be left behind. They viewed the movement from monolatry to monotheism not simply as development but as progress. Quite apart from any evolutionary point of view, it would be quite appropriate for us to ask whether the theological pluralists are asking us to move away from full monotheism into monolatry, which must be to move from a higher to a lower view of deity.

It may of course be argued that the present pluralist proposal is different and that there is no question of Christians being asked to accept a plurality of deities, even in theory, but rather to recognise that there are many ways to the one God, with Christ as simply one of those ways.

An obvious difficulty in this, of course, is that not all

contemporary religions are monotheistic or even theistic. Within Hinduism for example, there is considerable variety of belief and practice. Even Vedantic Hinduism, often regarded as its most sophisticated form, is pantheistic rather than theistic, so that its ultimate concept of deity is very different from biblical monotheism. How then can we say that Christ is one of the ways to God when there is no general agreement as to the nature of God?

This point is in fact recognised by Langdon Gilkey, one of the contributors to *The Myth of Christian Uniqueness*. He says, 'Each system of religious symbols forms a coherent, interrelated whole ... Thus each doctrine or symbol within any given system differs significantly from analogous symbols in other systems. As a result, no one doctrine in any such system of symbols ... can be abstracted out and be established as universal in all religions, a point of unity with other religious traditions. God is as similar – *and* as different – from the ultimate principals of Hinduism and Buddhism as are the Christ and Krishna or the Christ and a Bodhissatva'.[4] Later he says, 'there seems no consistently theological way to relativize and yet to assert our own symbols – and yet we must do both in dialogue.'[5]

After such clear-sightedness, he takes refuge in the strange irrationality of 'relative absoluteness'[6] and the idea that each particular religion is both true and relative because it is a true revelation for that community. This of course is an example of the subjective view of truth we have already considered in our previous chapter.

Paul Knitter contends for a similar position. He says, 'What we have here ... is the concept of limited uniqueness, if such a thing is possible', and he goes on to say, referring to Jesus, that this 'need not diminish or undermine the Christian's full personal commitment to him as the incarnation of God ... (but) his finality remains an open question'.[7]

'Relative absoluteness' – 'limited uniqueness' – such language does not encourage us to think that a coherent point of view is being expressed, let alone one that Christians can accept as true to their faith.

Particularly serious for Christians is the inevitable disjunction between God and Christ which follows if Christ is simply one way to God. Historic Christianity has made much of the fact that the One who brings us to God is himself God. The logic of modern pluralism must either be that Christ is a being inferior to God, or else that he is one of a number of 'incarnations' of God, which, at least in terms of their plurality, would be like the Hindu avatar doctrine.

Brian Hebblethwaite writes helpfully when he says, 'If the Incarnation is to be understood as God's self-presentation in person within the structures of his creation then its uniqueness follows immediately from the fact that God is one. God can doubtless be *represented* by innumerable other people; but if he is to come himself into our world, then he cannot split his own identity by identifying himself with two or more human beings, any more than one human being can be represented as two or more replicas.'[8]

If Christ is held either to be inferior to or to be a mere 'avatar' of God, what happens to the doctrine of the Trinity? It cannot survive in anything like its historic form.

Theological Pluralism and Historic Christianity are two different faiths

The Christian claim that Christ is unique is not unreasonable. From the evidence itself it is possible to make out a strong case for his uniqueness. In the final analysis, however, the issue is one of faith. The historic Christian faith has sometimes been called 'a presuppositional position'. What is meant by this? It means that it has a basic belief which lies behind its whole system of thought. This is true of faiths generally, and this is true also of many viewpoints that are not always identified as faiths by those who hold them.

Philosophers have often recognised the great importance of what Herman Dooyeweerd called a religious root, the basic presupposition of a particular faith. Without using Dooyeweerd's term, writers as diverse as Cornelius Van Til and Michael Polanyi have certainly recognised the idea and the fact. Such a 'faith' is a common human phenomenon, although it would not always be considered 'religious' on a narrow definition of that term.

A particular faith is not necessarily fixed and unalterable. As Lesslie Newbigin, expounding Polanyi's outlook, points out, reshaping may take place, 'sometimes by gradual adjustments, sometimes by dramatic changes which Thomas Kuhn calls "paradigm shifts".'[9]

The philosophy of science itself recognises such paradigm shifts, and Arthur Koestler in several of his books, most notably in *The Act of Creation*[10], has shown their operation also in the arts, so that they furnish a link between what C. P. Snow called 'the two cultures'. Such shifts, however, important as they undoubtedly are, pale into insignificance beside the radical 'paradigm shift' involved in a religious conversion in which the religious root undergoes a complete change. The great importance of such a change is of course recognised in the New Testament and is one of the chief tenets of evangelical Christianity.

There can be no doubt that the faith that Jesus Christ is both God and man and that he is the ultimate Revealer of God and the only Saviour and Judge of humanity is in fact a very different faith from that which accepts all religions, or even many religions, or even just two, as equally valid approaches to God. They do not have the same religious root. So, although theological pluralism may represent itself as a more moderate or more tolerant form of the historic Christian faith, they are in fact completely incompatible.

Langdon Gilkey, himself a theological pluralist, sees the implications of such a paradigm shift. It is, he says, 'a monstrous shift indeed ... a position quite new to the churches, even the liberal churches'.[11]

Now in the nature of the case it is not possible to establish by reason alone that the conviction that Christ is the unique Saviour and Lord is built on truth. There is plenty of evidence for this, especially in connection with the resurrection of Jesus, but it falls short of absolute demonstration. For the follower of the historic Christian faith, this conviction is in fact the basic premise of the whole of Christianity. Once accept this and theological reasoning may begin to demonstrate that it is the logical foundation of the whole Christian faith.

Every faith has its basic assumption which cannot itself be conclusively established by reason for those who do not share it. This is true, in fact, of all reasoning. We always have to commence with some presuppositions. The Austrian scientist, Godel, was awarded a Nobel Prize for showing from mathematics that the premises of demonstration cannot themselves be demonstrated.

What then in the final analysis has the historic Christian to say to the theological pluralist? He may argue his case with him, as we have sought to do in this chapter, but when all has been said, he will invite him prayerfully and with a readiness for a new understanding of truth, to read the New Testament again. He will then pray for him, because although the pluralist may not believe in conversion, the historic Christian does!

Our attitude to people of other faiths

We are to love them
The New Testament has commands to love which are universal in their scope. In fact, we are forbidden to be restricted in our love (Matt. 5:43-48). God's rain and sun come as blessings to all human beings and our love should be as wide as these loving providences.

We are to do good to them
Paul, writing to the Galatians, who were living in an almost exclusively pagan environment, said to them, 'As we have opportunity, let us do good to all people, especially to those who belong to the family of believers' (Gal. 6:10). The reference to believers is helpful because it shows that the doing good referred to there cannot be restricted to the proclamation of the gospel.

So we are to express our love for others in practical ways. In fact, whether or not our preaching of the gospel is seen to be simply a manifestation of religious intolerance may well depend almost entirely on whether our general attitude and actions express love and desire for the overall well-being of others.

We are to preach the gospel of Christ to men and women of all faiths

This is not only the clear command of Christ himself in the Great Commission (Matt. 28:18-20), but also arises as an implication of his uniqueness. If he and he alone is God incarnate, he claims the allegiance of all, and his servants must seek to persuade others of the need to submit to him. If the first Christians had not done so, would the church exist at all today? Evangelism can never be an isolated expression of love, but it is nevertheless the supreme expression of it, for God's greatest blessing for human beings is reconciliation through Christ.

This preaching must be both faithful and sensitive

This is true, of course, of all Christian work, following the pattern of Christ who was both 'merciful and faithful' (Heb. 2:17) in his service to God. We must be faithful. We cannot compromise the gospel which we hold as a sacred trust and which must be proclaimed.

At the same time, we must remember that there are mental and emotional obstacles in the minds of many members of other faiths arising from the fact that the Crusaders were professing Christians and that many Christians will be regarded as representatives of the religion of a former colonial power. This underlines for us the great importance of sensitivity to other cultures and to the misunderstandings and hurts of people of other religions which have arisen from their past contact with those they would have regarded as Christians.

The gospel preacher should seek to understand the religious faith of those to whom he preaches

We may take Paul's sermon in Acts 17 as a helpful model here. This sermon, while never quoting the Old Testament roots of the gospel, is consistently true to them, while at the same time Paul shows clear understanding of Stoicism and Epicureanism. His gospel proclamation makes contact with their beliefs and yet at the same time cuts across them. The Christian faith is theistic, for Christians believe in a God who is both transcendent (distinct from the universe he has made) and immanent (present within that universe). As a Christian theist he was able to relate positively to the transcendentalism of the Epicureans and the immanentism of the Stoics, while cutting across the Epicurean rejection of the immanence of God and the Stoic rejection of his transcendence.

There is a splendid example of this kind of approach in speaking to Moslems about the gospel of Christ in a chapter by A.J. Malik in *Asian Faces of Jesus*.[12] Here he deals with Christological issues that are great stumbling-blocks to Moslems, the issues of Christ as God's Self-Revelation, as God's Son, and as the One who died and rose from the dead, and he shows how these may be approached in a way faithful to Scripture and yet sensitive to the Moslem outlook.

We are to be good citizens and to live at peace with all men
We will therefore be concerned about good community relations and cannot be party to racist acts or demonstrate racist attitudes. In Britain today, a large percentage of the followers of other religions are of course members of races other than the race (or rather the mixture of races) that is indigenous to our country.

It is not surprising that Paul, as a Christian, was distressed amidst the idolatry of Athens (Acts 17:16ff.). It did not lead him however to acts of iconoclasm but to a responsible and, moreover, a courteous preaching of the good news of Christ.

We need also to note that the New Testament never reveals any attempt to spread the Christian faith by coercion or by any means other than persuasion. Forcible conversion of others is totally alien to biblical Christianity. In the nature of the case it must be so. Authentic Christian conversion is not mere subscription to a theological position (although, in basic terms, it implies this) but is the commitment of the will to Christ in living faith. The divinely ordained means for securing this is the truth, proclaimed in the power of the Holy Spirit and motivated by love.

Some practical implications of the historic Christian position
What then are the practical implications of this position?

What about dialogue?

A great deal depends on our motivation.

Do I dialogue with others because they are human beings too and because, if I am to show love to them, I need some understanding of them? Do I dialogue with them to understand their religious outlook because I wish to commend Christ to them?

If so, I will want to listen as well as to talk. This is not because I am uncertain of my own faith and hope to learn how to believe in, live for and worship God from them, but because I must understand them better if my witness is to be both sensitive to them and also faithful to Christ. Dialogue will not therefore be a substitute for preaching but a means to effective Christian witness.

What about making common cause on matters of common concern?

If it is a matter of social or political ethics, then this surely is right. We are citizens of an earthly as well as of a heavenly kingdom, and our concern for justice should lead us to support the rights of other members of the community, whatever their religion may be. William Carey, in India as a Christian missionary, worked with a Hindu reformer to secure the abolition of suttee.

What about the rights of people of other religions to worship in their own way? We are not citizens of a theocracy as the people of Israel were in the land of Canaan in Old Testament days. We expect the right as Christians to freedom of worship and freedom to witness within lands controlled by other religions. It would seem then a matter of simple justice that we should support freedom of religion within our own country. After all we do not believe in conversion by the suppression of the beliefs and practices of others.

What about religious education in schools?

There have been many changes in thinking about this during the past thirty years or so. Ronald Goldman's attack on the use of the Bible at primary level, later modified a little,[13] was followed by an increasing tendency to teach a multiplicity of faiths, including not only other religions but also other 'life-stances' such as humanism and communism. An important development too has been the celebration of the festivals associated with various religions.

Clearly there are good educational reasons for giving the teaching of the Christian faith the primary place in British schools, for much in British history and culture cannot be understood without it.[14]

Christian parents may feel that there is a difference between instruction about religious beliefs and participation in religious practice. In theory the first promotes understanding, while the second goes well beyond this. In practice though it is not always easy to draw the line if children are in fact learning by doing. Also what are we to think of role play, if this means acting the part of a religious worshipper?

It is obviously important for Christian parents to know what is happening and to watch the whole situation carefully and prayerfully. They could hardly be blamed if, in particular circumstances and in particular schools, they felt the whole matter too fraught with danger of compromise and decided to withdraw their children from Religious Education classes.

What about inter-faith worship?

Inevitably this has already been touched on in connection with religious education, as some elements in the celebration of festivals undoubtedly come into the category of worship.

We may distinguish three aspects of worship, the Object, the attitude and the expression of worship.

There is much difference of opinion and of emphasis in the expression of worship, even among Christians today, and few would consider there to be serious abandonment of principle in worshipping with other Christian believers who express their worship somewhat differently.

Without doubt, however, the expression of worship does reflect our understanding of the nature of the God we worship and even in Christian worship the expression may exhibit differences according to the emphasis of the pulpit teaching about the character of God. How much more will this be true in relation to other religions!

Clearly though the attitude is of even greater importance, for faith, obedience and sincerity are essential to true Christian worship, and mean that it is a way of life and not simply an activity at certain prescribed times. If true worship can never be a matter simply of the lips but must involve the submission of the whole life, how can this possibly be the case if the religious Object is not the God of Christ, or if there is such a combination of concepts and worship materials from different religions that the nature of the Object of worship is not clear?

Subjectively then the true attitude is vital, but objectively it is the Object of worship who is all-important. Baal-worship, whether sincere or insincere, was clearly totally unacceptable in itself. Not only so but even a somewhat Baalized concept of Jahweh and so of sacrifice is rejected (Ps. 50). Inter-faith worship draws perilously close to syncretism if it does not in fact pass over into it.

It is difficult to see how inter-faith worship can be reconciled with belief in the uniqueness of Jesus, for the God of Christ is the only God who exists and Christ is the only way to him. Paul's attitude to Christian participation in pagan worship (1 Cor. 10: 1-18) is clear. He was certainly deeply troubled at the thought that Christians might become involved in it. Can we be less concerned than he?

References

1. David Wright, 'The Watershed of Vatican II', in *One God, One Lord, in a World of Religious Pluralism*, Cambridge, Tyndale House, 1991, p. 171.
2. John Hick and P.F. Knitter (eds.), *The Myth of Christian Uniqueness*, London, SCM, 1986, p. viii.
3. D.M. Ball, 'My Lord and my God: The Implications of "I am" sayings for Religious Pluralism' in A.D. Clarke and B.W. Winter, *One God, One Lord,* 1991, pp. 53-71.
4. *The Myth of Christian Uniqueness,* p. 41.
5. *op. cit.,* p. 47.
6. *op. cit.,* pp. 46-50.
7. P.F. Knitter, *No Other Name? A Critical Survey of Christian Attitudes towards the World's Religions*, London, SCM, 1985, p. 386.
8. In a letter printed in *Theology 80* (Sept. 1977), p.386.
9. L. Newbigin, *The Gospel in a Pluralist Society*, London, SPCK, 1989, p. 44.
10. A Koestler, *The Act of Creation*, London, Picador, 1989.
11. *The Myth of Christian Uniqueness,* p. viii.

12. A.J. Malik, 'Confessing Christ in Islamic Context' in R.S. Sugirtharajah (ed.), *op. cit.,* pp. 75-84.

13. R. Goldman, *Readiness for Religion: A Basis for Developmental Religious Education*, London, Routledge and Kegan Paul, 1965, especially pp. 70-733.

14. One document arguing for this was the *Report of the Working Group on Religious Education and Religious Observance*, published in January, 1981 and subsequently accepted by the Strathclyde Regional Council Education Committee. This did not, however, rule out instruction in the beliefs and practices of other religions.

Chapter 15

THE PERSONAL ISSUE

Throughout much of this book we have been surveying the witness of the Bible to Jesus Christ. This teaching is deeply impressive. It is given through a great many different writers. Their books differ much in literary type, in style and in vocabulary. An extremely wide variety of words and phrases is used by the Bible writers to convey to their readers the meaning of his person. They embrace simple designations such as 'King' and 'Shepherd' which are meaningful even to children and profound descriptions such as 'Word' and 'Light' which provoke deep thought. Nothing is stereotyped. Yet, despite this, there is an amazing harmony in the teaching given.

It has been said that what marks out a true work of art in any medium, be it pencil, paint, stone, wood, cloth, language or music, is the fact that you may come to it time and time again and always find some new beauty in it. This makes the Bible God's own great work of art, and the nature of its subject is unmistakable. It is a portrait of the Lord Jesus Christ, with each biblical book adding its own brush strokes. Moreover, it is not simply a canvas portrait, nor even a piece of sculpture. To say that the portrayal of Christ given in the Bible is three-dimensional is totally inadequate, for to all the dimensions of earth is added the infinite dimension of heaven.

Yet even the concept of a work of art hardly does justice to the Bible presentation of Christ. An artist known to me told me how the artistic stimulus first came to him. As a child he was taken to the municipal art gallery in Glasgow. He enjoyed his visit and liked many of the pictures he saw. But then at last he stood before Rembrandt's *Man In Armour*. He was overcome with awe. He said to me, 'I felt this was not a portrait of the man, but the man himself.' It is Christ himself who confronts us within the Bible. We see him with the inner eye, we hear his voice with an inner ear. We cannot escape the challenge of the one who is not dead but lives for evermore, and whose majesty and glory and yet winsome humanness meet us in living power throughout the pages of Scripture.

What then is Christ for us today?

It may be said, of course, that Christ can be to us today whatever we wish him to be. If we follow the Deconstructionists[1] we will not ask what the writers of the New Testament held to be the historical facts about Jesus nor how they understood his significance. What matters will be his significance for us, which could be wildly different from their understanding of him.

As we have seen, however, their view is self-destructive, for it is based on a theory of literature which, if carried through logically, would mean that the Deconstructionists would be unable to argue that we should accept their own theory. It might be right for them but, on their own principles, it may not be for us.

If we reject Deconstructionism, then we are faced with a Jesus who comes before us as a real historical person, understood by his followers to be the divine Son of God and Lord of all, in which belief they maintained they were simply following what he believed about himself.

If, as we have argued, the accounts of his resurrection are to be treated as true, then real experience of Jesus as a living person is possible for us today.

It is important to say that we need the New Testament so that we may be sure that any alleged experience of Jesus is authentic. If it is truly Jesus we are experiencing, then he will be the Jesus whose life, death and resurrection are recorded in the New Testament, and who presents himself to us there as the Son of God and the one who claims absolute Lordship over us.

We will repeat the question: what is Christ for us today, or, as this book comes to its close, to make it more specific and personal, what is he to you? This question has to be faced and answered by us all. He is too unique and compelling a Figure to be ignored.

He is someone to trust
One of the saddest aspects of our present society is the widespread breakdown of trust between human beings. Society can only

function properly on a basis of confidence in others. Family life, business life, national and international life all run into great trouble when trust is undermined. What the economists call confidence in the pound or the dollar is so often really confidence in the British or the Americans whose actions determine the true value of their currency.

The enormous increase in the divorce rate speaks to us all too eloquently about this. We think of the colossal breakdown in confidence that lies behind most divorces, the deceit, the suspicion, the anxiety, the agony, all of which are either causes or symptoms of the destruction of trust between a husband and wife. In this sort of environment is it any wonder we are producing a generation with so many young people who feel they cannot really trust anybody?

So then Christ comes to you and me first of all as somebody to be trusted. He was constantly calling people to personal faith in himself. But you have perhaps learned from life's bitter experiences that it is unwise to trust anybody unless you have plenty of evidence of his or her trustworthiness.

Christ produces evidence so full, so persuasive, so deeply moving, that it should sweep away all reservations, all cynicism. The Bible shows him to be somebody who always put others before himself, who never made promises and failed to keep them, who showed depths of compassion and tenderness which outclass every other human being in history. Yet at the same time, he was so strong that people knew they could lean on him as hard as they wanted, and he would prove as steady and firm as a rock.

The final evidence of his complete trustworthiness comes to us in the central events of the story, in his sufferings and death and resurrection. He had dealt with disease and demon-possession and death. Now he would get to the root of the entire human problem and deal with sin itself by bearing it and the divine punishment it so justly deserved. Here is the final self-forgetfulness and the purest love. And beyond it lay the triumph of the resurrection and all the power of new life.

Trust is the only proper response to such a person, and not simply trust in this statement or that promise, nor for this purpose or that.

The trust for which he calls is full confidence in him, to save me from my sins, to guide me in life, to receive me to his presence when death comes. If faith's object is fully trustworthy then the more that faith considers its object the more it grows, embracing more and more spheres, more and more aspects of its relationship with that object. It cannot grow however until it is born, and it is born in personal commitment.

The evidence of Christ's trustworthiness surely moves us to make that personal commitment!

He is someone to thank

An atheist who was converted to Christ said that one of the worst features of being an atheist is that you have nobody to thank. Surrounded by blessings untold and attributing them all to nature or to the life-force or to evolution, and just nobody to thank! How different for the Christian! He begins his Christian life on a note of thanksgiving to Christ for saving him from his sins. To him this is the supremely wonderful thing that has made everything look different.

Then he discovers the power of the risen Christ to strengthen him when he is tempted, that the Christ who has saved him from sin is able to keep him from sin, because he now lives within him, and so he gives thanks for this. Then he finds that Christ guides him through Holy Scripture when he has problems, that Christ gives him power to speak about him to other people, and that he has promised to come back again to conduct him to heaven. All these facts add further notes or even movements to the great symphony of thanksgiving which is beginning to take shape.

His thanksgiving takes on more and more dimensions. He discovers that Christ is the Creator of the universe, so that he can thank him for material as well as for spiritual blessings. He discovers that the element of meaning in everything he sees is really derived from him who is the Word and the Wisdom of God.

Even troubles and problems and afflictions cannot rob him of his gratitude, for in them all he can see a divine thread of purpose. He knows that although they are not pleasant and he would rather be without them, Christ is on the throne of the universe and he has allowed them to come into life so that he can give him strength in adversity, comfort in sorrow, and courage in the face of danger.

He is someone to love

Human life is all about relationships. All of us know in our heart of hearts, no matter how materialistic we may be, that it is people who really matter and not things. That is really what the songs are all about, what the books are all about, what life is all about. If trust is a vitally important feature of human relationships, so is love. This word is used today so often as if it simply meant sexual love, and even then largely in terms of its physical side. Yet we all know that love is only worthy of that name when it is not self-seeking but self-denying and is concerned with the well-being of the person who is its object.

A good many songs have been written about unrequited love. It is a sad experience. The Son of God knows more about this than any other person. As he surveyed the city that would crucify him in just a few days, he cried out, 'O Jerusalem, Jerusalem, you who kill the prophets and stone those sent to you, how often have I longed to gather your children together as a hen gathers her chicks under her wings, but you were not willing' (Matt. 23:37).

Other songs have been written about a lover who proves unfaithful, whose love does not last or proves to be too self-centred. Some of us do not show much love unless we are loved in return. Our 'love' is more like a kind of blackmail to secure the attention of somebody else. Christ knows much about this too. His love is always pure, strong, persistent and utterly selfless, but he often poured and pours it out on those who give so little in return.

Love like that deserves and ought to have wholehearted, lifelong devotion from you and me. If through trust you have been brought into a new relationship with him, then all the conditions are there for an ever-deepening outpouring of love and devotion to him. His love for you does not vary. It is always absolute. If you trust him, and you ponder with thankfulness all he has done for you, then your love for him will grow and grow until it is the deepest fact of your life.

He is someone to serve

Psychologists tell us that the best way to a truly integrated personality and therefore to a satisfying life, is to find the centre of life outside oneself. Paradoxically, if we lose ourselves in serving a cause or a person, we find ourselves. Self-centredness makes for utter misery and is, both in itself and in its effects, a foretaste of hell.

Now the Lord Jesus Christ is one who calls us to serve him. He gives us work to do. Nothing could be a greater privilege. Not only what we think of as Christian service, activities like leading a service, preaching a sermon, singing in the choir, teaching a Sunday-school class, is service for Christ. Everything we do throughout the whole of life, down to the last detail of it, should be seen as service for him. In fact, to view life this way often leads to a drastic reappraisal of our sense of priorities.

It may be that you have never really thought about the claims of Christ upon your time and talents. If you are a Christian, it is not up to you to choose the course of your life, to decide what job you will do or how you will spend your leisure time. That is for him to decide. Ask him to show you and give yourself a chance to listen to what he says through the Bible and in prayer, and you will not lack the direction you need. It will not all come at once, but you can trust him to show you each stage of the pathway as you need to walk it.

Obedience is of vital importance in the Christian life. Some Christians ransack the Bible looking for promises and hardly give a thought to the commands staring them in the face on every page. The promises are given to enable us to carry out the commands. We shall not lack anything, for his service brings the truest fulfilment to those who serve him.

He is someone to worship

It is possible that somebody reading this chapter has an uncomfortable feeling. All that has been said may be true, but is it not possible for us, in each of these ways, to be still very much self-centred and self-occupied?

Take faith, for example. Perhaps our real aim in putting our trust in Christ is to get something for ourselves, something the Bible calls 'salvation'. We discover that thanksgiving makes us feel good and we enjoy the feeling. Love secures that we are loved ourselves and we may be doing our service for the 'perks', for what we may get out of it.

Now we may think these objections are a bit cynical, but they are not without point. It is possible to be self-centred in all these areas, so that we are really using Christ as a means to an end, and not treating him as an end in himself. The thought is horrifying. Martin Buber used to talk about the difference between an 'I - it' and an 'I - thou' relationship. In the first we really treat a human being as if he were less than human. We treat him as a means to an end. In the second we establish a true relationship which involves respect for the other's person-hood.

Now our relationship with Christ should be the greatest 'I - Thou' relationship of life. In fact, it might be better to call it the 'Thou - I' relationship. He does not exist to serve ends determined by our wants and needs. We exist to serve ends determined by him. What saves our trust, our gratitude, our love and our service from being completely vitiated by self, is the fact that they are all seen in the context of worship. We see that the Christ who offers himself to us is God and Lord. He is worthy and we are worthless. He will be the centre of the worship of the redeemed universe throughout all eternity and, by his grace and only by that grace, we shall take our places among the worshippers. Perhaps in heaven we may be hardly aware that we exist. What will dominate everything is the fact that he exists, and that he is all-holy, all-wise, all-loving. Worthy is his name!

References
1. See p. 35.

SUBJECT INDEX

Aaronic priesthood 97

Abba 83, 146, 209

Adoptionism 53, 54, 78, 237

Advent, Second 177, 182, 184, 190, 200, 201, 230

Alexandria, School of 115, 116, 141, 148, 236

Alpha and Omega, Jesus as 65

Angel of the Lord 107-109, 137

Anhypostasia, Enhypostasia 238

Antioch, School of 115, 116

Apollinarianism 232

Apologetics 191, 259, 260

Apologists, minimisers and maximisers 191-193

Aramaic 58, 83, 104

Arianism 152, 231

Ascension of Jesus 169, 175, 176, 179, 190, 199, 200, 230, 251, 263

Atheism 280

Atonement 72, 74, 193, 247

Attributes, Incommunicable 236

Avatars 263, 268

Baptism of Jesus 14, 26, 73, 147, 245

Being, Ground of Being 265

Bodhissatva 47, 267

Boyhood of Jesus 203, 238

Buddhism 47, 90, 261, 267

Captain of the Lord's host 107

Chalcedon, Definition of 162, 163, 225, 226, 130, 232, 245

Character of God 153

Character of Jesus 55, 102, 103, 149-168, 212, 250

Christ, Messiah, Jesus as 13, 16-18, 24, 27, 54, 80, 86, 90, 98, 104, 119, 120, 126, 167, 174, 213, 219

Christadelphians 132

Christology from Above 57

Christology from Below 57, 203

Christology, Functional 255

Christology, Ontological 255

Christology, the earliest 78, 79

Church, churches 87, 88, 177-179, 196, 244, 245

Compassion of Jesus 25, 203, 210

Confessions, Reformation 229

Conversion 185, 259, 260, 270, 272

Covenant 117, 226

Creation, New 199

Creator and Sustainer, Jesus as 59, 66, 83, 133-135, 215, 231, 280

Credal reinterpretation 233-235

Creed, Apostles' 198, 230

Creed, Nicene 230-232

Creeds 219-236

Crucifixion, death of Jesus 19, 30, 53, 54, 73-75, 78, 87, 139, 140, 144-148, 169, 170, 174, 193-199, 205, 213, 230, 278

Crusaders 271

Cultures, The two 112, 269

Davidic Kingship 20, 22, 96-100

Day of Questions 161

Dead Sea Scrolls 117

Death 169, 170, 173, 175, 211, 212, 279

Deconstructionism 35, 48, 113, 114, 118, 129, 278

Deism 41, 72-75, 265

Demythologising 252, 258, 264

Dereliction, Cry of 142, 148

Descent into hell 230

Divinity, meaning of 234

Docetism 146, 148

Doulos 56

Education, Religious 273, 274

Enemies 14, 15

Enlightenment 41, 116, 227, 265

Epicureanism 271

Epistemology 34, 228

Ethics, Christian 89, 227, 228

Eutychianism 233

Evangelicalism 204, 269

Evangelism 271, 272

Evolutionary Philosophy 254, 265, 266

Exaltation of Jesus 53, 54, 61, 81, 82, 88, 169-184, 196, 242, 243, 250, 251

Existentialism 72-75, 90, 256, 258

Exodus from Egypt 76, 124, 256

Exorcist, Jesus as 14, 211, 279

Faith 47, 76, 79, 86-89, 112, 114, 127, 142, 160, 191-193, 220, 226, 227, 256, 262, 268-270, 278-280

Fall, The 236

Feminist Theology 208-211, 223

Firstborn 59

Flesh of Christ 235, 236

Form Criticism 72

Fulfilment 92, 108, 128

Fulness 59

Galilean background 46, 207

Gethsemane 26, 246, 247

God-consciousness of Jesus 227

God, Doctrine of 124, 228, 253

God, Jesus as 28, 55, 57, 58, 62, 65, 79, 80, 83, 85, 108, 138, 216-218, 221, 225, 230-232, 234, 239, 242, 260, 263, 268, 283

God the Father 83, 91, 108, 155, 174, 201, 208, 216, 230-232

Godliness of Jesus 102, 103

Good, the 8, 5, 151

Gospel of Thomas 45

Gnosticism 59, 260

Graeco-Roman world 124

Great Commission 271

Greeks 23- 25

Healers, Jesus as 14, 190, 191, 211

Heavenly Session 175-178, 230

Hellenism 58

Henotheism 266

Hermeneutics, Interpretation 111-130

Herodians 14, 143

Hinduism 149, 263, 267, 273

History, OT 36-40

History, religious and theological 37, 38

Holy Spirit, Spirit of God 14, 50, 51, 72, 88, 95, 108, 137, 167, 174, 179, 180, 196, 198, 199, 201, 212, 230, 236, 241, 242

Homoiousios 232

Homoousios 231, 232

Humanity of Jesus 63, 79, 203, 204, 221, 222, 225, 238, 242, 245, 246, 249, 263

Humiliation of Jesus 60, 61, 131-148, 250, 251

Hypostasis, Hypostatic Union 238

'I am' sayings 27, 212, 217-218

I-It relationship 283

I-Thou relationship 283

Image and Glory of God, Jesus as 60, 226

Image of God in human beings 226

Immanence 340, 271, 272

Incarnation 60, 64, 72, 107, 137-142, 168, 190, 202-243, 245, 252, 263, 268

Inspiration, Biblical 9, 10, 51, 77, 78, 114, 192, 212, 225, 233, 234, 255, 256, 259

Islam 251, 272

Jehovah's Witnesses 132

Jesus, the name 63, 80

Jesus Seminar 44

Jesus, westernised 206

Jew, Jesus as a 1st Century 206

Judge, Jesus as 53, 66, 174, 183,
       201, 230, 248, 263, 269
Judgement 170, 183, 248
Kantianism
Kenosis 238, 239
Kerygma 73, 74, 207
King, Jesus as 14-19, 97-101, 104,
       106, 122-124, 136, 177, 178,
       200, 206, 221, 251, 251, 277
Kingdom of God, of Heaven 154,
       207, 208, 221, 251
Knowledge, limited and unlimited
       205, 240
Krishna 263, 267
Lamb of God 65, 89
Language learning 112, 113
Last Adam, Jesus as 59, 60
Lausanne Congresses on World
Evangelization 245
Law 149-153
Law, Mosaic 96, 119, 120, 126, 150,
       152-154, 157, 161, 162
Leader, Jesus as 53
Liberal Jesus 71, 206
Liberalism, Theological 116, 206,
       229, 234, 262, 269
Liberation Theology 203, 204, 206,
       223
Life, Eternal 182, 183
Light, Christ as the 277
Literalism 115
Lord, 18, 19, 28, 55-59, 65, 82, 83,
       85, 87, 88, 90, 124, 138, 168,
       174, 200, 207, 214, 215, 221,
       230, 283
Love 151, 153, 222, 244, 279
Male, Jesus as 208-211, 281
Maranatha 58, 80
Mary, The Virgin 236
Mediator, Jesus as 55
Messiah in OT and Judaism 61-63,
       103-105, 108-110, 119, 120,
       130, 174, 213, 224

Metaphysics, Methaphysical theist-
       ic arguments 228, 254-256
Midrash Pesher 117
Miracles of Jesus 14, 15, 25, 86,
       94, 172, 189-191, 199, 211-
       213, 222, 249
Monolatry 265
Monotheism 265-268
Moravians, Moravianism 227
Mystery 202, 222
Myth, mythology 41, 42, 72-75, 90,
       263-165
Nag Hammadi 45
Neoplatonism 229
Nestorianism 233
New Age Movement 187, 201
Non posse peccare, 163
Obedience of Jesus 63
Omnipotence of Jesus 66
Omnipresence of Jesus 240, 241
Omniscience of Jesus 66, 240-242
Original Sin 163-165
Pagan writers quoted in NT 246
Pantheism 265
Parables of Jesus 15, 25, 26
Paradigm shifts 111, 112, 269
Particularity, Scandal of 210
Paulinism 208, 234
Person, Jesus as One 221-224, 226,
       237
Pharisees 14, 18, 119, 120, 141,
       143, 150, 161, 195, 212
Philosophy, Greek 63, 130, 149,
       226-230
Philosophy, Modern 72-74, 109,
       185-190, 226-228, 256, 265,
       268
Pleroma 59
Pluralism, Theological 261-270
Polytheism 83, 124, 266
Posse non peccare 105
Post-Modernism 35, 48, 113, 129,
       187

Post-Structuralism 118
Prayers of Jesus 24, 146, 147, 180, 181, 204, 244
Preaching, Early Christian 51-55, 60, 75, 79
Prediction 122, 123, 128, 170, 171
Pre-existence of Jesus 74, 83, 107-109, 132-138, 216, 218, 237, 245
Presuppositions 268, 269
Priest, High Priest, Jesus as 63, 81, 96-98, 101, 122, 123, 181, 251
Process Philosophy 254
Process Theology, Christology 254
Promise 121-123
Prophecy 92-95, 108, 121-124, 127, 128, 170, 171, 249
Prophet, Jesus as 52, 65, 92-95, 101, 122, 123, 251
Prosopon 226
Protestant Churches 230
Pseudonymity 66
Psychology 131, 221, 226, 253, 264, 282
Quest of the historical Jesus 42, 49, 70-72, 205-208
Racism 272
Rationalism 116, 192
Redaction criticism 43
Redeemer, Jesus as 215
Reformers 115, 116
Religion 261, 262, 269
Religious, Non-Christian 244, 247
Religious root 268, 269
Renaissance 116
Resurrection of believers 60, 74, 182, 199
Resurrection of Jesus, the risen Jesus 19, 20, 54, 56, 72, 74, 75, 78, 92, 170-176, 178, 184, 190-201, 208, 211, 212, 230, 235, 251, 269, 279

Revealer, Jesus as 137, 138, 246-248, 272
Revelation, Divine 61, 108, 137, 246, 248, 256-258, 211, 212, 230, 235, 251, 269, 279
Ritschlianism 234, 255
Roman Catholic Church 230
Romans 19, 25, 52, 120, 160, 195
Sabbath 15, 161, 162
Sadducees 120
Salvation 203, 204, 246-248, 262
Samaritans 25, 160
Sanhedrin 143, 195
Satan, Evil One 14, 156, 164, 230
Saviour, Jesus as 20, 53, 55, 124, 142, 174, 200, 204, 209, 215, 246-248, 263, 269
Scepticism and Reductionism, Historical 34, 41-46, 74, 76
Scepticism and Reductionism, Theological 10, 73, 76
Science, Modern 181-190, 192, 253, 269
Seed, Jesus as 103, 110, 121
Sensus plenior 115
Septuagint 29
Sermon on the Mount 21
Servant of God, Jesus as 17, 52, 65, 100, 101, 110, 139, 140, 174, 213, 239
Service, Christian 282
Shepherd, Jesus as 16, 26, 122, 218, 277
Similitudes of Enoch 105
Sinlessness of Jesus 41, 72, 102, 103, 148, 157, 158, 162-68
Situation Ethics 151, 152, 148
Sociology 226, 253
Son of God, Son 13, 17-20, 26-28, 44, 52, 57, 64, 70, 80-87, 90, 91, 98, 105, 106, 121, 145, 148, 191, 215-219, 229, 231, 278, 281

Son of Man 16, 17, 27, 29, 64, 65,
      84, 90, 103-105, 122, 174,
      219, 251
Sophia, Wisdom, God as 209
Speech-Act Theory 223
Spiritualisation 115
Spiritualism 47
Stoicism 271
Structuralism 35, 112, 113, 118
Sufferings of Jesus 16, 63, 101,
      139, 144, 148, 158, 220,
      230, 279
Supernatural, supernaturalism,
      natural, naturalism 69, 185-
      201, 251-254, 263-265
Symbolism 65, 89, 105, 263-265,
      267
Synoptic Gospels 11, 27, 28, 44, 64,
      70, 81, 84, 155, 157, 218
Teaching of Jesus 14-18, 21, 22,
      25-28, 87, 88, 212
Temptation of Jesus 21, 29, 63,
      156, 157, 164-168, 220, 221,
      239, 242
Terminological seedbed 124-126
Theism 271, 272
Third World Christologies 206,
      207, 213, 272, 276
Transcendence 131, 132, 249, 250,
      255, 271, 272

Transfiguration 17, 26, 29, 81
Trinity 72, 173, 174, 179, 239,
      240, 263
Two natures of Christ 62, 63, 144,
      162-168, 200, 225-243,
      248, 253
Typology 123, 124, 127-129, 249-
      252
Union with Christ 175, 237
Uniqueness of Jesus 244-260
Verbal adaptation 125
Verbal assonance 126
Victor, Christ as 215
Vine, Jesus as the 26
Virgin Birth, Virgin Conception
      20, 21, 163, 190, 198, 203,
      230, 236-238, 245, 251
Vishnu 263
Westminster Confession of Faith
      119
Wisdom, Jesus as 125, 126, 280
Word, Jesus as the 28, 61, 95, 121,
      130, 132, 134, 135, 137,
      138, 235, 277
World Council of Churches 263
Worship 282-283
Worship, Inter-Faith 274, 275
Yugoslavia, Former 245
Zeus 263

SCRIPTURE INDEX

Genesis
1-3 59
1:1 94
2:17 170
3:15 103, 122
6:2 105
12:1ff. 121
12:7 103
14 97
16:13 107
18:22 107
19:1 107
32:24-30 107
48:15f. 107
49:10 98

Exodus
3:11-15 76
3:14 27, 217
6:2-3 76
20 168

Leviticus
16 96

Numbers
23:19 103
31:16 95

Deuteronomy
5:29 141
14:1 106
17:14-20 98
18:15-18 122
21:15-17 66
23:4-5 95
30:8-16 126
34:10-12 65

Joshua
5:13-6:2 107
24:14 168
24:15 266

Judges
13:18 109

1 Samuel
4:21f. 56

2 Samuel
7 98
7:14 106

1 Kings
11:6 48
11:38 98
11:41-42 49
14:19 49
14:29 49
15:1-5 48
15:3 98
15:9-15 48
15:11 98
15:25-26 48
16:21-28 48
16:29-22:40
17:17-24

2 Kings
4:31-37 211
4:32-37 172
17:7-23 168

1 Chronicles
9:1 168
29:29-30 49

2 Chronicles
13:22 49
33:10-20 49

Job
1:6 105
2:1 105
38:7 105

Psalms
1 102
2 13, 67, 99
2:7 106
8 81
8:4 16, 103
16 171
33 28, 124
40:6-8 103
50 275
50:7-15 109
69:1-3 145
72 99
80: 104
81:13f. 141
89:27 66, 106
102:25-27 62
105:15 93
110 67, 97

Proverbs
8 124

Isaiah
1:2 106
1:10-17 109
6:5 1236
7:10-18 100
9:6 100, 109
11:1-10 100
11:1-9 29
11:1ff. 29
11:1 130
29:13 109
32:1-8 100
40:3 13
42 140
42:1-9 100
42:1-3 110
42:1ff. 29
44:6 65

48:12 65
49 140
49:1-13 100
49:1 101
49:6 110
50:4-9 100
50:6 140
51:9-11 90, 124
51:17 145
51:9-11 90, 124
52:13-53:12 17,
65, 100, 140 171
52:13 17, 101,
171
53:7 101
53:9 55
53:10-12 17
53:10 101
53:12 101, 171
53:22 55
61:1-4 100
61:1-3 109
61:1ff. 29, 101
63:1-6 100
63:1-3 109

Jeremiah
7:21-26 109
11 101

Ezekiel
34:11 122

Daniel
7:13ff. 104
7:13-14 16, 80,
84, 176
8:17 104

Hosea
6:4 153
6:6 109
10:4 94

Hosea, cont.
11:1-4 153
11:1 106
11:8-9 141, 153
12:3-5 107

Amos
5:21-27 109

Micah
1:10-16 126
5:2 109, 122

Malachi
3:1-4 109
3:1 13

Matthew
1:20 20
1:25 21
2:23 126
3:15 155
3:17 155
4:1-11 156
5:1-12 126
5:3 120
5:17 153
5:21-22 168
5:43-48 270
7:21-23 245
7:24-27 56
7:28-29 21
7:28 22
8:10 160
8:17 148
9:9 22
11:1 22
11:27 27, 85, 219
11:28-30 209
12:8 22, 85
12:18-21 29
12:28 241
12:41 22
12:42 22

13:53 33
15:24-26 160
15:39
16:13ff. 87
16:16 145
16:21 145, 170
16:27 183
17:5 155
17:22f 170
18:20 174
19:1 22
20:17-19 145, 170
20:18 29
21:11 93
22:23-34 143
22:41-46 85
23:2-4 129
23:23-24 129
23:37 142, 281
26:1 22
26:29 200
26:36-56 146
26:64 177, 200
27:19 158
27:35 30
27:46 148, 212
28:18-20 271
28:20 179

Mark
1:1 13, 51
1:2-3 13
1:4 14
1:7-8 14
1:11 13, 14, 155
1:13 14
1:14-15 14
1:14 17
1:16-20 14, 143
1:17 17
1:33 14
1:34 19
1:41 25, 140

1:43 140
2:2 14
2:6-7 14
2:13f 143
2:13 14
2:14 17
2:16 14
2:18-20 144
2:19-20 145
2:23-3:6 129, 161
2:23-28 15
2:23-24 162
2:24 14
2:27 162
2:28 85, 162
3:1-6 143
3:5 141
3:6 14, 143
3:7-8 14
3:11 19
3:13-19 14, 143
3:19 15
3:22-30 14
3:33-35 177
4:17 145
4:35-5:43 15
4:41 15
5:35-43 172
6:3-4 15
6:6 142
6:10-11 15
6:14-29 15
6:34 25
6:37-44 16
7:24-8:10 16
7:37 157
8:1-10 16
8:2 25
8:17-18 16
8:22-26 16
8:27-38 16
8:31 19
8:32f 17

8:34 17
9:1 17, 29
9:2-8 17
9:7 13, 17
9:9 19
9:19 142
9:21 205
9:31 19
9:34 17
9:38 17
10:13 17
10:17-18 85, 161
10:28 17
10:32-34 145
10:34 19
10:35-45 17
10:35ff. 17
10:38-39 147
10:38 145, 146
10:41 17
10:45 19
10:46-52 17
11:1-7 17
11:9-10 17
11:12-33 18
11:12-14 94
11:20-21 94
11:27-12:44 214
11:27-12:37 161
12:6 13, 18
12:17 45
12:28-34 153
12:35-37 18, 19, 85, 109
12:38-44 18
13:26 19, 84
13:32 13, 85, 205, 240
14:3-9 19
14:12-16 19
14:24 19
14:25 19
14:28 19

Mark, cont.
14:32-50 146
14:33 146
14:34 146
14:36 91, 146
14:61f. 19
14:62 19, 29
15:2 19
15:21 19
15:25 30
15:34 148
15:38-39 52
15:43 19
16:9-20 19, 176
16:19 176

Luke
1:35 163
2:1-4 30
2:11 24
2:41-52 24, 241
2:52 203
3:21 24, 180
3:22 23
3:23 24
4:1-2 156
4:1 241
4:14 242
4:17-20 100
4:18-19 29
4:18 25
4:24-30 25
4:24-29 160
5:12 25
5:16 24
6:5 85
6:12 24
6:20 25
6:24-25 25
6:46 215
7:1-5 25
7:11-17 172
7:13 24
7:35 209

7:36-50 25, 211
8:2-3 25
8:14 25
9:9
9:28f. 180
9:31 26
9:35 23
9:51-19:28 25
9:51-55 160
9:51 26
10:1 24
10:21 25
10:22 27, 85,
  219
10:25-37 25
10:33ff. 25
11:1 180
11:37-53 129
12:13-21 25
12:33 25
12:50 145
13:6-9 94
13:34 26, 209
14:2 25
14:13 25
15:11-32 25
17:16 25
17:21 177
18:15-17 25
18:18-19 85
18:31 26
19:1-9 25
19:10 122
19:41-44 25
20:41-44 85
21:1-4 210
21:20-24
21:29 200
22:31-32 180
22:33 147
22:37 101, 148
22:39-53 146
22:40-46 180

22:42 239
22:44 204
23:13-15 157
23:27-29 25
23:33 30
23:34 245
24:5-6 170
24:13-35 26
24:16 173
24:27 92
24:39-43 200
24:39 172
24:44-47
24:50-51 176

John
1:1-18 28, 95,
  126, 133, 137
1:1-2 132
1:1 94, 124,
  134, 138, 235
1:4 64
1:14 64, 124,
  134, 235
1:18 64, 133
1:21 65, 94
1:25 65
1:41-49 27
1:41 64
1:45 64
1:49 64
1:51 27
2:4 159
2:11 26, 241
2:19-22 144, 211
2:19-21 173, 217
3:3-8 49
3:13-14 27
3:13 216
3:14 169
3:16 64
3:18 64
3:35 216
4 160

4:6 28
4:10-14 217
4:22f.
4:25-26 27
4:32-34 157
4:34 85, 204
5:17f. 218
5:19-27 215
5:21-29 217
5:22-23 201
5:23f. 204
5:26ff. 64
5:27 27
5:30 85, 239
6:14 94
6:27 27, 217
6:30-35 94
6:33 216
6:35 217
6:38 85, 216
6:50f. 216
6:51 132
6:53 27
6:62 27
7:5 171
7:32 143
7:37 212
7:45f. 212
8:23 133
8:28 27, 169
8:29 157
8:34-36 217
8:46 157
8:48 143
8:57-59 29
8:58f. 218
8:58 217
8:59 143
9:16 161
10:17f. 217
10:17-18 211
10:18 173
10:22-33 27

John, cont.
10:29f. 218
10:30f. 218
10:31 143
11:1-44 172
11:4 218
11:25 64
11:33 28
11:34 205
11:35 28
11:38 28
11:47-57 143
12:23-29 155
12:24 183
12:32-34 169
12:33-34 27
12:41 136
12:44 218
13:3 133
13:12-17 159
13:31 27
14:3 174, 182
14:6-11 218
14:6 114
14:18 179
14:23 218
14:27 217
14:28 133
14:30-31 157
15:11 217
15:12, 13 154
15:23f. 218
16:3 218
16:7 174
16:15 218
16:27-28 216
16:28 133
17 133, 180
17:5 27, 133,
    216, 242
17:20 180
17:24 133,
    216, 242

18:1-8 217
19:18 30
19:26 159
19:28 28, 147
20:10-18 211
20:15 159
20:17 216
20:19-29 195
20:19-20 200
20:27 172
20:28 28, 138
20:30f. 64
20:30-31 26, 86
20:30 94, 241

Acts
1:1-2 196
1:9 176, 199
1:11 200
2:23-24 173
2:23f. 54
2:24 201
2:24-32 171
2:32f. 137
2:33 51, 88, 179,
    196
2:36 53, 54
2:40 51
2:42 54
2:47 178
3:6 88
3:13 52
3:16 88
3:20-21 78
3:22-24 95
3:22 52
3:24 93
3:26 52
4:11f. 53
4:25-26 109
4:27 52
4:30 52, 88
5:31 53
7:55 88

7:56 81
9 56, 173
9:3ff 88
9:4 177
9:10ff. 88
10:14 215
10:36 53
10:38 153, 158
10:42f. 52
10:42 201
13:46-47 110
15:13-21 195
16:14 49
17:2-3 170
17:16ff. 272
17:26 60
17:28 246
20:7-12 172
20:35 88
22 56
26 56

Romans
1:4 57, 174
3:9-20 168
4:25 174
5:12ff 60
5:18 67
8:3 163, 164
8:9 179
8:11 173
8:15 91
8:28-30 60
8:29 57
8:32 57
8:34 181
9:1-29 220
9:4 105
9:5 58
9:30–10:21 221
10:5-10 126
10:9 87
10:16 148
11:36 80

14:10-12 80
15:1-3 159

1 Corinthians
1:24 124
2:1-5 48
3:6-9 177
7:10-11 89
8:6 59, 134
10:1-18 275
10:13 167
10:14-22 168
10:31–11:1 159
11:23 89
13 153
15 60, 182
15:1-3 48
15:3f. 87
15:3-4 174
15:5-7 195
15:5-8 171
15:17 174
15:35ff. 182
15:42-44 173, 183
16:22 58, 80

2 Corinthians
1:18-20 121
1:21-22 167
4:4 60
4:6 56
4:7 104
5:10 80
5:17 66
8:9 133
11:3-4 47
12:9 242

Galatians
1:1 173
1:19 195
2:16 168
3:15-16 103
4:4 57, 236, 239
4:6 91

Gal., cont.
4:12-15 48
6:10 270

Ephesians
1:19f. 173
1:20 176
1:22 178
2:20-22 177
3:20 242
4:25 168
4:28 168
4:31 168
5:3 168
5:5 168
5:18 179
5:25-33 177
6:2 168
6:10-21 167

Philippians
2:1-13 159
2:5-11 60
2:5-8 238
2:7 164, 238
2:9-11 215, 242
3:20-21 201
3:21 173, 175,
   182

Colossians
1:13 80
1:15-17 59
1:15 66, 106
1:16-17 80, 134
1:16 131, 215
1:17 59, 135
1:19 59
2:9 59
2:10 136, 215
2:15 215
3:4 182
3:16 179
4:11 29, 80
4:14 29

1 Thessalonians
4:15-18 182

2 Thessalonians
1:7-8 183
2:13-14 49

2 Timothy
2:24-26 110

Titus
2:13 58

Hebrews
1:1–2:4 221
1:1f. 95
1:1-2 61
1:2 81, 134
1:3 135, 177
1:4 67
1:5 105, 109
1:8 109, 177
1:9 109
1:10-12 62
2:5-18 221
2:6 81
2:17f. 221
2:17 63, 271
2:18 158
4:14-16 221
4:14 81, 221
4:15 158, 163
5:6 97
5:7-10 63
5:8-9 63
5:8 158
5:9 158
5:10 97
6:6 82
6:9 67
6:20–7:19 97
7:3 81, 97
7:7 67
7:19 67
7:22 67

7:25 181
7:28 81
8:6 67
9:15 247
9:23 67
9:24 176
10:1-4 247
10:5-7 103
10:8 247
10:9 247
10:11-14 181
10:18 247
10:26 247
10:27 170
10:29 82
11:35 67
11:40 67
12:3-4 143
12:24 67
13:20 175

James
1:1 56
1:22ff. 56
2:1 56

1 Peter
1:3 81, 173
1:10-12 95, 137
1:12 54
1:21 55
1:25 54
2:18-25 159
2:21-25 55
2:25 122
3:15 55
3:18–4:6 230
3:21-22 176
4:11 55
5:4 122

2 Peter
1:1 55
1:4 235
1:8 55

1:11 55
1:16 54
1:17 81
2:5 93
2:20 55
3:18 55

1 John
1:1 64
2:1 181
2:6 159
3:5 158, 163
4:7–5:3 153
4:8-10 64
4:8 153
4:9 64
4:15 87
4:16 64, 153
5:11 64
5:13 86

Revelation
1 173
1:8 65
1:12f. 178
1:13 65, 80
1:17-18 172
1:18 212
1:20 178
3:14 106
5:1-7 32
5:6 65
11:15 200
12:9 165
22:17 183
22:20 58, 183

PERSONS INDEX

Alexander, T. D. 110
Apollinarius 232
Arius 231
Athanasius 61, 132, 231, 235, 255
Balchin, John 90
Ball, David 262
Barth, Karl 76, 163
Beasley-Murray, George 43
Blomberg, Craig 45, 223
Blum, E. A. 66
Bornkamm, Gunther 49
Bousset 58, 66
Bray, Gerald 243
Bridge, Donald 28, 65
Bruce, F. F. 29, 66, 168
Brunner, Emil 198
Bultmann Rudolf, 36, 42, 72-5, 252, 258, 264-5
Byung Mu Ahn 207
Calvin, John 61, 90
Carey, William 273
Carson, D. A. 129
Chardin, Teilhard de 254
Chesterton, G. K. 125
Chomsky, Noam 112
Churchill, Winston 36
Collingwood, R. G. 48
Copernicus 111
Craig, William 66, 77, 172
Cranfield, C. E. B. 29, 49
Cyril of Alexandria 232
Davey, F. N. 71
de Burgh, W. G. 9
Denney, James 55, 66, 71
Derrida, J 48, 113
Dibelius, Martin 72
Dilthey, W. 48
Dodd, C. H. 29, 91, 117, 216
Dooyeweerd, Herman 112, 253, 268
Drane, John 49
Duncan, John 47

Dunn, James D. G. 79
Elliot, J. H. 118
Erasmus 116
Eusebius of Caesarea 231
Eutyches 233
Fabella, Virginia 210
Fee, Gordon 241
Fiorenza, Elizabeth S. 208
Foucault, M 48
France, R. T. 80, 110
Funk, R. W. 49
Gandhi 8, 149
Gartner, B. 117
Gerhardsson, B. 29, 117
Gilkey, Langdon 267, 269
Goldman, Ronald 273
Gooding, David 109
Gregory of Nazianzus 232
Gundry, Robert H. 172
Gunton, Colin 79
Guthrie, Donald 28, 49, 66, 67
Guttierrez , G. 223
Harnack, Adolph 176, 229, 234
Harris, Rendel 117
Harrison, E. F. 66
Hebblethwaite, Brian 268
Hegel, G.W.F. 41, 256
Heidegger, Martin 72, 74, 258
Heisenberg, 201
Hengel, Martin 83
Hick, John 262
Hiebert, D. E. 66
Hooker, Morna 110
Hoskyns, E. C 71
Hunter, A. M. 91
Irenaeus 61, 67, 255
Irving, Edward 163
Jeremias, J. 83, 224
Johnson, A. R. 110
Jones, Henry, 234
Jones, Peter 201

Kahler, Martin 71
Kant, Immanuel 34, 35, 69, 254, 256
Kappen, Sebastian 207
Kasemann, Ernst 42, 49
Keim, K. T. 89
Kelly. J. N. D. 230
Kierkegaard, Soren 77
Kirk, A. 223
Knitter, Paul 262, 267
Knox, John 79
Koestler, Arthur 112, 269
Kuhn, Thomas 111, 269
Lewis, C. S. 26, 189, 199
Lindars, B. 66
Lovestam, E. 118
Luther, Martin 61, 255
Mackay, Donald 201
Mackintosh, H. R. 212
Malik, A. J. 272
Marshall, I. Howard 6, 213
Martin, Ralph P. 29, 49
Mayor, J. B. 66
McCann, J. C. 109
McDermott, B. O. 209
McFarlane, Graham 168
McQuarrie, John 90, 234
Metzger, Bruce 66
Mitchell, D. C. 109
Moberly, R.W.L. 121
Moreland, J. P. 49
Morison, Frank 193, 197
Motyer, J. A. 109
Nestorius 232
Newbigin, L. 128, 269
North, C. R. 110
Papias 40, 52
Pittenger, Horman 254
Plato 11, 115
Polanyi, Michael 112, 268
Polycarp 67
Polycrates 67
Pratt, Richard 49
Ramsay, Sir William 176

Reimarus, Hermann 41
Renan, Ernst 8
Ricoeur, Paul 113
Ritschl, Albrecht 234, 255
Robinson, John A. T. 49, 73, 78,
    131
Sailhamer, J. H. 110
Sampson, Philip 48
Sanders, E. P. 119
Schlatter, Adolf 71
Schleiermacher, Friedrich 227
Schweitzer, Albert 49, 71, 205
Selwyn, E. G. 230
Sider, Ronald J. 223
Smalley, S. S. 66
Snow, C. P. 269
Socrates 11
Spinoza 227
Storr, Antony 168
Stott, John R. W. 148
Strauss, David 8, 41, 42, 189,
    252, 264
Stuhlmacher, P. 89, 219
Sturch, Richard 249
Tatian 12
Thucydides 33
Tillich, Paul 148, 201, 264
Torrance, T. F. 128
Van Til, Cornelius 268
Vermes, Geza 46
Warfield, B. B. 243
Watson, F. 48
Weiss, Johannes 71
Wells, David 10, 44, 49, 254
Wenham, David 163
Whybray, N. 109
Wilkins, M. J. 49
Wilkinson, L. 48
Wilson, G. H. 109, 118
Witherington III, Ben 45, 209
Wright, David 262
Xenophon 11
Young, William 128

SELECT BIBLIOGRAPHY

N. Anderson, *The Mystery of the Incarnation,* London, Hodder and Stoughton, 1978

D. Bridge, *Jesus the Man and His Message*, Christian Focus, 1995

D. Bridge, *Why Four Gospels?*, Tain, Christian Focus, 1996

F.F.Bruce, *The Real Jesus*, London, Hodder and Stoughton, 1985

A.D.Clarke and B.W.Winter (eds.), *One God, One Lord in a World of Religious Pluralism,* Cambridge, Tyndale House, 1991

J.D.G.Dunn, *Christology in the Making: A New Testament Enquiry into the Origins of the Doctrine of the Incarnation,* London, SCM, 1980

J.B.Green and M.Turner (eds.), *Jesus of Nazareth: Lord and Christ: Essays on the Historical Jesus and New Testament Christology*, Carlisle, Paternoster, 1994

A. Grillmeier, *Christ in Christian Tradition,* London, Mowbrays, 1975

C.E. Gunton, *Christ and Creation*, Carlisle, Paternoster, 1992

C.E.Gunton, *Yesterday and Today: A Study of Continuities in Christology,* London, Darton, Longman and Todd, 1983

C.F.H.Henry (ed.), *Jesus of Nazareth: Saviour and Lord,* London, Tyndale Press, 1966

J.N.D.Kelly, *Early Christian Creeds*, London, Longmans, Green, 2nd edn. 1960.

J.N.D.Kelly, *Early Christian Doctrines*, London, A. and C. Black, 2nd edn. 1960

G.E.Ladd, *I Believe in the Resurrection of Jesus*, London, Hodder and Stoughton, 1975

P. Lewis, *The Glory of Christ*, London, Hodder and Stoughton, 1992

A. McGrath, *The Making of Modern German Christology*, Oxford, Blackwell, 1986

A.McGrath, *Understanding Jesus,* Eastbourne, Kingsway, 1989

I.H.Marshall, *I Believe in the Historical Jesus*, London, Hodder and Stoughton, 1977

I.H.Marshall, *The Origins of New Testament Christology*, Leicester, IVP, 1977

H.D.McDonald, *Jesus - Human and Divine*, London, Pickering and Inglis, 1968

B.O.McDermott, *Word Become Flesh: Dimensions of Christology*, Collegeville, , Liturgical Press, 1993

John McQuarrie, *Jesus Christ in Modern Thought*, London, SCM, 1990

Frank Morison, *Who Moved the Stone?*

Stuart Olyott, *Son of Mary, Son of God: What the Bible teaches about the Person of Christ,* Welwyn, Evangelical Press, 1984

W.Pannenberg, *Jesus, God and Man,* Philadelphia, Westminster Press, 1968

Robert L. Reymond, *Jesus, Divine Messiah: The New Testament Witness*, Phillipsburg, Presbyterian and Reformed, 1990

Harold H. Rowdon, *Studies in Christology presented to Donald Guthrie*, Leicester, IVP, 1982

P.E.Satterthwaite, R.S.Hess, G.J.Wenham (eds.), *The Lord's Anointed: Interpretation of Old Testament Messianic Texts*, Carlisle, Paternoster, 1995

W.M.Thompson, *The Jesus Debate: A Survey and Synthesis*, New York, Paulist, 1985

J.Webster, *Believing in the Incarnation Today,* Basingstoke, M.M. and S., 1983

A.Wessels, *Images of Jesus: How Jesus is Perceived and Portrayed in Non-European Cultures*, London, SCM, 1990

M.J.Wilkins and J.P.Moreland (eds.), *Jesus under Fire: Modern Scholarship Reinvents the Historical Jesus,* Grand Rapids, Zondervan, 1995

B.Witherington III, *The Jesus Quest: The Third Search for the Jew of Nazareth*, Downers Grove, IVP, 1995

C. Wright, *What's so Unique about Jesus?*, Eastbourne, Marc, 1990

Christian Focus Publications publishes biblically-accurate books for adults and children. The books in the adult range are published in three imprints.

Christian Heritage contains classic writings from the past.

Christian Focus contains popular works including biographies, commentaries, doctrine, and Christian living.

Mentor focuses on books written at a level suitable for Bible College and seminary students, pastors, and others; the imprint includes commentaries, doctrinal studies, examination of current issues, and church history.

For a free catalogue of all our titles, please write to
Christian Focus Publications,
Geanies House, Fearn,
Ross-shire, IV20 1TW, Great Britain

Other titles by Geoffrey Grogan,

Wrestling With The Big Issues

In this much appreciated book, Geoffrey Grogan examines the principles and methods used by Paul to assess and solve the doctrinal and practical problems that appeared in the early Christian Church. Most of these problems have reappeared throughout church history, and can be found today in evangelical churches. Geoffrey Grogan is convinced that the answers to many of today's difficulties are to be found in applying to current situations the Spirit-inspired instructions of the apostle.

Howard Marshall says about *Wrestling With The Big Issues*: 'This book is remarkable for being written by a New Testament scholar in such a simple and relevant way that any reader will be able to understand what is being said and see how Paul's letters still speak to Christians today.'

Sinclair Ferguson comments that 'Geoffrey Grogan brings to his teaching, preaching and writing a life-time of study. He combines careful exposition with practical care.'

And Clive Calver says that 'Geoffrey Grogan possesses the uncanny knack of setting truth on fire: here the personality of the apostle shines through its pages; the life of a man who Christ used to transform the history of his church.'

ISBN 1 85792 051 1   256 Pages

In the Focus on the Bible commentary series, Geoffrey has also contributed the commentaries on Mark and 2 Corinthians.

Books by Donald Bridge

JESUS - THE MAN AND HIS MESSAGE

What impact did Jesus make on the circumstances and culture of his time? What is it about him that identifies him both as a unique Saviour and the greatest example of gospel communication?

Donald Bridge challenges the way we view Jesus, and our portrayal of him to the world around us. He argues that walking with Jesus today means reading his words, welcoming the impact of his personality, embracing the provision he makes for us, and sharing his good news with others.

Donald Bridge combines a lifetime of study of the Gospels with an intimate knowledge of the land where Jesus lived and taught. He has been both an evangelist and a pastor, as well as working for several years in the Garden Tomb, Jerusalem.

176 PAGES   B FORMAT
ISBN 1 85792 117 8

SPIRITUAL GIFTS AND THE CHURCH
Donald Bridge and David Phypers

First published in the 1970s, when the Charismatic Movement became prominent in British church life, this classic study of gifts, the individual and the church has been revised and expanded in light of developments since then. The authors, Donald Bridge and David Phypers, give a balanced view of a difficult and controversial issue.

The baptism of the Spirit, with its associated gifts, is a subject which has perplexed and fascinated Christians. It is unfortunately one which also divides Christians who disagree over the extent to which gifts should appear in the Church.

Donald Bridge is an evangelist and church consultant and David Phypers is a Church of England pastor.

192 PAGES   B FORMAT
ISBN 1 85792 141 0

Reformed Theological Writings
R. A. Finlayson

This volume contains a selection of doctrinal studies, divided into three sections:

General theology
The God of Israel; God In Three Persons; God the Father; The Person of Christ; The Love of the Spirit in Man's Redemption; The Holy Spirit in the Life of Christ; The Messianic Psalms; The Terminology of the Atonement; The Ascension; The Holy Spirit in the Life of the Christian; The Assurance of Faith; The Holy Spirit in the Life of the Church; The Church – The Body of Christ; The Authority of the Church; The Church in Augustine; Disruption Principles; The Reformed Doctrine of the Sacraments; The Theology of the Lord's Day, The Christian Sabbath; The Last Things.

Issues Facing Evangelicals
Christianity and Humanism; How Liberal Theology Infected Scotland; Neo-Orthodoxy; Neo-Liberalism and Neo-Fundamentalism; The Ecumenical Movement; Modern Theology and the Christian Message.

The Westminster Confession of Faith
The Significance of the Westminster Confession; The Doctrine of Scripture in the Westminster Confession of Faith; The Doctrine of God in the Westminster Confession of Faith; Particular Redemption in the Westminster Confession of Faith; Efficacious Grace in the Westminster Confession of Faith; Predestination in the Westminster Confession of Faith; The Doctrine of Man in the Westminster Confession of Faith.

R. A. Finlayson was for many years the leading theologian of the Free Church of Scotland and one of the most effective preachers and speakers of his time; those who were students in the 1950s deeply appreciated his visits to Christian Unions and IVF conferences. This volume contains posthumously edited theological lectures which illustrate his brilliant gift for simple, logical and yet warm-hearted presentation of Christian doctrine (I Howard Marshall).

272 pages   ISBN 1 85792 259 X   large format

MENTOR TITLES

Creation and Change by Douglas Kelly (large format, 272 pages)
A scholarly defence of the literal seven-day account of the creation of all things as detailed in Genesis 1. The author is Professor of Systematic Theology in Reformed Theological Seminary in Charlotte, North Carolina, USA.

The Healing Promise by Richard Mayhue (large format, 288 pages)
A clear biblical examination of the claims of Health and Wealth preachers. The author is Dean of The Master's Seminary, Los Angeles, California.

Puritan Profiles by William Barker (hardback, 320 pages)
The author is Professor of Church History at Westminster Theological Seminary, Philadelphia, USA. In this book he gives biographical profiles of 54 leading Puritans, most of whom were involved in the framing of the Westminster Confession of Faith.

Creeds, Councils and Christ by Gerald Bray (large format, 224 pages)
The author, who teaches at Samford University, Birmingham, Alabama, explains the historical circumstances and doctrinal differences that caused the early church to frame its creeds. He argues that a proper appreciation of the creeds will help the confused church of today.

MENTOR COMMENTARIES

1 and 2 Chronicles by Richard Pratt (hardback, 520 pages)
The author is professor of Old Testament at Reformed Theological Seminary, Orlando, USA. In this commentary he gives attention to the structure of Chronicles as well as the Chronicler's reasons for his different emphases from that of 1 and 2 Kings.

Psalms by Alan Harman (hardback, 420 pages)
The author, now retired from his position as a professor of Old Testament, lives in Australia. His commentary includes a comprehensive introduction to the psalms as well as a commentary on each psalm.

Amos by Gray Smith (hardback, 320 pages)
Gary Smith, a professor of Old Testament in Bethel Seminary, Minneapolis, USA, exegetes the text of Amos by considering issues of textual criticism, structure, historical and literary background, and the theological significance of the book.

Focus on the Bible Commentaries

Exodus – John L. Mackay*
Deuteronomy – Alan Harman
Judges and Ruth – Stephen Dray
1 and 2 Samuel – David Searle*
1 and 2 Kings – Robert Fyall*
Proverbs – Eric Lane (late 1998)
Daniel – Robert Fyall (1998)
Hosea – Michael Eaton
Amos – O Palmer Robertson*
Jonah-Zephaniah – John L. Mackay
Haggai-Malachi – John L. Mackay
Matthew – Charles Price (1998)
Mark – Geoffrey Grogan
John – Steve Motyer (1999)
Romans – R. C. Sproul
2 Corinthians – Geoffrey Grogan
Galatians – Joseph Pipa*
Ephesians – R. C. Sproul
Philippians – Hywel Jones
1 and 2 Thessalonians – Richard Mayhue (1999)
The Pastoral Epistles – Douglas Milne
Hebrews – Walter Riggans (1998)
James – Derek Prime
1 Peter – Derek Cleave
2 Peter – Paul Gardner (1998)
Jude – Paul Gardner

Journey Through the Old Testament – Bill Cotton
How To Interpret the Bible – Richard Mayhue

Those marked with an * are currently being written.

Rev Geoffrey Grogan is Principal Emeritus of Glasgow Bible College. His theological studies were undertaken there and at the London Bible College. He served the College as a full-time lecturer for fourteen years before going south in 1965 to teach at LBC. In 1969 he returned to Glasgow as principal. He has served on four missionary councils, on the Strathclyde Education Committee and the Management Committee for the Cambridge University Diploma in Religious Studies. He has written books on the *Trinity*, the *Person of Christ, Paul,* and commentaries on *Isaiah, Mark and 2 Corinthians.*